RUSSIAN LITERATURE

IN TRANSLATION 2

SIDNEY MONAS, EDITOR

Mandelstam in his thirties. From *Delos*, no. 1 (1968): 39 (the collection of Clarence Brown).

COMPLETE POETRY OF

OSIP EMILEVICH

# Mandelstam

TRANSLATED BY BURTON RAFFEL

AND ALLA BURAGO

WITH AN INTRODUCTION

AND NOTES BY SIDNEY MONAS

STATE UNIVERSITY OF NEW YORK PRESS

ALBANY 1973

Published by
State University of New York Press, Albany

© 1973 State University of New York

All rights reserved

No part of this book may be used or reproduced in any manner whatsoever without written permission. No part of this book may be stored in a retrieval system or transmitted in any form or by any means including electronic, electrostatic, magnetic tape, mechanical, photocopying, recording, or otherwise without the prior permission in writing of the publisher.

For information, contact State University of New York Press, Albany, NY
www.sunypress.edu

Mandel'shtam, Osip Emil'evich, 1891-1938?
  Complete Poetry of Osip Emilevich Mandelstam.

(Russian literature in translation, 2)
I. Raffel, Burton, tr. II. Burago, Alla, tr.
III. Monas, Sidney. IV. Series.

978-1-4384-7166-2   (paperback : alk. paper)

PG3476.M355A27     891.7'1'3     76-38004

Complete Poetry of Osip Emilevich Mandelstam

First Edition

Published by State University of New York Press
99 Washington Avenue, Albany, New York 12210

Copyright © 1973 State University of New York
All rights reserved

Library of Congress Cataloging in Publication Data
Mandel'shtam, Osip Emil'evich, 1891–1938?
Complete poetry of Osip Emilevich Mandelstam.

(Russian literature in translation, 2)
I. Raffel, Burton, tr. II. Burago, Alla, tr.
III. Monas, Sidney. IV. Series.
PG3476.M355A27    891.7'1'3    76-38004
ISBN 0-87395-210-3 cloth
ISBN 0-87395-211-1 microfiche

Printed in the United States of America

# Contents

| | |
|---|---|
| Translator's Preface by Burton Raffel | vii |
| Preface by Sidney Monas | ix |
| Introduction by Sidney Monas | 1 |
| *Stone* (1913) | 29 |
| *Tristia* (1922) | 83 |
| *Poems* (1928) | 121 |
| Uncollected and Unpublished Poems | 143 |
| Twenty-Two Unpublished Poems (1909–1910) | 299 |
| Two Later Unpublished Poems | 313 |
| Notes by Sidney Monas | 317 |
| Appendix 1: Two Chapters by Nadezhda Mandelstam | 339 |
| Appendix 2: Finding-List of Poems with Titles | 351 |

# Translator's Preface

This book follows scrupulously the order and the texts established by Gleb P. Struve and Boris A. Filipoff, the editors of Osip Emilevich Mandelstam's *Collected Works,* 2d ed. (Washington: Inter-Language Literary Associates, 1967), vol. 1 (poetry).

Mandelstam published two books of poetry, *Stone* in 1913, and *Tristia* in 1922. In 1928 he published a kind of collected *Poems,* the third section of which incorporated poems written between 1921 and 1925; he also added poems to the two earlier collections. Much the largest part of his life's work in poetry is the category here termed "Uncollected and Unpublished Poems." For the period from 1926 to Mandelstam's death, this is quite simply all that has survived; it was not prepared for publication by the author and clearly incorporates poems both good and bad. This is even truer of the uncollected and unpublished poems for the period from 1908 to 1926, many of which are clearly poems Mandelstam rejected, and rightly rejected, as not meriting book publication. For a book like this one, however, which attempts to give Mandelstam's complete *oeuvre* in poetry, even these inferior poems have substantial merit—and everything by a poet as fine as Mandelstam is in some sense important, even if only as a document of failure.

These translations follow the original pretty much line by line, and always stanza by stanza, strophe by strophe. I have not hesitated to reorder lines, where the syntax of English would not permit more exact tracking of the Russian. Not much of the form and structure of the original is preserved, though I have sneaked in as much rhyme (often internal rhyme) as I could manage. Still, much of the tone, the rhetoric of Mandelstam is here: I have been as careful as I knew how not to violate that. Translation is a giddy art, and translation of a poet as great and as difficult as Mandelstam is a perpetual tightrope act—but translation need not be rape.

I have not tried to translate either Mandelstam's children's poetry or his humorous verse, two very special genres almost impossible to translate and, in Mandelstam's case, not I think either terribly illuminating or of great intrinsic importance. The total of these poems, numbered from 396 to 457 in Struve's and Filipoff's edition, comes to sixty-two items.

I should like to record, finally, how deeply, powerfully depressing it has often been for me, a poet and a Jew, and of Russian-born parents, to re-experience Mandelstam's inner life. The exhaustion and tears, here, are not Mandelstam's alone.

BURTON RAFFEL

# Preface

Osip Emilevich Mandelstam was born in Warsaw in 1891, the son of a struggling Jewish leather merchant from Riga. He grew up in Saint Petersburg, studied at the Tenishev School, then in Paris and Heidelberg and the University of Saint Petersburg, though he never took a degree. In 1912 he became one of the Acmeist poets, along with Anna Akhmatova and Nikolai Gumilev. Later, he became quite close to Marina Tsvetaeva, with whom he spent some time in the Crimea in 1916. During the period from 1916 to 1919, the years of the war, the February Revolution, the October Revolution and the outbreak of Civil War, his wanderings were complex and his adventures and misadventures came rather thick. In 1921, he married Nadezhda Iakovlevna Khazin. From 1924 to 1930, he lived in Leningrad, under increasing pressure from writers more officially favored than he. In 1930, he went on a long trip to Armenia arranged by Nikolai Bukharin and returned to Moscow in 1931. From this time on, publication became increasingly difficult, and by 1934 virtually impossible. On the night of 13 May 1934 he was arrested, presumably because of a sardonic poem on Stalin that he had written. He was grilled in the infamous political prison, the Liubianka, and later sent into exile in Cherdyn, where he attempted to commit suicide. He was allowed to choose a somewhat more lenient place of exile, and he and his wife lived in Voronezh between 1935 and 1937. After having been allowed briefly to return to Moscow, he was rearrested the night of 2 May 1937 and sent, this time alone, to a transit camp near Vladivostok in the Far East. The official date of his death was cited as 27 December 1938; but there is still considerable doubt as to when, exactly, and even where he died.

During his lifetime, he published only three volumes (not counting light, children's verse) of his poetry, a few separate poems, some essays, autobiographical sketches, and one work of short fiction.

That, in brief outline, is the biography that has been so movingly described in some of its details by his widow, Nadezhda Mandelstam, in her book *Hope against Hope,* soon to be supplemented by a second volume of her reminiscences. His work is difficult, varied, complex. In sections of her memoir that were not included in the English translation, Nadezhda Iakovlevna has made very clear why, for a proper understanding of Mandelstam, it is necessary to read the bulk of his poetry, including the variants and draft versions which more and more in his mature period he came to consider as poems in their own right.

The translators, with great skill and patience, have managed to render into English virtually *all* of Mandelstam's serious poetry that is extant. I believe that they have nobly served not only Russian, but world literature.

As editor, I would like to acknowledge my indebtedness to Professors Gleb Struve and Boris Filipoff, without whose magnificent three-volume Russian edition of Mandelstam the present volume would scarcely have been possible. For the twenty-four poems of Mandelstam that did not appear in the Struve-Filipoff edition, I would like to thank the *Vestnik Russkogo Studencheskogo Khristianskogo Dvizheniia* [Messenger of the Russian Student Christian Movement], nos. 97–98 (1970), where they first appeared in print. I would like to thank Professor Clarence Brown for his help and cooperation; and also Professors George Ivask, Igor Chinnov, and Elisabeth Markstein. I am grateful, too, to Elizabeth Coccio of State University of New York Press; and I own a rather special debt of gratitude to Gianna Kirtley and to Carol Monas.

Above all, I would like to express my respect for and gratitude to Burton Raffel and Alla Burago, with whom it has been an extraordinary pleasure to work.

SIDNEY MONAS

# An Introduction to Mandelstam

*by* SIDNEY MONAS

## The Hunger in Space

"Just as a person does not choose his parents," Mandelstam wrote in 1921, "a people does not choose its poets." [1] Russia would certainly have avoided him if it could. Even today, long after his posthumous rehabilitation, most of his poems are unpublished in the USSR. A collected volume announced in 1959 has still not appeared.

Abroad he has fared better. There is now the full, if not complete, three-volume Russian collection of his works, edited by Gleb Struve and Boris Filipoff.[2] There have been numerous translations, including a small volume in German by a poet close to his sensibility, Paul Celan.[3] There is a growing realization that not only was he an important poet of the twentieth century, but perhaps as much as Rilke or Pound or Yeats or Eliot, *the* poet. Yet it is astonishing how reluctantly he has been accepted even by Russians abroad.

1. From an essay entitled "Thrust," in Osip Mandelstam, *Sobranie sochinenii* (Washington, D.C., 1971), 2:228. This second edition, in three volumes, edited by Gleb Struve and Boris Filipoff, published by Inter-Language Literary Associates, 1967–1971, will hereafter be referred to as Mandelstam, followed by the volume and page numbers.

2. This marvelous, old-fashioned, scholarly edition (see fn. 1) is put together with great care, love, and respect. It contains, in addition to all the previously published works of Mandelstam, unpublished poems, drafts, newspaper pieces (his interview of December 1923 with Ho Chi Minh, for instance), essays on Mandelstam by such distinguished scholars as the editors themselves, George Ivask, Emmanuel Rais, and others. It contains biographical reminiscences (some first published elsewhere) by Akhmatova, Tsvetaeva, and others. It contains some Mandelstam letters, his literary translations, light verse, children's verse, album-verse. It contains some marvelous pictures and copious notes. It is not systematic, and it is, of course, of necessity incomplete. But it is a great pleasure and a genuine monument of Russian scholarship.

3. See the excellent bilingual edition of Paul Celan, translated by Joachim Neugroschel in *Speech-Grille* (New York, 1971). There is an excellent and eloquent essay on Celan by Dietlind Meinecke, *Wort und Name bei Paul Celan* (Berlin and Zurich, 1970), which unfortunately, however, shows little awareness of Celan's indebtedness to Mandelstam. One of Celan's best known earlier poems, while somewhat more melodramatic than Mandelstam, is typically Mandelstammian in its imagery and development. I refer to the *Todesfuge*:

> Schwarze Milch der Fruehe wir trinken sie abends
> wir trinken sie mittags und morgens wir trinken sie nachts
> wir trinken und trinken . . .
>
> [*Speech-Grille*, p. 28]

Celan's conception of the Word is also basically Mandelstammian.

He was not, after all, shot by the Bolsheviks in the last days of the Civil War, like his friend Gumilev. He was even rumored to have had some enthusiasm for the regime in its early days. His first three volumes always had their admirers, as did of course the unpublished poem on Stalin for which he was exiled to Voronezh.[4] But the *Voronezh Notebooks,* heroically preserved by his remarkable widow, and by Akhmatova, with the help of a few brave friends—"late Mandelstam," difficult, obscure, obsessive—that was more problematic.

In much of Russian literature and literary criticism in the years between 1907 and 1917 there is a sense of impending catastrophe, and a certain longing for it. Expectations were apocalyptic, and both Esenin and Mayakovsky at somewhat different angles on the edge of their seats predicted the coming Revolution. In Mandelstam's poems, however, there was a *stillness,* the sense of an ominous interval, like the unease of a Chirico shadow among geometrically balanced traditional shapes, like a sailboat that has come about, and before its sails quite catch the wind on the new tack.

This nervous little man, schlemiel, luftmensch, Christian and Jew, with a sweet tooth and a dread of dentist's drills, prophet at war with linear time, artiodactyllic inhabitant of near-arctic Saint Petersburg longing for the *mezzogiorno*—he could feel the encroachment on his chosen city of the new "Assyrian," the new "Egyptian" age, for which man would not be the measure but the raw material. Like a true Joseph, he moved into Egypt. He was a "Holy Fool," a *iurodivyi* of seventeenth-century Russia, a "bird of God" (he loved swallows and identified himself with the goldfinch); he was one of those imitators of Christ, God's fools, who were during Russia's times of troubles alone privileged to criticize the State. Like Ovid, he was an exile dreaming of Rome; like Dante, he wrote poems to "the measure and rhythm of walking." All poets were exiles, "for to speak means to be forever on the road."[5] But Mandelstam thought of himself also as a *colonizer.*

It is in his essay on Chaadaev, this push for exploration and settlement—in that essay where he portrays so brilliantly the basic inner impulse of the lonely, austere, brilliant nineteenth-century figure from whom almost all of modern Russian thought descends.[6] In Mandelstam's portrait: Chaadaev was the first Russian to go to Europe and *return.* Mandelstam read Chaadaev's *Philosophical Letters* in the context of the work of Kliuchevsky, a history

---

4. See poem no. 286.
5. Mandelstam, 2:375; English translation from Osip Mandelstam, "Talking about Dante," trans. Clarence Brown and Robert Hughes, *Delos,* no. 6, p. 75.
6. Mandelstam, 2:284–92.

professor at Moscow University, who wrote eloquently of Russia's historic colonization of the steppe and forest lands of the vast Eurasian spaces.[7] In the *Philosophical Letters,* Chaadaev had written bleakly of Russia's separateness, an orphan among nations, belonging neither to East nor to West; a country without a history, whose sole historical attainment had been "the occupation of space."[8] But Chaadaev's account had to be seen as the projected negative of an implied positive picture. Occupied space had now to be colonized with values; implanted with the warmth of a splendid teleology —to become one with mankind; One Body; the Kingdom of God on Earth.

It is also in his essay on the nineteenth century. Here Mandelstam begins by quoting the fragment, written in slate pencil on a slate board and posthumously discovered, by Gabriel Derzhavin, Russia's greatest poet of the eighteenth century and a man who had served as minister of justice under Catherine II.[9] The River of Time in its flowing sweeps everything away, and into the Abyss of Oblivion it pours Tsardoms, Tsars, People; and should it be that through the sounding of Lyre or Horn, *Something should yet remain*—why, then, Eternity seizes it by the Throat; nor does it escape the Common Fate. There, wrote Mandelstam, expressed in the quaint, personified language of the expired eighteenth century was the lesson of the nineteenth: Relativism. The Absolute was dead, and the world was growing colder. The appalled reaction of Derzhavin had its less obvious counterparts in the sciences, each of which tended to separate itself off into a mere methodology, in utilitarianism, in what Mandelstam called "Buddhism" in both science and art—the creation of artificial, abstract, self-contained, "objective" worlds—meaning positivism in science, theosophy in religion, and a Flaubert-Goncourt kind of realism in art.[10] But the century had, still, the potentiality of its eclecticism: the sense of freedom to choose equally among

---

7. V. O. Kliuchevsky, *Sobranie sochinenii,* 8 vols. (Moscow, 1956–1959). Two volumes of his famous *Kurs russkoi istorii* [Course of Russian history] have been translated into English: *Peter the Great* (New York, 1961), and *Russia in the Seventeenth Century* (Chicago, 1971). Michael Karpovich, a student of Kliuchevsky's and the teacher in turn of *most* American historians of Russia (at least those now over forty), describes an interesting meeting with Mandelstam in Paris in 1908 in "Moe znakomstvo s Mandel'shtamom," *Novyi Zhurnal* 49 (1957), pp. 258–61.

8. Peter Chaadaev, *Philosophical Letters & Apology of a Madman,* trans. with an introduction by Mary-Barbara Zeldin (Knoxville, 1969), p. 36.

9. On Derzhavin, see Mandelstam's essay, "The Nineteenth Century," in Mandelstam, 2:276–77. See also J. V. Clardy, *G. R. Derzhavin* (The Hague, 1967), and H. Koehle, *Farbe, Licht und Klang in der malenden Poesie Deržavins* (Munich, 1966).

10. Mandelstam, 2:280–83. Mandelstam's conception of "Buddhism" is related in great part to Schopenhauer and comes by way of Herzen's well-known essay, "Buddhism in Science," in A. Herzen, *Selected Philosophical Works* (Moscow, 1956), pp. 71–96. Herzen had considerable impact on Mandelstam in his youth.

all the products of time. No friend to what he called "the century of pancomprehensibility, the century of relativism with its monstrous capacity for reincarnation," he saw it nevertheless as providing materials for defense against the monumental "Egyptian and Assyrian" cultures to come:

> In relation to this new age, with its immense cruelty, we are colonizers. To Europeanize and to humanize the twentieth century, to heat it with a theological warmth—that is the task of those who have managed to emerge from the wreckage of the nineteenth century, thrown ashore by the will of the fates on a new historical continent.[11]

Most dramatically, this thrust of the self-proclaimed colonizer appears at the end of what is probably Mandelstam's greatest short essay, "The Word and Culture," just before his declaration that "classical poetry is the poetry of revolution." He elaborates here on the eclecticism of the modern poet.

> It is something quite the opposite of erudition. Contemporary poetry for all its complexity and inner violence is naive. . . . For [the contemporary poet] the entire complexity of the old world is a kind of Pushkinian reed. On it, ideas, scientific systems, political theories are played, in precisely the same way as, during the time of his predecessors, nightingales and roses were played on it.

Then, quite unexpectedly, and without even beginning a new paragraph, comes this extraordinary statement: "They say the cause of revolution is hunger in the interplanetary spaces. We need to sow wheat out there, in the ether."[12]


## The Blessed, Crazy Word

"Crazy," or "senseless," as in the repeated line of poem number 118:

> We'll meet in Petersburg
> as if we'd buried the sun there,
> and for the first time we'll say
> the blessèd senseless word.

A *iuridovyi* always was a little cracked. He speaks the word as it occurs to him; he speaks in tongues—glossolalia—and the word is blessed precisely

---

11. Mandelstam, 2:283.
12. Ibid., p. 227.

because it is free from the expected logic of the occasion, from the Reality Principle.

The whole poem hinges on "as if" (*slovno*) a notion inseparable in the Russian from "the word" itself (*slovo*). "Burying the sun" means to go on a binge, a celebration, especially in summertime Saint Petersburg where the sun shines all night. But not in November, when it has to be a celebration "as if,"

> In the black velvet of Soviet night,
> in the velvet of universal emptiness,
> women's eyes sing on, belovèd eyes, blessèd women,
> immortal flowers bloom on.

Women, their eyes, flowers, and singing are all blessed, like the word—blessed by their fullness of physical being, blessed by their exemption from the logic of the situation.

The theater, the opera, is part of the celebration, a warming of the hands, away from the boredom, the cold and the dark. It pursues a drama different from the angry singing of the motorcar in the darkness outside. It permits a certain imaginary defiance:

> I need no night pass,
> I'm not afraid of sentries . . .

Nothing could have been more "as if" than that. It was 1920, and everyone needed a pass, and Mandelstam was frightened stiff of the sentries, especially the sailors in leather jackets.

"Blessèd" words; as the gods are blessed in Homer, because they are immortal. "Blessèd" words, as in poem number 86, "Solòminka," where a euphonious list of mysterious ladies is reeled off: Lenore, Solòminka, Ligeia, Seraphita.

Lenore is of Buerger's Romantic ballad, and of Poe's "Raven"; Ligeia, of Poe's gruesome story, who comes back to life under strange circumstances; Seraphita belongs to a Swedenborgian tale of Balzac's; Solòminka is the diminutive of the Russian word for "straw" (*soloma*), but also the Russian diminutive form of Salomé, who not only danced for the head of John the Baptist but provided a name to a Georgian beauty with whom Mandelstam was in love. The names have their own historical-literary associations and their own meanings; they have also their physical qualities, their "sound" qualities, which are part of their ambience and their living, immortal nature.

Mandelstam compared the physical nature of the word to a paper lantern with a candle inside. Sometimes the candle inside was the meaning and the paper and frame were the sound structure; and sometimes the paper and frame were the meaning and the candle was the sound.[13]

The word was a Psyche, or soul, and immortal. The word was not its object-meaning, or even the sum of its object-meanings, though sometimes it could be felt "hovering over its object like a soul over the recently deceased body of the beloved." The word was a Psyche and could choose its own meaning.[14] Nevertheless, the meanings it had chosen were there, sealed into its image—the word had a history; and conscious meaning could not, without impoverishment, simply be thrown overboard, as Khlebnikov and the Futurists attempted to do.

Not only did the word have *a* history, but for Russia it was history. For when Chaadaev had declared that Russia had no history, he had overlooked language. Russia's history was in its language. And the nature of its language was Hellenic—not in the sense that it derived from the Greek, but in that it "preserved the gift of free incarnation."[15]

The capacity of the Russian word-Psyche to choose its body freely—the "Saint George's Day" of language![16]—this was the secret basis of kinship with the Greek. And it was based on freedom from the usages of State and Church—from "the King's English," the Royal Society Dictionaries and their attempts to unify, to standardize, to *mechanize* the patterns of meaning. There had been of course the Byzantine monks—they were, Mandelstam wrote, medieval Russia's equivalent of the intelligentsia—and the clerks of Ivan IV's chancery. But the results of their work had been shaky; they had created no sense of communality, no family sense of kindred. Russia had not even an Acropolis. And it was in the seminar of philology rather than in the large formal lecture of political science that the communality created by Russian history was to be discovered.[17]

While it was the constant effort of the priest, the administrator, and the *intelligent* to reduce the word to its ready-made meaning, to its object-meaning, its "mechanical" or "translators' " meaning, it was the poet who kissed it awake and transformed the frog into a prince, the sleeping beauty into a living girl.

13. Ibid., p. 256.
14. Ibid., p. 226, p. 222.
15. Ibid., p. 245.
16. Saint George's Day, in November, celebrated the gathering of the harvest. Traditionally, before the seventeenth century, peasants were free to move from one estate to another for a certain period of time after Saint George's Day, which was thus a symbol of peasant freedom. It was the increasing restrictions and the final abolition of this freedom that marked the beginning of serfdom in Russia.
17. Ibid., p. 246, p. 251.

What distinguishes poetry from mechanical speech is that it rouses us and shakes us awake in the middle of a word. Then the word turns out to be far longer than we thought, and we remember that to speak means to be forever on the road.[18]

To speak, speech—for Mandelstam the impulse to poetry, its "command." The basic metaphor here is *movement,* motion, as in the question Mandelstam poses as to "how many sandals Alighieri wore out in the course of his poetic work, wandering about on the goat paths of Italy?"[19] Or in the need for physical motion manifest in his own response to the presence of poetry. "Restlessness was the first sign," Nadezhda Iakovlevna writes, "that he was working on something, and the second was the moving of his lips."[20] Physical motion and the shape and poise of the body to accommodate that motion is a theme that runs throughout Mandelstam—the movement of the poet's lips, the syllogism of Dante's step on the goat paths of Italy, the complex pattern of a horse's hooves on the cobblestones of provincial Russia ("Whoever Finds a Horseshoe," poem no. 136). For him inspiration began as a buzzing, jangling, humming sound, in which he had to distinguish the words, a concentration that induced motion, sometimes strained and, viewed from the outside, grotesque and anguished.

> His head was twisted around so that his chin almost touched his shoulder; he was twirling his walking stick with one hand and resting the other on one of the stone steps to keep his balance. . . . When he was "composing" he always had a great need of movement. He either paced the room (unfortunately we never had very much space for this) or he kept going outside to walk the streets. The day I came across him sitting on the steps, he had just stopped to rest, tired of walking around.[21]

This, a man old before his time, toothless, eyelids painfully inflamed, with an improperly mended broken arm, suffering from angina pectoris. . . .

"The quality of poetry," Mandelstam himself wrote,

> is determined by the rapidity and decisiveness with which it instills its command, its plan of action, into the instrumentless, dictionary, purely qualitative nature of word formation. One has to run across the whole

---

18. "Talking about Dante," p. 75.
19. Ibid., p. 68.
20. Nadezhda Iakovlevna Mandelstam, *Hope against Hope: A Memoir,* trans. Max Hayward (New York, 1970), p. 186.
21. Ibid., p. 184.

width of the river, jammed with mobile Chinese junks sailing in various directions. This is how the meaning of poetic speech is created. Its route cannot be reconstructed by interrogating the boatmen: they will not tell how and why we were leaping from junk to junk.[22]

The whirring, humming, buzz, the tangled movement of inspiration, the strain and physical anguish of bodily adaptation. . . . But, as Nadezhda Iakovlevna writes,

> the process of composing verse also involves the *recollection* of something that has never before been said, and the search for lost words is an attempt to *remember* what is still to be brought into being ("I have forgotten the word I wished to say, like a blind swallow it will return to the abode of shadows").[23]

The poetic need for surprise, astonishment, wonder, is a notion essential to Mandelstam, as is the rather Augustinian conception of "re-membering" or "re-collecting."[24]

Indeed, the Logos of the Book of John is very much intertwined with Mandelstam's conception of the word, and for that matter so is Christianity in general. Yet he resists the institutionalization of language through the Church as well as through the State or the Party or the Intelligentsia.

> The speed at which language develops is incommensurable with the development of life itself. Any attempt to adapt language mechanically to the needs of life is doomed to failure before it begins.[25]

Hellenism, the Word, Christianity: all three, closely linked.

Hellenism means the humanization of the cosmos, sowing wheat in the interplanetary ether to allay the hunger in space.

> Hellenism—that is the conscious encirclement of man with the utensil [*utvar'*]; instead of impersonal objects, the transformation of these objects into the utensil, the humanization of the surrounding world, heating it with the most delicate teleological warmth. Hellenism—that is a system in the Bergsonian sense of the word, like a sheaf of phenomena

---

22. "Talking about Dante," p. 66. For a strikingly similar account of lyric composition, see Northrop Frye, *Anatomy of Criticism* (Princeton, 1957), pp. 275–77.
23. *Hope against Hope,* p. 187 (the italics are mine).
24. Saint Augustine. *The Confessions.* bk. 10. The origin is, of course, Platonic.
25. Mandelstam, 2:247.

freed of temporal dependence, coordinated in an inner liaison through the human I.[26]

"Christianity," writes Mandelstam, "is the Hellenization of death."[27] Except for the brilliant Russian essay by George Ivask entitled "The Christian Poetry of Mandelstam," it is a subject that critics have spent more energy evading than confronting.[28] Even Nadezhda Iakovlevna—though her husband's Christianity is mentioned in passing from time to time in her splendid book, and though she would not seem to have been unsympathetic to it—tends to avoid the issue. Mandelstam himself is extraordinarily reticent about it, and concerning his conversion there is none of the drama and pageantry surrounding that of, say, Pasternak. It is difficult to note at which point in his life he became a convert. In "The Hum of Time," he writes of "the Judaic chaos" of his family background, the incomprehensibility of the books at the bottom of his parents' shelf and his own incapacity to learn Hebrew.[29] But it is clearly a buzzing, humming chaos, next to the *"silentium"* from which life springs. His first overtly Christian poem, dedicated to Kartashev (no. 100, see the note on p. 322) consists entirely of Jewish imagery. There are earlier references to "a thin cross" (no. 19), to the historical and esthetic eloquence of Christianity (nos. 38, 39, 43, 46, etcetera) and a poem that deals directly with a powerful (if still somewhat ambivalent) religious experience (no. 30). Still, there is no doubt that Ivask is right, and Mandelstam, in his festive, sacrificial manner, resembling Jacob Boehme, thought of Christianity as at once a joyful game that Christ had freed man to play with God and a Road to Calvary: Mandelstam is the most Christian of modern poets.

Even his early ambivalent but passionate involvement with the Revolution is permeated with Christianity, "for every cultivated man is a Christian now," he wrote. And more strikingly:

an heroic era has opened in the life of the word. The word is flesh and bread. It shares the fate of bread and flesh: suffering. People are hungry. The state is even hungrier. But there is something hungrier yet: time.

26. Ibid., pp. 253–54. The meaning of *utvar'* is very imperfectly rendered by the English "utensil." It has the same etymological root as *tvorit'*, "to create." It means also "valuables," in the sense that the silverware belonging to a house may be referred to as its "valuables." In that sense, too, it conveys the meaning of "fixture" and "ornament."
27. Mandelstam, 2:318.
28. Iurii Ivask, "Khristianskaia poeziia Mandel'shtama," *Novyi Zhurnal* 103 (1971), pp. 109–23.
29. Clarence Brown, ed. and trans., *The Prose of Osip Mandelstam* (Princeton, 1965), p. 88.

Time wants to devour the state. The threat sounds like that trumpet-voice scratched by Derzhavin on his slate board. Whoever will lift high the word and show it to time, as the priest the Eucharist, will be a second Redeemer. There is nothing hungrier than the contemporary state, and a hungry state is more terrifying than a hungry man. Compassion for the state which denies the word—that is the social path and the great deed [*podvig*] facing the contemporary poet.[30]

## The Fourth Estate

Mandelstam called himself a *raznochinets,* that curious Russian word; plural, *raznochintsy.* In poem number 260, Burton Raffel translates it as "middle-class intellectuals," but no single phrase is altogether adequate. It means literally, "people of different ranks," and it was first used in legal documents in the eighteenth century to indicate people outside the established castes—not nobles or merchants or priests or artisans, though possibly their fathers had been—and later, it came to have the connotation, "educated commoners," or "classless intellectuals." In the 1860s, the educated elite was laced with *raznochintsy,* who, new to the universities and the learned professions, new to science and literature, provided a somewhat raw tone and style for the intelligentsia, a style markedly different from that of the "esthetic" and aristocratic 1840s, whose representatives tended to think of the men of the 1860s with nervous distaste, because though comrades in the cause, they "smelled of crushed bugs."[31]

"A *raznochinets,*" writes Mandelstam in his autobiography, "has no biography other than the books he has read."[32] And he proceeds with a masterful portrait of his family and of himself by way of the family bookcase: the unintelligible and horizontally piled Hebrew books of his father on the bottom shelf, that compressed "Judaic chaos," which he resists and resents but which yet presses upward with its black-and-yellow insistence, its exotic and creative intensity. The next shelf belongs to Schiller and the German Romantics, whom Mandelstam's father read when, sent to a Berlin Yeshiva at the age of fourteen, he broke with home by reading them instead of Talmud and Torah. His father's voice, with its "languagelessness," its lost

---

30. Mandelstam, 2:225–26.
31. The remark attributed to Herzen after his meeting with Chernyshevsky in London. The classic literary account of the difference in style between the men of the 1840s and those of the 1860s is of course I. S. Turgenev's *Fathers and Sons.* For an excellent analysis of their political differences, see Franco Venturi, *Roots of Revolution* (New York, 1966).
32. Brown, *The Prose of Osip Mandelstam,* p. 122.

and touching "no-tongue," fills the room. Neither German nor Russian, and having broken with Hebrew and Yiddish; a struggling leather-merchant, affluent enough to maintain an apartment in Saint Petersburg, a summer place in Pavlovsk, to send his son to the fashionable Tenishev School (ten years later Vladimir Nabokov went there) and to send him abroad for three years, once to Paris and once to Heidelberg; but insecure, unestablished, literally "outside the Pale." And then there is his mother's shelf: the impressive Isakov edition of Pushkin, and beside it, symbol of the intelligentsia psyche of the 1880s, that apotheosis of mediocre secular martyrdom, the poet Nadson. Mandelstam's mother spoke a clear, distinct Russian—with an impoverished vocabulary, but unmistakably *hers,* for unlike the tongue-tied father, she was "intelligentsia" from Vilno.

Mandelstam's relations with his family were not easy, and to those unfamiliar with the drama of Jewish family life (a drama since exhausted to the point of banality in the context of American literature) seemingly grotesque and bizarre. It is unlikely that a *raznochinets* would be more at ease in the bosom of his family than in the bosom of society, for every family is a government in its own way, but he is not necessarily a Nechaev. Mandelstam's relationship to his family was sometimes, as he himself put it, "Terrible, terrible. . . ." That did not mean it was not close.

At a certain age, Karl Kautsky's Marxism colored the cosmos for Mandelstam as vividly as Tiutchev's poetry.

> I perceived the entire world as an economy, a human economy—and the shuttles of English domestic industry that had fallen silent a hundred years ago sounded once more in the ringing autumn air! Yes, I heard with the sharpness of ears caught by the sound of a distant threshing machine in the field the burgeoning and increase, not of the barley in its ear, not of the northern apple, but of the world, the capitalist world, that was ripening in order to fall![33]

He loved many things that were not to the taste of the ascetic Nadson-worshipping intelligentsia: beautiful women, wine, chocolates, opera, church architecture. Still, he knew a *raznochinets* when he saw one, and he saw one not only in the mediocre, grim-faced Nadson, but in Francois Villon ("Brother Francois!") and above all in Dante, whose apotheosis in the capuche with the aquiline profile had led too many people astray.

> Dante is a poor man . . . an internal *raznochinets* of an ancient Roman line [like Pushkin's Evgeny in "The Bronze Horseman"]. . . . He does

---
33. Ibid., p. 111.

not know how to act, what to say, how to make a bow. . . . The inner anxiety and the heavy, troubled awkwardness which attend every step of the unselfconfident man . . . who does not know what application to make of his inner experience or how to objectify it in etiquette, the tortured and outcast man. . . . If Dante were to be sent out alone without his *dolce padre,* without Virgil, a scandal would inevitably erupt. . . . The gaucheries averted by Virgil systematically correct and straighten the course of the poem . . . an awkwardness overcome with torturous difficulty. . . . The shade that frightens old women and children was itself afraid, and Alighieri underwent fever and chills all the way from marvelous fits of self-esteem to feelings of utter worthlessness.[34]

And even in Nadson he saw, or perhaps better, "heard," *something*—the pathos of his mother's generation in the hum of time, and he acknowledged a kind of relationship to a poet whom the "esthetes" of the Symbolist generation turned away from in contempt.[35]

The Symbolists either fled everyday reality, like De l'Isle-Adam's hero, Axel, who thought living was something the servants could do for him, or regarded it with horror, like Blok in his brief, simple, powerful poem that begins: "Night. A street. A street-lamp. A drugstore." In contrast to the exaltation of Symbolist esthetics, Mandelstam and to a somewhat lesser degree his Acmeist colleagues were, as Nadezhda Iakovlevna put it, "of the earth, earthy. . . ."[36] He celebrated the "thing" as *utvar'*—the humanized utensil—earth, stone, as building material, even the dead weight of which tended to predispose it to be used in building ("Heaviness and Tenderness, sisters . . ." in no. 108).[37] "M. never talked of 'creating' things," Nadezhda Iakovlevna writes, "only of 'building' them."[38]

This feeling of "being the same as everyone else" ("though perhaps not quite as well-made as others . . ."),[39] this sense, "natural for any poet, of a common bond with the street, with ordinary people," never left Mandel-

---

34. Mandelstam, "Talking about Dante," p. 73.
35. On the remoteness of the Symbolists from daily life, see Edmund Wilson, *Axel's Castle* (New York, 1959).
36. The title of Nadezhda Iakovlevna's chapter 56 is translated by Max Hayward as "The Earth and Its Concerns" (*Hope against Hope*, p. 260).
37. It should be remembered that Mandelstam's first book of poems was called *Stone,* or *Kamen'* in Russian, which may have been a pun also on the Latin *camenae,* another word for "the muses."
38. *Hope against Hope,* p. 264.
39. Ibid.

stam and was very different from the feeling of a professor or a man of letters.

> Poetry is quite different: the poet is linked only with readers sent his way by Providence and he does not have to be superior to his age, or to the people he lives among.[40]

The Symbolists were "teachers" with a cultural mission, but Mandelstam colonized with his own body. He had no aspiration to be part of a priesthood, an aristocracy; and no inclination, as so many of his generation, who, reacting against "bourgeois democracy" and the First World War tended toward a mystique of the strong and authoritarian personality. Mandelstam, who preferred Christianity to Judaism, because he felt the Trinity provided some shelter from the overwhelming force of a unitarian and totalitarian God, considered himself "a pedestrian," walking with peasants. And the fact that he felt he spoke *with* men rather than *for* them, gave him the poet's sense of confidence, of being right. He knew what he heard. In Voronezh, where he was sent for the political crime of writing a sardonic poem about Stalin, this frail, stricken, hungry, sick man walked with a posture that made the street urchins think he was a general.[41]

Mandelstam favored the Revolution—"but without the death penalty."[42] His encounters with the Socialist Revolutionary adventurer-assassin Bliumkin have been told several times and have assumed a legendary quality.[43] The hero of Mandelstam's one piece of prose fiction, Parnok, vainly attempts to save someone from a revolutionary lynch mob, as Mandelstam tried to save Bliumkin's intended victim. But it was not so much the violence of the Revolution that repelled him—and certainly not its assault upon private property—but rather the tendency within it for the Party, and the intelligentsia dazzled by the Party, to constitute itself a power over language and therefore over the truth.

> Social differences and class antagonisms pale before the division, now, into friends and enemies of the word. Sheep and goats, really. I sense

---

40. Mandelstam, 2:265. The essay is called "On the Interlocutor" [*O Sobesednike*].
41. "The little boys would ask him: 'Are you a priest or a general, mister?' and to this M. always replied: 'A little bit of both.'" Nadezhda Mandelstam, *Hope against Hope*, p. 195.
42. Ibid., p. 101.
43. Ibid., pp. 101–9; see also the memoirs of Ilia Ehrenburg, *People and Life* (New York, 1962), pp. 192–93. Ehrenburg was also one of the first Soviet writers to write about Mandelstam openly and with unfeigned praise after Stalin's death. See also his *Memoirs, 1921–1941* (New York, 1964).

the almost physically unclean goat-spirit emanating from the enemies of the word. . . .[44]

Although the *topoi* of his poems, the commonplaces, the epithets, were often classical, they were at the same time pastoral and everyday. Sheep and shepherds, weaving, the spinning wheel, baking, sailing, plowing, beekeeping, building, woodcutting, well dipping—workmen's motifs. True, he could see in the "aristocratic" game of tennis a parable of love and war (no. 51); but so could he in "democratic" football sense the presence of Judith and Holofernes (no. 167). Attacked again and again for his nonexistent allegiance to the Old Regime, he responded defiantly:

> I drink to soldiers' star-flowers, to everything I was blamed for:
> to lush furcoats, to asthma, to Petersburg days and their bile,
> to pine-trees' music, to petrol in Elysian Fields,
>
> . . . . . . . . . .
>
> . . . . . . . . . .
>
> I drink: to which? I still don't know, wine
> from the Pope's cellars, or a lovely Asti spumante . . .
>
> [No. 233]

"Soldiers' star-flowers" is a euphemism for "officers' epaulettes," which were abolished by the Revolution (only to be restored later by Stalin)—it was the sort of thing Mandelstam the man of the Old Regime was supposed to favor. The accusation of "lush furcoats" was a recurrent motif in the accusations against him;[45] "asthma" meant the "decadent" Proust, whose great novel he admired—in other words, all the "forbidden delights." Yet the poem ends with an equation between "Chateauneuf du Pape," the most aristocratic of wines, and "asti spumante," the poor man's champagne.

In 1924, Mandelstam, already hounded and persecuted, contrasted the "obedient" typewriter of writers courting the regime, trying to play to the tune of the stripped-down Soviet sonata, to his own loyalty to "a marvelous oath to the fourth estate":[46]

> Who else can you kill? Who else make famous?
> What kind of lies will you invent?

---

44. Mandelstam, 2:223.
45. *Hope against Hope,* p. 193; see also Appendix 2 of this volume.
46. In Russian, the lines read literally: "Should I then betray to shameful gossip, my wonderful pledge to the Fourth Estate and oaths enormous to the point of tears?"

> There's the typewriter: quick, rip out a key—
> There's a fishbone in there . . .
>
> .  .  .  .  .  .  .  .  .
>
> .  .  .  .  .  .  .  .  .
>
> But the typewriter's plain sonatina—that's only
> the shadow of those mighty ones and all their mighty music.
>
> [No. 140]

Between these two poems, the latter written in 1924, the former in 1931, lay a long period of grim poetic silence, during which Mandelstam, harassed and persecuted, failed to hear the hum of poetic inspiration. The "block" was broken by a trip to Armenia, arranged by Mandelstam's "protector," Nikolai Bukharin, himself to fall victim some years later to Stalin's terror. On his return from Armenia, Mandelstam wrote a marvelous, therapeutic rhetorical sketch clearly unpublishable at the time, which he called "Fourth Prose," in part because he saw this vehement fragment as a rebellious fourth estate of words, a *Pugachevshchina* that had risen up inside him to overthrow discretion and restraint, a Luciferian *non serviam*: "I divide all the works of world literature into those written with and without permission. The first are trash, the second—stolen air." [47]

From that day, until the day of his final arrest in 1937, he wrote steadily.

## The Hum of Time

He saw it, felt its pressure, smelled it, above all he *heard* it. As Victor Terras has put it, he had "'absolute pitch' for time." [48] *Shum vremeni*—"the *hum of time*"—as he called his autobiography; the golden fleece spun out on the wheel and the hum that fills the room even when the wheel is still. In a phrase, a line, a strophe, a paragraph, an aphorism, he could characterize a century, an epoch, a cultural milieu. Thus, the eighteenth century, in his essay on André Chenier: "like a dried-out lake; no depth, no moisture; what was submerged, now all surface." [49] At the center of his concern was the dying nineteenth century, the century of relativism and tolerance, which

---

47. Mandelstam, 2:182. There is an English translation by Clarence Brown in M. Scammell, ed., *Russia's Other Writers* (New York, 1971), pp. 130–45.
48. "The Time Philosophy of Osip Mandel'shtam," *Slavonic and East European Review* 48, no. 109 (July 1969):346.
49. Mandelstam, 2:293.

had nevertheless summoned up a monstrous and barbaric successor, the new Assyrian-Egyptian age. He was fond of the image (gleaned from Pushkin's "Feast in Time of Plague") of the banquet in a dying city. He evokes it at the end of his autobiography, and immediately after that the shade of a nineteenth-century figure with whom he felt a close kinship, the aristocratic esthete Konstantin Leontiev, who had died the year Mandelstam was born.

> If I had a vision of . . . Leontiev yelling for a cabby on that snow-covered street . . . it was only because he of all Russian writers is most given to handling time in lumps. He feels centuries as he feels the weather, and he shouts at them. . . . Looking back at the entire nineteenth century of Russian culture—shattered, finished, unrepeatable, which no one must repeat, which no one dares repeat—I wish to hail the century as one would hail settled weather, and I see in it the unity lent it by the measureless cold which welded decades together into one day, one night, one profound winter, within which the terrible State glowed, like a stove, with ice. And in this wintry period of Russian history, literature taken at large, strikes me as something *patrician* [italics mine], which puts me [i.e., a *raznochinets*] out of countenance: with trembling I lift the film of wax paper over the winter cap of the writer. No one is to blame in this and there is nothing to be ashamed of. A beast must not be ashamed of its furry hide. Night furred him. Literature is a beast. The furriers—night and winter.[50]

That palpability is not nineteenth-century time; it is its own thing, its own system of relevancies, not the straightforward linear march of progress, the ineluctable, constant surge that wears everything down, even the cliffs of Dover, that frightened Derzhavin and the Tennyson of "In Memoriam," not the time that is measured in the spacial terms of clock faces and calendars; it is Bergsonian, twentieth-century time; time as *durée;* time as a system of inner connections.

But it does not merely toss down, into the abyss, peoples, tsars, and tsardoms. It is a creative element: or rather it is the background against which creation takes place. In the famous "Slate Ode" (no. 137), Derzhavin's gloomy poem immediately sets up a dialogue with Lermontov's "star speaking with star," and the stars themselves become a projection of the writing scratched on slate—a projection of man's creativity in time. The flow of the river of time does not merely corrode—in corroding, it shapes. Flint is the

---

50. Clarence Brown, *The Prose of Osip Mandelstam*, p. 132. On Leontiev, see my essay: Sidney Monas, "Leontiev: A Meditation," *The Journal of Modern History* 43, no. 3 (1971):483-94.

pupil, water the teacher. And if there is a destructive, masculine time; there is by its side the feminine creatrix.

If a man is true to his humanity, he is enriched by time:

> All voyage long the heavy sea-waves boomed,
> and then, leaving his ship, all sea-worn, canvas-stretched,
> Odysseus came home, full of space and time.
>
> [No. 92]

It is almost as though he had been woven by the waiting Penelope.

Under attack by his fellow writers, some of them already close to speaking in an "official" tone, Mandelstam, accused of being out of step with his epoch, a child of the past, found a curious if partly ironical identity in the "dying time." In the series of poems, among his very greatest, beginning with number 130, in which time as a "regal shepherd's helper" coaxes an unsuspected freshness out of stale bread, to the rekindling of fire in the eyes of dying time in number 141, he is the "stepson" of "my lord and master time" (*vek-vlastelin*), his eyelids are inflamed as are those of the patrician past, now dying, whose eyes are apples—apples that come from the mocking revolutionary song about the bourgeois: "*Akh, ty iáblochka, kuda kátish'sia?*" ("Ah, little apple, where are you rolling now?") In number 135, the poet grieves over disjuncture, rupture, discontinuity, and "my time" (*our* time, the age) becomes a dying beast with its backbone broken:

> You stare behind you with a senseless
> smile, cruel, weak,
> like a wounded animal
> staring back at his paw-tracks.

In number 227, under greater pressure still, the age becomes an incompetent wolfhound that doesn't know a sheep from a wolf and attacks the lamb it was meant to guard.

As a boy, Mandelstam used to attend concerts at the huge glass-domed railroad station in Pavlovsk, that zany triumph and juncture of nineteenth-century art and technology, where, as he wrote, "the change of conductors seemed to me a change of dynasties."[51] The world of the timetable had infected literature:

> The railroad has changed the whole course, the whole structure, the whole rhythm of our prose. It has delivered it over to the senseless muttering of the French *moujik* out of *Anna Karenina*. Railroad prose, like

---

51. Brown, *The Prose of Osip Mandelstam*, p. 69.

the woman's purse of that ominous *moujik,* is full of the coupler's tools, delirious particles, grappling-iron prepositions.[52]

Mandelstam wanted Russian prose off that track. "Destroy your manuscript," he advised,

> but save whatever you have inscribed in the margin out of boredom, out of helplessness, and, as it were, in a dream. These secondary and *involuntary* [italics mine] creations of your fantasy will not be lost in the world but will take their places behind shadowy music stands, like third violins at the Marinsky Theatre, and out of gratitude to their author strike up the overture to *Lenore* or the *Egmont* of Beethoven.[53]

Prose, liberated, would assume the condition of music. But in the poem called "Concert at a Railway Station," number 125, there is an elegy—echoing Lermontov as in the "Slate Ode," and also Tiutchev—a grieving for the entire age. The "roses rotting in hot-houses," suggest, among other things, the *rosalia,* or Roman spring festival for the dead. Among the farewells of his *Tristia,* farewell to the dying time grieves lyrically.

Mandelstam disliked timetable time, and would have no clocks in the meager apartments he and his wife inhabited before their exile to Voronezh, where of course they had no apartment. But for a long time, hounded by the threat of arrest, ironically, they would spend much time in railroad station waiting rooms, where the police would not think of looking for them (no. 224).

At a time when other writers out of timid conformity would have nothing to do with him, Mandelstam—especially during his stay in Armenia—became acquainted with a young biologist, and through him with a number of life scientists. He became fascinated with evolutionary theory and was convinced that literary criticism should take biological science as a model. Perhaps his previous reading of Spengler and Bergson had prepared him a little for that. But his "absolute pitch" for time held him here, too, in good stead, and although his approach to Darwin, Lamarck, Linnaeus, Passy, is that of a poet and he conceives their work poetically, his essay "Around Naturalists" is a most remarkable venture.[54]

---

52. Ibid., p. 188.
53. Ibid., p. 187.
54. Mandelstam, 2:162–68; the Russian title is *Vokrug Naturalistov.* Stanley Edgar Hyman, who in *The Tangled Bank* (New York, 1962), attempts to deal with Darwin (among others) as a sensibility through his language, and especially his tropes, might have learned from Mandelstam.

Lamarck particularly fascinated him. He saw in Darwin's great predecessor a figure of classic dimension, who combined the eighteenth-century personifying moralism of a La Fontaine with the tragic sense and cosmic scope of a Shakespeare. He found the Darwinian view of "evolution" (a word Mandelstam disliked) sympathetically "Dickensian"—that is to say, playful and optimistic—but he preferred Lamarck's "tragic" view. "What Lamarck feels is precisely the *gaps* in nature."[55] For Lamarck, the environment is not a mere "surrounding," but a *call,* a summons; and there are creatures who respond, yet fail the call. In his great poem "Lamarck" (no. 254), Mandelstam takes us *down* the ladder of evolution into the muteness, the strained and straining silence of nature.

The emergence of a new species, in Lamarck's view as interpreted by Mandelstam, is not a question of progress or evolution—it is a breakthrough, a new creation. It is something like the creation of a poem as described in the passage from "Talking about Dante" quoted earlier in this essay. It is a product of choice, or of a pattern of choices, something like the poet hopping among the "mobile Chinese junks," or something like the chess master about to make an inspired move.

As much interested in geologic as in biologic time, Mandelstam (who came to geologic theory by way of the fifth chapter of Novalis' *Heinrich von Ofterdingen*) believed that,

> a stone is a kind of diary of the weather, a meteorological concentrate as it were. A stone is nothing but weather excluded from atmospheric space and put away in functional space. . . . Meteorology is more basic than mineralogy: it encompasses it, washes over it, it ages and gives meaning to it. [It] is not only the past, it is also the future: there is periodicity in it.[56]

In this sense, Mandelstam believed, "A mineralogical collection is a most excellent organic commentary to Dante."[57]

For what is basic to Dante's poem, according to Mandelstam, is not its rootedness in the scholastic philosophy of Dante's time, but its synchronism, its quality, *like that of a stone,* of an "Aladdin's lamp penetrating into the geologic murk of future times." And Dante's basic metaphor—defined metaphorically by Mandelstam—"designates the standing-still of time."

---

55. Mandelstam, 2:164.
56. "Talking about Dante," p. 103.
57. Ibid., p. 102. See the remarkable passages by Novalis (Hardenberg), not only the chapter from his novel cited in the text, *Gesammelte Werke* (Zurich, 1945), 1:190-229, but also in *Gesammelte Werke,* vol. 3, *Freiberger Studien* (1946); also 4:74-79.

Its root is not in the little word "how," but in the word "when." His *quando* sounds like *come*. Ovid's rumbling is closer to him than the French eloquence of Virgil. . . . If the halls of the Hermitage should suddenly go mad, if the paintings of all schools and masters should suddenly break loose from the nails, should fuse, intermingle, and fill the air of the rooms with futuristic howling and colors in violent agitations, the result then would be something like Dante's *Comedy*.[58]

Mandelstam credits Dante not only with the most extraordinary metaphors of weaving (dear to Mandelstam himself) but with having anticipated the modern polyphonic orchestra, counterpoint and dissonance included: "he was forced to resort to a glossolalia of facts, to a synchronism of events, names, and traditions separated by centuries, *precisely because he heard the hum of time* [italics mine]."[59]

The sense of time that rises above time—like gothic architecture, like the needle point of the Admiralty tower pointing like a mast at the sky, like the Greek word, like that point in the performance of the Eucharist when time comes to a stop:

> It takes the world in its hands, like a simple apple.
>
> . . . . . . . . . . . .
> . . . . . . . . . . . .
> . . . . . . . . . . . .
> . . . . . . . . . . . .
>
> And like eternal noon the Eucharist endures—
> All partake, are blessed, play, sing . . .
>
> [No. 117]

Similarly, in the poet's own life, the poet's first awareness of himself as distinctively a poet:

> My breath, my warmth has leaned
> against the glass windows of eternity,
>
> And the glass is printed with a design
> no one can know, suddenly.

---

58. "Talking about Dante," p. 103.
59. Mandelstam, 2:409. In the Russian, the word *obertony* is used, which Clarence Brown quite correctly translates as "overtones." But I wish to emphasize the correspondence with Mandelstam's basic metaphor, *shum vremeni*.

> Let this moment trickle uselessly down:
> that lovely design is fixed forever.
>
> [No. 8]

In this sense, he is at once "no man's contemporary" (no. 141), and unuprootedly "a contemporary . . . a citizen of the Mosseamstress Era . . ." (no. 260). Perhaps the most complex, if not the most affirmative, expression of the poet's social role as a link with eternity, as the ritual of the Eucharist is a link with eternity, as in the extraordinary poem, "Whoever Finds a Horseshoe" (no. 136).

> We see a forest and say:
> there's a sea-going wood . . .

But the pine tree does not live on in the mast, nor does the spark-strewing run of the horse live on in the horseshoe hanging over the door, which has become a fetish, which has been reduced to mechanical meaning—"good luck"—but which does not hold the flow of the horse's motion over the cobblestones. It is the poet who provides this vital link with the past, the poet who brings the trees to life from the mast, the horse in motion from the horseshoe. Society, without the poet, repeats the last real poet it had:

> Human lips with nothing left to say
> keep the shape of the last word spoken,
> and arms keep the feeling of weight
> though the jug splashed half empty, carrying it home.
>
> [No. 136]

The poet, like a gold coin—legal tender to be exchanged for a living past —is cut down

> . . . like a clipped coin
> and I am no longer sufficient unto myself.
>
> [No. 136]

## Petropolis

For all the pastoral *topoi* and metaphors of his usage, Mandelstam is preeminently an urban poet, a poet of the human *polis,* a *political* poet. He is as aware as any of the "Wasteland" aspect of the modern city—the "desolation and glass" of Petersburg. Unlike T. S. Eliot, however, who sees

> Falling towers
> Jerusalem Athens Alexandria
> Vienna London
> Unreal [60]

he sees the "granaries of faith" (no. 124), the latency of stone which cries out to be built:

> Mighty Notre Dame, the more I study
> your monster's ribs, the more
> I think: someday I'll build beauty
> out of an evil mass, I will, I too.
>
> [No. 39]

He sees the thrust of the Admiralty Tower, which itself reminds him of a ship's mast, and he writes:

> Four elements united, rule us, are friendly,
> but free man made the fifth.
> This chaste-constructed ark: isn't the
> superiority of space denied?
>
> [No. 48]

For the great writers of classic Russian literature, Saint Petersburg, "the most intentional city in the world," [61] as Dostoevsky called it, had been a place of illusion and hallucination, madness, schizophrenia, the dissociation of personality, in which the dream of reason had produced monsters. It was so, too, for Andrei Biely, whose modernist novel, *Peterburg,* had made inventive use of the literary myth of Saint Petersburg, the "abstract" and "unreal" city. For Mandelstam, however, the city was *"deeper* than delirium" (no. 45) and included the two-hundred years of European culture that had come to Russia by way of "Peter's creation" (no. 45), culture that he valued not because it was European, but because he felt it was the only link with the eternal that man could grasp. Petersburg, like Acmeism, the literary movement that was born, grew, and died there, was a longing for world culture.

Attending services at the Uspensky Cathedral in the Moscow Kremlin in 1916 with Marina Tsvetaeva, with whom he was then in love, Mandelstam could write:

> And this tender Cathedral is in Moscow, but is Florence.

---

60. T. S. Eliot, *The Complete Poems and Plays* (New York, 1952), p. 48.
61. F. Dostoevsky, *Notes from the Underground* (New York, 1960), p. 6.

> And Moscow's five-domed cathedrals,
> Russian-souled, Italian-souled,
> make me think of Eos, Goddess of Dawn,
> but with a Russian name, and wearing a fur-coat.
>
> [No. 84]

But on the whole, Moscow was hostile to him, and he disliked it. It smelled of the murdered Tsarevich (Dmitry, said to have been murdered on orders from Boris Godunov) and of the pseudo-Dmitry, who also for reasons of state and after he had killed Boris was murdered, too. He disliked the messianic doctrine of Moscow as "the third Rome," and he shuddered at the new Assyrian-Egyptian age he felt gathering there. His friend and hero Chaadaev, as he well remembered, had headed his letters from Moscow, "Necropolis."

Moscow had been known as a city of wood, and in his later poems Mandelstam associated wood with huge buckets the Mongol khans used to lower disobedient Russian princes into wells as punishment; with execution blocks and ax handles for beheading. For him, Asia was far more strongly *there* than Rome or Florence.

For Petropolis—lovingly Mandelstam bestows its Greek name—the city of stone, there is a different feeling. Not that stone is better than wood. Both are material. Both are there to be fashioned. Both aspire. But Petropolis has the shape of a boat, of an ark, ready to take off in an argonauts' voyage against space; it is launched into the universe. Mandelstam's feeling is complex. Few of his Petersburg poems are without irony, and in his autobiographical prose the irony predominates. Even the image of the ark manages to suggest as well the ship image from Biely's *Peterburg*—the ship, that is, of the damned soul of the Flying Dutchman. And in 1916, Mandelstam, addressing the sea goddess, stone-helmeted Athena, for the first time associates Petropolis with dying, and with Proserpina, goddess of the earth and queen of the dead (no. 89). Petersburg has become "transparent"—that is to say phantasmal; belonging already to the kingdom of the dead. So, Petersburg, too, is a Necropolis. And in a poem of 1918, Mandelstam addresses a now "transparent" star:

> At that terrible height a monstrous ship
> spreads huge wings, and flies—
> Oh green star, your ruined and beautiful
> brother, Petropolis, is dying.
>
> [No. 101]

It is the city's lodestar, its "guiding" or "brother" star—the projection of its hopes and aspirations, precisely the wheat sown by the city in the ether of space.

Behind Petropolis are Greece and Rome. The dome of Saint Peter's, which is compared to a swallow's nest—and if we take the full elucidation of the myth of Procne the self-sacrificing, the giver-over of self, and Mandelstam's idea of the swallow as word-soul, we begin to see the meaning of this great "nest"—the freedom in space of Kazan Cathedral, designed by a Russian serf who had lived in Rome: these are among the felt presences. And one might add the classic shawl slipping from the shoulders of Akhmatova, as in a play by Euripides or Racine. Unlike any other Russian writer he stresses in dealing with Petropolis, not its *artifice,* but its human aspiration to burst bonds, to shake free of dead weight, to unload, to soar.

> Nature is Rome, too, is reflected, now, in Rome.
> We see its secular power
> in transparent air, like a light-blue circus,
> in the forum of fields, in the colonnade of groves.
>
> [No. 65]

The city is thus *like* nature, and *not* "unnatural."

As for the pathetic impermanence of these seemingly mighty structures, the death and decay of imperial centers, of aspirations laid in the dust, Mandelstam makes quite clear what "Rome" means to him:

> It's not Rome, as a city, that lasts forever,
> but man's place in the universe.
>
> Kings try to take it,
> priests use it as an argument for war,
> and without it houses, and altars,
> are contemptible rubble, pitiful, wretched.
>
> [No. 66]

In Mandelstam's only fictive story, "The Egyptian Stamp," which may be taken to mark the end of Russian realism, as Gogol's "Overcoat" which it so much resembles, marked its beginning, the lamblike, sacrificial hero fails, though he tries hard, to prevent a lynching:

Petersburg had declared itself Nero and was as loathesome as if it were eating a soup of crushed flies. Nevertheless, he telephoned from a pharmacy, telephoned the police, telephoned the government, the state, which had vanished, sleeping like a carp. He might with equal success have telephoned Proserpine or Persephone, who had not yet had a telephone installed.[62]

It is in the telephoning that Rome lives, not in the "innumerable swarm of human locusts" that have by now destroyed their victim in the fish-well boat on the blackened banks of the Fontanka Canal.

## The Judas of the Future

Mandelstam, who was fond of birds, identified himself particularly with the goldfinch—perhaps because it had associations with the town of Voronezh, with Kol'tsov, nineteenth-century lyricist, who had lived there and written of goldfinches, because the bird was an indomitable dandy and held its head high and sang through all adversity. In Russia, boys are fond of birds and often catch them and keep them in cages. One such goldfinch provided Mandelstam with a series of poems.

More and more, he worked in "series," preserving draft versions, allowing associations to proliferate, keeping as it were, in Clarence Brown's phrase, the full "phonic shadow." In Mandelstam's extraordinarily self-revealing essay, "Talking about Dante," he wrote: "Draft versions are never destroyed." For the critic, the alert reader, "in order to arrive at the target one has to accept and take account of the wind blowing in a different direction." It was, he wrote, like "tacking in a sailboat." [63]

Mandelstam also made distinctions between himself and the goldfinch: "'They cannot stop me moving about,'" he told Nadezhda Iakovlevna, "'I have just been on a secret trip to the Crimea.'" And he said about the changing of the seasons: "'This is also a journey . . . and they can't take it away from us.'" [64]

But the noose was tightening. In Voronezh, the Mandelstams were completely isolated. Mandelstam's health was failing—his heart bad, his eyesight dim, his poorly mended arm aching. Perhaps, if he wrote a poem "to order," as so many of his friends had done, an ode to Stalin, his fortunes might be mended. Or if not his, Nadezhda Iakovlevna's. What Akhmatova had called "the relatively vegetarian," or early, period of repression was over,

---

62. Clarence Brown, *The Prose of Osip Mandelstam*, p. 167.
63. P. 82. The remark about draft versions never being destroyed, taken from the same passage, finds curious echoes in Michael Bulgakov's novel, *The Master and Margarita*. Mandelstam did know Bulgakov and visited him occasionally.
64. *Hope against Hope*, p. 197.

and the Great Purge was in full swing. The radio was full of the most fulsome rhetoric, praising Stalin. On 16 January 1937, just before he resolved to write an ode to Stalin—as a kind of transition from the goldfinch cycle to the Stalin cycle—he wrote this poem:

> And what do we do with these crushed plains,
> the drawling hunger of this miracle?
> Anyway, that openness we see
> in them we see for ourselves, falling into sleep, we see—
> and the question keeps growing—where are they going? where are they from?—
> And isn't he crawling slowly along them,
> Him, the one we cry out at in our sleep—
> Him, the Judas of the future?
>
> [No. 350]

The Russian text says, literally, "the Judas of peoples to come." "That openness" is not merely the flatness of the "crushed plains"—the vastness of steppe and sky beyond the Voronezh hills—but the historical and cultural "openness" of Eurasia ("where are they going? where are they from?") which along with the vast spaces and possibilities of the American continent comes as close in terms of historical space and historical experience to the metaphysical sense of what Heidegger in his essay on Rilke called "the Open" as the nonmetaphysical imagination can grasp.[65] It is across the horizon of this openness that Judas crawls. And there can be little doubt as to his historical identity. And it is now not "that openness we see . . . [as we are] falling into sleep," but rather "the one we cry out at . . . Him. . . ."

Two days later, Mandelstam wrote

> No comparisons: everyone alive is incomparable.
> With sweet fright
> I'd agree with the steppe's smooth equality, and
> the sky's circle was like a sickness.
>
> I'd turn to the servant-air
> waiting for news, for something,
> and get ready to leave, and I'd drift down an arc
> of journeys that never begin.
>
> Wherever I've got more sky—I'll wander there, yes—
> but this bright boredom won't let me leave

---

65. Martin Heidegger, *Poetry, Language, Thought,* trans. Albert Hofstadter (New York, 1961), pp. 106–16.

> these young Voronezh hills, won't let me go
> to those universal hills—there, clear, distinct, over in Tuscany.

[No. 352]

At first glance, the statement that "everyone alive is incomparable" seems like a good Acmeist affirmation. "Equality" refers not only to the flatness of the steppe, but to revolutionary aspirations, distinguishing them from the gradated hierarchies of feudal Europe. "The sky's circle" is confining, like a sickness; yet the poet "agrees"; he might inwardly, in spite of his fear, assent. His getting ready to leave, and his drifting "down the arc of journeys" is, of course, in imagination. Where he'd go would be where horizons were broader. The view from the Florentine hills would be immeasurably broader than that from "these young Voronezh hills"—*because* they are universal, they have universal human significance, they have culturally and historically acquired universality. Mandelstam's nostalgia is not for a physical landscape but for a view of cultural breadth; scope. But he is held down, imprisoned, by the force—not the force of gravity (heaviness and tenderness are still sisters; to have weight means to cry out to be built) but the force of the figure looming on the horizon—"the Judas of peoples to come," who will betray the building.

And so, the Mandelstam who in 1921 was ready to greet the revolution in the manner of Hoelderlin greeting the return of the gods—

> our blood, our music, our political sense—all this will find its continuation in the tender being of a new nature, a nature-psyche. In this kingdom of the spirit without man every tree will be a dryad and every phenomenon will speak of its own metamorphosis—.[66]

that Mandelstam in 1937 felt something like a shadow pass obliquely across his grave: "And what's mine has picked itself / up and gone . . ." (no. 346). In several poems he wrote of "Precious world-yeast" (i.e., poetry) and the grim shadow passing obliquely across a grave. Clarence Brown and Nadezhda Iakovlevna have both described the "phonic shadow" of Stalin as it fell over the last poems in the *Second Voronezh Notebook*—the syllables that echoed *"os"* as in *osa* ("wasp") and *os'* ("axle")—central to the only thing both Mandelstam and Stalin had in common, their first name, Joseph, of which both *Osip* and *Iosif* are variants.[67] Among these poems are some of Mandelstam's best. Meanwhile, notebook and pencil lay on the

---

66. Mandelstam, 2:222.
67. Clarence Brown, "Into the Heart of Darkness: Mandelstam's Ode to Stalin," *Slavic Review* 26, no. 4 (December 1967):584–604.

table. Mandelstam rarely used them except at the *end* of the process of composition; and he had in the past felt somewhat sardonic toward Pasternak who complained of needing at least the space and peace and quiet of a writing desk in order to compose; Mandelstam, on the contrary, composed in his head, pacing his room or the streets, his body tense and his lips moving; in his poetry, "moving lips" and not pad and paper were the symbol of poetic composition. "But for the sake of the 'Ode' he changed all his habits, and while he was writing it we had to eat on the very edge of the table, or even on the window sill." [68]

"'Now, look at Aseyev,'" he said to Nadezhda Iakovlevna, "'he's a real craftsman, he would just dash it off without a moment's thought.'" [69]

Finally, he wrote the Ode. It did not help him, though it may have lightened the lot of Nadezhda Iakovlevna and provided her with the opportunity to save many of the poems. The Ode itself has not survived. "'It was an illness,'" Mandelstam later said to Akhmatova.[70]

One of the poems that emerged from the Stalin matrix was a vision of himself as Prometheus, which he rejected: "No, never again—tragedies don't come back . . ." (no. 356). Or, if they do, it is as farce; or at the very least as proletarian: "Those lips lead me down into the essence / of Aeschylus the wood-loader, of Sophocles the wood-cutter . . ." (no. 356). One recalls that although he never read James Joyce, he anticipated *Ulysses* if not altogether *Finnegans Wake*.

"'Why is it that when I think of *him*,'" he asked Nadezhda Iakovlevna—she repeats the question in her chapter on the Stalin Ode—"I see heads, mounds of heads? . . . What is he doing with all those heads?'" [71]

It was the Tatar conquerors of Russia who piled pyramids of heads outside the cities as landmarks to the folly of opposition to their rule. It was part of the Muscovite history from which Mandelstam had shrunk, and from which he had turned briefly to tragic, brief Petropolis. And yet—

> Hillocks of human heads into the horizon,
> and I am diminished—they won't notice me,
> but I'll come back, resurrected in tender books and
> children's games, saying: See? The sun is shining.
>
> [No. 341]

Perhaps he will come back.

---

68. Nadezhda Mandelstam, *Hope against Hope*, p. 199.
69. Ibid., p. 200.
70. Ibid., p. 203.
71. Ibid.

*Stone* (1913)

1

An apple drops to the ground,
toneless, precise
—and all around
the song of the trees, the forest silence . . .

                                                                           1908

---

2

Christmas trees burn in the woods
like tinsel; wolves
like toys stare, in the bushes,
with terrible eyes.

Oh the sadness of my too-much seeing,
oh my silent freedom
and the forever-laughing crystal
of heaven's dead and frozen arch.

                                                                           1908

---

3

You appeared out of the half-
dark hall, suddenly, wearing a shawl—
we disturbed no one,
we woke no servants . . .

                                                                           1908

# 4

To read as children read,
to think as children think,
to blow away everything large,
to rise up out of sorrow.

I'm tired to death of life,
I don't want any,
but I love my miserable country
having known no other.

In a garden, far away, I swung
on a wooden swing,
and I still remember the dark, tall trees
through a feverish mist.

                                                    1908

---

# 5

Your face
is more delicate than delicate,
your hand
is whiter than white,
you live
in some far-away world
and everything
that's you is inevitable.

Your sorrow
is inevitable
and your forever-burning
fingers,
and the gentle sound
of your voice,
which never gives up,

and the distance
in your eyes.

1909

---

# 6

Pale-blue enamel
April-like,
and birch trees lifting branches
as darkness drops.

A fine and finished design, delicate,
a thin-etched net, set, hard
like lines on china,
traced clear

As the Artist
draws it across the sky,
knowing a moment's momentary power,
careless of sad death.

1909

---

# 7

Pure, clear cups:
the noble harmony, the deep peace
of my household gods, set
far from astral music.

My household gods are always still,
rapturous: in scrupulous niches,
as the sun fades to make meditation
possible, I listen to their silence.

What toy-like destinies,
what timid laws
these fine-chiseled bodies order,
so cold, so fragile!

Some gods need no glorification:
you and the god are equal,
your careful hand
is allowed to move them, here, there.

                                        1909

---

8


My body, is mine, to do what
with, this indivisible whole, this mine?

Who shall I thank—tell me: who—
for the quiet joy of breath, of life?

I am gardener, but I am flower,
I'm not alone in this world dungeon.

My breath, my warmth has leaned
against the glass windows of eternity,

And the glass is printed with a design
no one can know, suddenly.

Let this moment trickle uselessly down:
that lovely design is fixed forever.

                                        1909

## 9

More sorrow than can be spoken
woke two round eyes;
the flower vase stirred
and splashed out crystal.

All over the room,
languor—oh, a sweet medicine!
Such a tiny kingdom
devoured immensities of sleep.

A drop of red wine,
a bit of May sun—
and, breaking a thin biscuit, the
white of the slimmest of fingers.

1909

## 10

Stretching silk
on a mother-of-pearl shuttle,
begin, oh supple
fingers, your fascinating lesson!

Hand-ebbs, hand flows—
monotonous movements
you use to conjure
some sun-filled moment of fright

When a wide palm
blazes like a seashell,
then dim, rolls into shadow,
then disappears in a rose-colored flame!

1909

11

There's no need to talk,
no need. There's nothing to be taught.
And the dark beast-like soul
is sad and good and beautiful:

Not wanting to teach,
not knowing how to speak, and
swimming like a young dolphin
along the grey-haired, whirling gulfs of the earth.

*1909*

---

12

When blow falls on blow
and a mortal, untiring
pendulum swings over my head,
wanting to become my fate,

To lurch, to stop—hard!—
the spindle falling:
there's no way to come together, no way to compromise,
and no one gets to run.

Pointed patterns wind around
each other, and faster and faster
poisoned darts fly up
from brave savage hands . . .

*1910*

## 13

Snow beehives grow slower,
window crystals turn transparent,
and a turquoise veil
lies carelessly across a chair:

A self-intoxicated fabric
pampered by caressing light,
knowing sensations of summer,
untouched by snow and cold—

And if the frost of eternity
flows in icy diamonds
this: contains the quick flickering
of blue-eyed transient dragon-flies.

1910

---

## 14
## Silentium

She's still unborn,
she's music, she's word, and so
she's the unbreakable link
among all living things.

The sea's breasts breathe slowly,
but the light is as bright as madness
and pale lilac foam
turns in a dull blue beaker.

May my lips find the
muteness of the First Day—
like a crystal note
pure from the beginning!

Aphrodité: be foam again.
Word, return to music
and you, heart merged with life's original way,
feel shame for all ordinary hearts.

                                        1910

---

## 15

The sail stretches its delicate ears,
staring eyes go empty
and a silent choir of midnight birds
sails over the soundlessness.

I'm as poor as nature
and as simple as the sky,
my freedom is as ghostly
as the singing of midnight birds.

I see a stagnant moon
and a sky deader than canvas:
oh emptiness, I accept
your morbid wild world!

                                        1910

---

## 16

The sea-guest blew in
like the shadow of sudden clouds
and, slipping by, rustled
along embarrassed shores.

A huge sail soars sternly;
the pale white wave

drops back—and again
she's afraid to touch the shore.

And a boat, rustling in the waves
like leaves . . .

                                                    1910

---

## 17

I grew out of a dark, vicious
swamp, rustling like a thin reed,
breathing a forbidden life
languidly, passionately, sweetly.

No one sees me
drooping into my cold, marshy home,
welcomed by the quick whispers
of autumnal time.

I like this cruelty, this insult,
and in this dream-like life
I envy everyone in secret,
I'm secretly in love with all of you.

                                                    1910

---

## 18

How clear, how dark the huge pond,
how white a languid window;
but my heart—why so slow,
so stubbornly heavier and heavier?

So heavy that it goes to the bottom,
wanting the fine sand,
and then like a straw, it escapes from deep, deep down,
floating easily up again.

Stand at the head of your bed, smile as if you meant it,
sing yourself to sleep, yourself, all your life—
lie in your melancholy, pretend the whole thing,
and speak softly, warmly to your proud boredom.

1910

## 19

Twilight smothers my bed,
my breath comes hard . . .
Perhaps what I really love
is a thin cross and a secret road.

1910

## 20

What slow-stepping horses,
what dark-lit lanterns!
Surely these strange people know
where they're leading me.

And I let them lead,
I'm cold, I want to sleep;
the road turned, I was thrown
toward approaching starlight.

My hot head swaying,
the tender ice of a foreign hand,

silhouettes of dark fir trees
I've never seen.

1911

## 21

A thin beam sows light
thin in a damp forest.
I carry sorrow, slow,
like a gray bird in my heart.

And the wounded bird?
The sky is silent, has died.
Someone has pulled the bells
out of the blurred tower,

And the sky stands
mute, deserted,
like the empty white tower
filled with silence and mist.

The endlessly tender morning,
half-awake, half-dream—
oblivion unquenched—
the foggy chiming of thoughts . . .

1911

## 22

The heavy air is damp, hollow;
it's good, there's nothing frightening in the forest.

Walking alone: a light cross
I carry without a murmur.

And censure goes soaring up,
like a wild duck, to indifferent Russia—
I live gloomily, but
loneliness isn't my fault!

A shot. Ducks' wings heavily
over the sleepy lake,
pine trunks stupefied
with doubly reflected life.

A strange sheen in the colorless sky,
misty world pain—
Oh let me be hazy too,
let me keep from loving you.

1911

---

23

A bad day,
the grasshoppers' chorus is asleep,
and the shadow of the dark cliffs
hangs gloomier than tombstones.

The ring of flying arrows,
the cry of prophetic crows . . .
I'm in a nightmare,
moment flashes after moment.

Pull away the edge of phenomena,
break the earth's cage,
let the fierce hymn burst out,
the brass crashing of rebel secrets!

Oh, the pendulum of souls swings
strict, stern, deaf, straight,

and fate knocks passionately
on our forbidden door . . .

							1911

## 24

A black wind whispers
with barely-breathing leaves
and a trembling swallow
draws a circle in the dark sky.

Twilight
and the fading beams
argue quietly in my loving
dying heart.

And a copper moon comes to stand
up over the darkening forest.
Why is there so little music
and so much silence?

							1911

## 25

Why is there so much song in my soul,
why are there so few good names,
why is spontaneous rhythm only an accident,
an unexpected wind from the north?

It will whirl up dust,
it will rattle all the paper leaves
and never come back—or else
come back completely changed.

Oh broad Orpheic wind,
you'll vanish into the seaworld
and, loving an uncreated world,
I forget that unneeded "I".

I wandered around and around, and in a toylike
thicket found an azure grotto . . .
Can I really be real,
can I really die some day?

1911

## 26
## Seashell

Night, maybe you don't need
me: I'm cast up on your shore,
out of the world abyss,
like a seashell without pearls.

You whip foam out of the waves,
indifferent; you sing because you sing;
but you'll learn to love, you'll learn to welcome
a superfluous seashell and its lies—

You'll lie near it, on the sand,
you'll wrap it in your cloak,
you'll tie the enormous bell of sea-swells
around and around it,

And you'll fill the fragile seashell,
like some dead heart's house,
with the whisper of foam,
with mist, and wind, and rain . . .

1911

## 27

Oh sky, sky, I'll dream of you!
You can't have gone all blind,
day can't have burned away, like a white page:
a whiff of smoke, a wisp of ash!

1911

## 28

I shiver, cold—
I want to be numb!
But gold dances in the sky:
I'm ordered to sing.

*Yearn, musician, worry, and*
*love, and remember, and weep,*
*and catch the feathery ball*
*tossed from a dim planet!*

So that's it—our real link
with the secret world!
What aching misery,
what horrible luck!

And what if the glittering star
hanging over that modish shop
stabs deep into my heart,
suddenly, like a long pin?

1912

## 29

I loathe the light
of the monotonous stars.
Greetings, O my ancient madness—
an arc-pointed tower!

Be lace, stone,
turn to spiderweb:
stab the sky's empty breast
with this thin needle.

I'll have my chance, too—
I can sense wings beating wide.
Yes: but where will the arrow
of living thought go flying?

Or else, path worn out, time
worn out, I'll come back:
there, I could not love.
Here, I'm afraid to love . . .

1912

---

## 30

I could not feel your image
in the fog, your shaky, painful image.
"Lord!"—I said
by mistake.

And like a huge bird
God's name flew out of my breast.
A thick fog swirls in front of me,
and behind me there's an empty cage.

1912

## 31

No, not the moon shining for me, but a bright
clock-face—and it is my fault
that I feel the milkiness of the feeble stars?

And Batyushkov's arrogance revolts me:
"What time is it?" they asked him,
and he answered, "Eternity."

1912

## 32
## Pedestrian

Mysterious mountains
bring me unconquerable fear;
flying swallows delight me;
I love bell-towers soaring high!

And like some ancient pedestrian
walking bending boards, across an abyss,
I hear snowballs growing
and eternity ticking in a stone clock.

If only, if only! That ancient traveller,
seen for a moment against faded leaves: no, not me.
Sorrow really sings, in me;

There's an avalanche, a real avalanche!
And my soul—it's all in those bells,
but music can't save me from the abyss!

1912

## 33
## Casino

I don't like to plan happiness;
sometimes nature can be a dull stain.
And just a little drunk, I'm intended
to live all the thin colors of a thin life.

A shaggy cloud, a wind pulling it,
an anchor slipping down to a seabed,
and hanging like limp canvas
my soul flaps over this damned abyss.

But I love the dune casino,
seeing wide out of a foggy window,
a thin ray on a wrinkled tablecloth,

And greenish water all around me,
and wine in crystal, like a rose—
and how I love to watch a swooping gull!

1912

---

## 34

Falling is how it feels to be afraid,
and fear is feeling empty.
Who rolls rocks down on us—
rocks that claim to be free?

Walking wooden like a monk
you measured cobblestones, once,
cobblestones and coarse, hard dreams—
full of hunger for death and the yearning of flung-out wings . . .

So damn the Gothic castle
if the ceiling fools you
and they're not burning cheerful logs!

Not many live for eternity—
but think about here, about now,
and it turns frightening, the walls won't hold!

1912

## 35
## Tsarskoe Selo

FOR GEORGY IVANOV

Tsarskoe Selo, let's go!
Where cavalry soldiers
smile from their stiff saddles,
free, stupid, and drunk . . .
Tsarskoe Selo, let's go!

Parks, and palaces, and barracks,
and cotton batting blowing down streets,
and when the prince shouts, "Hey, you fellows!"
they bellow out, by rote, "Your health, your health!"
Parks, and palaces, and barracks.

One-storied houses
where generals with one broken-record
idea waste away exhausted days
reading dull magazines and Dumas's dull books . . .
oh, great rich mansions—not just houses!

A steam-engine screams . . . here's the prince,
his people are in a glass pavilion!
Dragging his sword, cursing, combing
his hair, an officer comes out:
oh yes, it's the prince all right . . .

And then, she's going home—
yes, yes, to the kingdom of etiquette—

and everyone feels secret fear, seeing the coach
with what's left of a grey-haired maid of honor
who's going home . . .

1912

## 36
## Gold-Piece

All day long, damp autumn air
in my lungs, and pain, and noise, noise:
I want my supper, I've got gold
stars in my black purse!

The yellow fog makes me tremble
as I walk down into a little cellar:
I've never ever seen
such a restaurant, such people: rabble!

Clerks, bureaucrats, Japanese,
theorists of other people's money . . .
a man behind the counter
biting gold-pieces—everyone drunk.

"Change, please,"
I ask earnestly,
"but no paper money,
I can't stand three-ruble notes!"

What's this drunk mob to me?
My God, how did I get here?
Don't I have the right to ask:
"Change my gold, change it!"

1912

## 37
## The Lutheran

Walking near the Protestant chapel, Sunday,
I met a funeral.
My mind was somewhere else, I saw
their stern faces, their troubled faces.

Their German words did not register,
but the thin harnesses shone,
the holiday roadway was a dull mirror
for lazy horseshoes.

And in mobile darkness, in a slow-moving carriage,
there where sorrow had hidden (a silent
hypocrite, tearless, reluctant to say even
hello), I saw, quickly, a buttonhole for fall roses.

Like a black ribbon they dragged on,
tear-bleared ladies, foot after foot,
red-cheeked under their veils, and the stubborn
coachmen drove into the distance behind them, on and on.

Dead Lutheran, whoever you were,
they buried you simply, easily.
Their eyes were blurred, as they ought to be, with tears,
and bells rang, but not too loud.

And I thought: Who needs eloquence?
Are we prophets? or the fathers of prophets?
We're indifferent to heaven, not afraid of hell,
and in this never-shining noon we burn like candles.

1912

# 38
# The Church of Hagia Sophia, Constantinople

Saint Sophia, where God Himself
ordered men and kings to halt!
And your dome, an eye-witness said, hangs
from heaven by a chain.

And every age can study Justinian,
when Diana of Ephesus
let them steal a hundred
and seven green marble columns, for alien gods.

Your builder built with open hands
and exalted soul—but what was in his heart
when he set your porticoes and apses
pointing out to east and west?

A beautiful temple, bathing in peace,
forty windows each a triumph of light;
under the dome, the under-arches show
four archangels, the loveliest of all.

A wise, a round building
to outlive nations and time,
and the seraphim's hollow sobs
will never warp the dark gilt.

1912

---

# 39
# Notre Dame

Here a Roman judge judged people not Roman,
and here a cathedral, now; joyful and new-born

like Adam, once, splitting out nerves, the
delicate cross-vaulting flexes muscles, plays.

Outside, a secret plan, visible, now:
the saddle-girth arches hold in
the huge mass, hold up the walls,
and bold battering rams of vaults just stand, still.

Primordial labyrinth, inscrutable forest,
rational abyss of the gothic soul,
Egyptian power, Christian modesty,
and a thin reed—an oak, and everywhere a king—a steep slope.

Mighty Notre Dame, the more I study
your monster's ribs, the more
I think: someday I'll build beauty
out of an evil mass, I will, I too.

1912

## 40

Tense silence is too much—
souls' imperfections are vexing, after all!
And in the confusion someone says he performs
poetry and everyone leaps: please!

I should have known this invisible presence:
a nightmare man reading Ulalume.
Meaning is—vanity; the word—is noise,
since the sound is a seraphim's servant.

Edgar singing the House of Usher on a harp,
the madman sipped water, came to, turned silent.
I walked outside. Autumn silk whistled—
silk scarf tickling warm on my throat . . .

1912

## 41
## An Old Man

Dawn already, the seventh
hour and a siren singing.
Old man, you who resemble Verlaine:
now's your time!

A sly, a child-like green fire,
a tiny green fire, in his eyes;
a turkish shawl
around his neck.

He curses, mumbles
incoherent nonsense;
he wants Confession—
but first he wants to sin.

Maybe he's a soured laborer,
maybe he's a free-liver in deep trouble—
but his eye, blackened in night's bowels,
blooms like a rainbow.

And keeping the holy sabbath
he shambles along,
and pleasant disaster
looks out at every gate;

And home—swearing,
white with anger,
his inclement wife comes
to meet a drunken Socrates.

1913

# 42
# Petersburg Strophes

FOR N. GUMILEV

A snowstorm whirled over yellow
government buildings, and whirled on,
and the lawyer climbs back into the sleigh,
pulling his coat closed with a broad sweep.

Ships are wintering. In direct sun
thick cabin-glass lights up.
Monstrous, like a docked battleship,
Russia rests, heavily.

And over the Neva, half the world's embassies,
and the Admiralty towers, and the sun, and silence!
And the State's coarse purple, rough
like a hair-shirt, is thin, worn.

Thick discomfort presses down on a northern snob—
Onegin's ancient boredom;
out on Senate Square—a snowdrift,
bonfire smoke, faint cold of bayonets . . .

Skiffs ladle water, gulls
visit the hemp warehouse
where muzhiks straight off the opera stage
ramble, selling hot honey tea and rolls.

Cars fly in a line, into the fog;
a finicky, frugal pedestrian—
type of eccentric Evgeny—is ashamed of poverty,
breathes gasoline and curses at fate!

1913

## 43

*Hier stehe ich—ich kann nicht anders*

"Here I stand—I can do nothing else,"
no light will brighten the dark mountain,
and stocky Luther's blind spirit
soars up over Peter's dome.

                                                    1913

---

## 44

Easy living drives us insane.
Wine in the morning, to start with, and hangovers
at night. How hold onto useless pleasure,
oh drunken plague, your color, your glow?

Shaking hands: an agonizing rite,
and night kisses in the streets,
and rivers flow heavy
and lanterns burn like torches.

We wait for death like a fairy-tale wolf,
but the first to die, I'm afraid, oh
I'm afraid, will be him with an anxious red mouth
and bangs hanging down over his eyes.

                                            November 1913

---

## 45

. . . The courage of midnight girls
and crazy stars jumping wild,

and then a tramp hangs on you,
begging inn money.

Tell me: Who will dull my mind
with wine
if Peter in fact created reality,
the Bronze Horseman, and hard granite?

Signals from the fort: I hear them,
I notice how warm it is.
The cannon ball carried,
I guess, into the cellars.

And deeper than the delirium
of an inflamed skull
are stars, and sober talk,
and a west wind off the Neva.

1913

---

## 46
## Bach

Churchgoers, here, are children of dust,
boards instead of ikons,
and Bach's chalk marks
only the numbers of psalms.

What discord heard in wild
taverns, and in churches!
But O most sober-minded Bach,
you rejoice like Isaiah!

Playing chorales for your grandfather, exalted
squabbler, did you, really
did you try to prove
spirit was real?

What's music? Sixteenth notes,
polysyllabic shouts from an organ,
it's all your grumbling, only your grumbling,
O stiff-necked old man!

And up on his black pulpit
the Lutheran pastor
mixes his words
with yours, you angry speech-maker.

                                                    1913

## 47

In peaceful suburbs
gardeners rake snow with shovels;
I walk with bearded
muzhiks, a casual pedestrian.

Kerchieved women flash by,
crazy little mutts yelp,
and the red roses of samovars
burn in taverns and houses.

                                                    1913

## 48
## The Admiralty Tower

The northern capital, a poplar tree droops, dusty,
a transparent clock-dial tangled in leaves,
and through dark foliage a frigate, an acropolis
shines in the distance, brother to water, brother to sky.

An air-boat, a mast no one can touch,

a measure for Peter's heirs,
and his lesson: a demigod's whim is not beauty,
but the predatory eye of a carpenter, is.

Four elements united, rule us, are friendly,
but free man made the fifth.
This chaste-constructed ark: isn't the
superiority of space denied?

Capricious jellyfish cling, angry;
anchors rot, abandoned like ploughs—
and there, the three dimensions burst their bonds
and universal oceans open.

              1913

## 49

A band of thieves played dominoes
all night, in the tavern.
The waitress brought an omelette;
monks drank all the wine.

Chimeras argued, up on the tower:
which of them was a freak of nature.
In the morning a gray preacher
called people to buy, buy.

Dogs play in the market,
the moneychanger's lock clicks.
Everyone steals from eternity,
and eternity—is like sea-sand:

It dries and falls from a wagon—
there's never enough padding for the sacks,
so monks tell lies about the tavern,
angry at the way they slept!

              1913

## 50
## Silent Movie

The movie. Three benches.
Sentimental fever.
A rich woman, noblewoman,
helpless in a rival's schemes.

Love's escape, unrestrained,
purity, innocence!
She loved the navy lieutenant
like a brother, nobly.

And he, natural son of a count
with gray hair, wanders around in the desert—
that's how it starts, this low-romance
of a beautiful countess.

She wrings her hands
like a Spanish gypsy. Frenzied.
Farewell! Mad sounds
of a piano brought to ground.

But enough courage, still,
in her weak and trusting heart,
to steal State papers
for the enemy's General Staff.

And a monstrous engine
rushes down a chestnut lane,
and the film unwinds, the heart
beats harder, but more gaily.

A travelling dress, a suitcase,
a car, a coach, a carriage,
only afraid of pursuit,
drained by a dry mirage.

Bitter, bitter nonsense:
no goal worth the means!
He'll live off his father's estate,
she'll live in a prison for life!

1913

## 51
## Tennis

Rough country cottages
where organ-grinders loaf,
and a ball flies by itself,
like magic bait.

Someone—who?—has choked down passion,
wrapped himself in snow,
and plays Olympic duels
with a frisky girl.

Lyre-strings are cracked, too cracked and old:
an Englishman, forever young,
set strings on a golden racket
and tossed it into the world!

Performing the game-rite,
lightly armed
like a Greek soldier,
in love with his enemy!

May. Scraps of storm clouds.
Green non-life withers away.
Everything is cars. Horns.
The lilac smell of gasoline.

The gay sportsman sips
spring water from a dipper;
and the war goes on,
bare elbows flash!

1913

## 52
## The American Girl

American, female, twenty years
old, impelled to get to
Egypt, forgetting the *Titanic*'s counsel, where it sleeps
darker than a crypt, deep in the ocean.

Factory whistles sing, in America,
and red skyscraper chimneys
surrender their smoked lips
to cold clouds.

Ocean's daughter stands in the Louvre,
beautiful as a poplar;
like a squirrel she climbs
the Acropolis, to pound sugary marble.

She reads *Faust* in the train
and understands nothing
and regrets that Ludwig
no longer sits on his throne.

1913

## 53
## Dombey and Son

When I hear English spoken,
more piercing than whistles,
I see Oliver Twist
and piles of ledgers.

Ask Dickens
what London was, then:
Dombey's City office
and the yellow Thames.

Rain and tears. Dombey Junior
is a blond and delicate little
boy, the only one who never understands
the gay clerks' jokes.

Broken chairs in the office,
sums of shillings and pence;
like bees escaped from a beehive
ciphers swarm around the year.

And dirty lawyers sting,
there in the tobacco haze—
and like a sagging old rag
bankruptcy hangs in their noose.

Law stands at the enemy's side:
nothing can help!
His daughter sobs, hugging
checked trousers.

1913

## 54

The bread's poisoned, the air's drained.
How hard to bind up wounds!
Sold into Egypt, Joseph
was never more miserable!

Bedouins under starry skies
close their eyes and ride,
composing loose ballads
about days vaguely experienced.

Inspiration is easy:
one dropped a quiver in the sand,
another traded his horse—a mist
of events fades away,

And when it's honestly sung,
lungs and heart full, in the end
everything disappears—all there is
is space, and stars, and the singer!

    1913

---

## 55

Valkyries soar, violins sing.
The opera puffs heavily away.
Coachmen holding fat fur coats
wait for their masters on marble stairs.

Down slides the hermetic curtain;
one idiot claps and claps, in the balcony;
cabmen dance around bonfires.
"So-and-so's carriage!" They go. The end.

    1913

## 56

Let's talk about Rome—glorious city!
Firmly established by the victory of domes.
Here's the apostles' creed:
dust flies, rainbows hang.

On the Aventine hill they're waiting for the king, endlessly—
twelve holiday evenings—
and strict canonical moons
can't swerve the calendar.

An enormous moon up over the Forum
drops brown ashes on the
world, my head's uncovered—
oh, this cold Catholic haircut!

                                                                    1913

---

## 57
### 1913

No victory, no war!
Oh iron ones, how long
are we condemned
to preserve the Capitol?

Or has Roman Thor
—the popular anger—lied,
and that oratorical tribune's
sharp beak just rests, now?

Or is the sun's decrepit
carriage carrying only bricks,
and Rome's rusty keys dangling
in a premature child's hands?

                                                                     1914

## 58

. . . Oh the moon doesn't grow
even a single blade of grass;
all the moonmen
weave tiny baskets—
weave tiny baskets
out of straw.

It's always twilight, on the moon,
houses are tidy;
not houses, really—
pigeon-houses.
Blue houses—
marvelous dovecotes . . .

                                                           1914

---

## 58a
## [A Variant]

All that stuff about the moon,
don't believe that nonsense about the moon,
it's all a fairy-tale . . .

        Oh the moon doesn't grow
        even a single blade of grass,
        all the moonmen
        weave tiny blankets,
        weave tiny baskets
        out of straw.

        It's always twilight, on the moon,
        houses are tidy,
        not houses, really—
        pigeon-houses,

        blue houses,
        marvelous dovecotes.

        No roads, on the moon,
        benches everywhere.

        They water sand
        with a big watering-pot—
        every step is a little leap
        over three benches.

        On the moon, where I live,
        I've got blue fish,
        but they can't swim
        on the moon,
        there's no water on the moon
        and fish fly . . .

1914/1927 *

\* A variant of No. 58, subsequently revised by Mandelstam in 1927.

---

# 59
# Akhmatova

With a half-turn, oh sorrow,
you note the indifferent.
The imitation classical shawl turned to stone
falling off a shoulder.

Ominous voice—bitter rhapsody—
soul unchaining the womb:
like Rachel, once, standing
an indignant Phaedra.

1914

## 60

Hooves repeating, over and over,
simple times, rough times.
Wrapped in heavy fur-coats, yardmen
sleep on wooden benches.

A knock on iron gates, and
royal-lazy, the doorman
climbs up, and his savage dog-yawn
makes me think of Scythians!

Like Ovid, his love turning
stale, blending Rome and snow in his songs,
singing ox carts
in the barbarians' plodding lines.

1914

---

## 61

Running out into the *piazza* the column
of columns made a half-circle, and was free—
and the Lord's temple sprawled
like a gossamer garden spider.

So the architect was no Italian,
but a Russian in Rome: So?
You walk through the grove of porticoes
like a foreigner, always the same,

And the small-bodied temple
is a hundred times livelier
than some giant pressed, like a cliff,
helplessly into the ground!

1914

## 62

Orioles sing in trees, and metrical
verse is measured in vowels.
Once a year Nature has quantity
too, like Homer's lines.

A day, that day, cavernous like a caesura:
peaceful, sluggish; ox at the grass,
air too heavy to be blown through a reed
for as long as a single full note.

1914

## 63

"Ice cream, ice cream!" Sun. Sponge cake,
airy. Clear glass, ice-water.
Daydreams flying to the milky Alps,
to a world of chocolate, where rose-dawns break.

But once the tiny spoon rings on glass, how sweet
to sit in the cramped summerhouse, surrounded by dusty acacias,
to take delicate edibles in intricate little cups
from the hands of the Graces of rolls-and-buns . . .

Then, then comes the sweetheart of street-organs, the roving refrigerator
with its many-colored box,
and the urchin stares, greedy,
at all the frozen wonders,

And even the gods can't tell what he'll take:
a diamond cream? a wafer filled with jam?
But the thin ice quickly melts,
glittering, in the sun—oh the divine ice.

1914

## 64

Values stride across centuries of dull
mistakes, immovable, fixed.
Writers of exalted poems
are flattened with distaste, but it's wrong, it's wrong.

Pitiful Sumarokov
babbled as the script required, and
then, like a prophet's royal staff,
solemn pain blossomed, here, for us.

What can you do in a theater of half-words,
half-masks, heroes and kings?
Ozerov's appearance
is the last ray of tragic dawn, for me.

1914

---

## 65

Nature is Rome, too, is reflected, now, in Rome.
We see its secular power
in transparent air, like a light-blue circus,
in the forum of fields, in the colonnade of groves.

Nature is Rome, too, and again, well, why
should we bother the gods, if we don't really have to?
We have animals' smoking guts, to predict battles,
we have slaves to preserve silence, and rocks to heap into buildings!

1914

## 66

Let all the flowering city-names
stroke the ear with their tiny, brief importance.
It's not Rome, as a city, that lasts forever,
but man's place in the universe.

Kings try to take it,
priests use it as an argument for war,
and without it houses, and altars,
are contemptible rubble, pitiful, wretched.

1914

## 67

I've never heard Ossian's tales, or
tasted ancient wine—
Why do I think I see Scotland's
bloody moon, and a forest clearing?

And hear, or seem to hear, crows and harps
shouting back and forth, in an ominous silence,
and soldiers' plaid scarves fluttering
in the wind, flashing by in moonlight!

A lovely inheritance:
other singers' wandering dreams.
It's easy to hate our own dull
neighborhood, our own dull people.

And how many treasures will bypass
grandsons, descend to great grandsons, maybe,
and again some poet will put together
someone else's song, and call it his own.

1914

## 68
## Europe

The sea tossed up the last continent
like a starfish or a Mediterranean crab.
Grown used to broad Asia, to America,
the ocean grows feeble, lapping at Europe.

Her live shores, jagged;
her airy peninsula-carvings;
those faintly feminine bays,
Genoa's lazy arc, Biscay.

Conquerors' land, age-old;
rags and tatters of the Holy Alliance;
Spain's heel, Italy's medusa,
and tender, kingless Poland.

The caesars' Europe! And since Metternich
aimed his goose-quill at Bonaparte—
now, as not in a century, now as I watch
your mysterious map slides, shifts!

                                    1914

---

## 69
## The Staff

My staff, my freedom,
center of my being:
Will my truth be the people's
truth, now, soon?

Until I found myself
I never bowed to the earth;
I smiled, took my staff
and went all the way to Rome.

Snow on rich black fields
may never melt, but
my people's sadness, here in my house,
is as foreign as ever, to me.

The burning sun of truth
will melt snow from cliffs.
They're right to trust me with the staff,
my people, for I have seen Rome!

                                                    1914

---

## 70
## 1914

The Greeks gathered, planning war
on the lovely island of Salamis,
torn away by enemy hands but visible
from Athens harbor.

And friendly islanders
fit out our ships.
The English never loved this sweet
European land, never!

Oh Europe, Hellas reborn,
keep the Acropolis safe, save Piraeus!
We need no gifts from this island—
a forest of ships, all unwanted!

                                                    1914

# 71
# On Pope Benedict XV's Encyclical

There is a freedom
inhabited by spirit—the fate of the best.
The Roman priest survives, eagle-
eyed and with ears wonderfully tuned.

The dove never trembles
at Churchly thunder.
Apostolic harmony: *Roma!*
Hearts open in smiles.

Under heaven's eternal dome
I say this name
again—though he who told me of Rome
has vanished in sacred dusk.

September 1914

---

# 72
# Ode to Beethoven

A heart so harsh that sometimes,
love it or not, leave it alone!
And in deaf Beethoven's dark room
a fire burns.
Tormentor, I could not understand
your violent happiness.
And now the performer discards
an incinerated notebook.

[When thunder hums on the earth,
and a stormy river roars
louder than thunder, louder than wind-toppled trees,] *
who's walking there, soized gloriously?
Walking so quick, so rash,
green hat in hand,

[the wind lifting
the skirt of his clumsy coat.] †

With whom drink fuller, drink deeper
of the cup of tenderness?
Who burns brighter,
sanctifying the struggle of will?
What Flemish peasant-son
invited the world to *ritornelle*
and never let the dance be over
till all the wild drunkenness was out?

Oh Dionysos, naive as a husband,
grateful as a child!
Fate came to you marvelously and you endured
indignant, or you joked!
What lonely anger went with you
when you permitted princes to buy off
genius, when you wandered, half seeing,
to some pointless piano lesson.

For you, a monk's cell—
where universal happiness can hide;
for you, the prophetic joy
of fireworshippers' songs;
fire blazes in man,
no one has ever quenched it.
Oh unknown god, the Greeks never dared
name you, but they worshipped!

Flame of majestic sacrifice!
Half the sky is burning,
the Tsar's royal-silk temple
shreds over our heads.
And in this fire, where we
see nothing,
you stood in the throne room
and pointed to the triumph of pure-white glory!

1914

\* † Lines in brackets were omitted in later printings.

## 73

Fire burns
my dry life
and I sing, now,
no stones, but trees.

Light, coarse:
all of a piece,
oak-cores,
fishermen's oars.

Hammer in the posts,
hammer, hammers,
banging the drum for this wooden heaven
where everything is light, light.

1914

## 74
## The Abbot

Oh fellow-traveller of the eternal novel,
Flaubert's abbot, Zola's:
red cassock, round
hat-brim against noon heat;
walking by, still,
in midday mist, along the unploughed edges,
dragging the dregs of Roman power
through ripe fields of rye.

Silent, decent,
he needs to eat, to drink
with us but hide the radiance
of his shining head in worldly stances.
As he drops asleep
on his featherbed he reads Cicero:

birds prayed, in their own Latin, like that,
in the old days.

I bowed, he replied
with a small, civil nod,
and then in conversation observed
"You'll die a Catholic!"
Then he sighed, "How hot it is, today!"
And tired from talking
he walked toward the park and the great chestnut trees
and the castle where he regularly lunched.

1914

## 75

There's still a marvelous tree
blowing on Mount Athos,
singing God's name
on the steep green slope.

The *muzhiks*-of-God's-own-name
rejoice in every cell:
the Word—is pure joy, is the
healing of all anguish!

Monks are scolded
loudly, all over the country,
but there's no need for us to save ourselves
from beautiful heresy.

Every time we love
we fall again.
We destroy some nameless One
and the name of Love, together.

1915

## 76

From Tuesday to Saturday
a desert stretches.
Oh drawn-out transmigrations!
Four thousand miles—a single arrow.

And swallows, too, flying
the ocean to Egypt,
hung four days,
not scooping water with their wings.

1915

## 77

How sweet to stare at a candle
and dream an imaginary freedom.
"First stay with me,"
Good Faith cried in the night,

"I'll crown you with my
crown, that's all,
so you can bow
to Freedom, as to Law, loving . . ."

"I'm married to Freedom,
and to Law, and so
I'll never lift off
this featherweight crown."

Us? Us? Doomed,
abandoned: are we
to die regretting the firm beauty
of Good Faith?

1915

## 78

Insomnia. Homer. Sails stretched taut.
A flock of ships, and I've counted
half its length: cranes
that floated over Greece.

A wedge of cranes in the distance—
crowned heads covered with god-foam—
sailing where? Without Helen
would you think of Troy, oh Greeks?

Homer. The sea. Love moves everything.
Can I listen? Not Homer, now;
he is still. And the black sea shouts
near my pillow, crashes and roars.

1915

## 79

Old women sheep, black Chaldeans,
hell-fiends in hoods of darkness,
retreat into the hills with their grudge,
like plebeians angry with Rome.

Thousands of them—shifting
hairy knees like wooden poles,
shaking, running in curls of foam
like balls in some immense gambler's wheel.

Needing a king, and their own black plateau,
the seven-hilled Rome of sheep,
and dogs barking, and bonfires sparking,
and bitter house-smoke, barn-smoke.

And bushes march at them, like a wall,
and soldiers' tents run, run,

a holy rout.
Fleece hangs like a heavy wave.

                                                    1915

---

## 80

Horses graze, neighing happily,
and the valley takes on a Roman rust;
time's transparent rapids sweep away
the dry gold of a classical spring.

I'll think of Caesar's fine features,
this autumn, trampling oak leaves
thick on deserted paths—
that feminine face, that crafty little nose-hook!

Here, far from Capitol and Forum,
where Nature withers, peaceful,
I hear Augustus' name and, on the world's edge,
hear years rolling like a majestic apple.

Let sorrow be lucid, in my old age:
I was born in Rome, Rome is mine again.
Cheerful old Autumn was my she-wolf
and Caesar's month, August, smiled at me.

                                                    1915

---

## 81

I'll never see the famous *Phèdre*
in the ancient high-tiered theater,
in the smoky gallery,

by guttering candle-light.
Indifferent to actors' fussing bustle,
garnering a harvest of applause,
I'll never hear the operatic verse,
double feminine-rhymed, aimed at footlights:

How I hate these shawls . . .

Racine's theatre! A powerful curtain
hangs across that other world,
hangs between it and us,
wrinkled, ruffling, heavy.
Classic shawls slip from shoulders,
pain-melted voices turn strong
and syllables hot with indignation
mould the right mournful stamp.

A festival of Racine, and I was late!

Dusty playbills rustle again,
and faint smells of orange peel,
and like a voice from a hundred-year lethargy
my neighbor says:
"Melpomené's tragic madness has drained me,
all I want is peace.
Shall we leave, before this jackal-audience
rips the Muse to bits?"

If the Greeks could see our plays . . .

1915

*Tristia* (1922)

## 82
## Theseus, Hippolytus, and Phaedra

—Oh these lace-rich shawls, this dress,
everything gnaws at my disgrace!

   —Stony Troezen town
   will see a famous disaster,
   the king's royal stairway
   will turn red with shame,

   .  .  .  .  .  .

   .  .  .  .  .  .

   and a black dawn will rise
   for a mother in love . . .

—If I could hate, oh if I could hate—
but—my lips confessed almost by themselves.

   —In the white noon Phaedra
   burns black.
   Funeral torches smoke
   in full daylight.
   Your mother, Hippolytus: fear her.
   Phaedra is the night is watching you
   here in full daylight.

—I stained the sun with black love,
[death will cool my love, with this pure phial.] *

   —We're afraid: who would dare
   to help Theseus in his pain?
   He stung the night
   and night attacked him.
   But we take corpses into the house
   and sing a funeral song
   and we will calm the sun
   that is black with wild, with sleepless passion.

1916

* The line in brackets was omitted when first published.

## 83
## Menagerie

This raped moment in time begins
with a disowned word, "peace."
Lamps burn in caves
and in mountain countries the air—is ether,
which we did not know how to breathe,
which we did not want to breathe.
Reed-pipes sing, once more,
in their goat voices.

Once the ox and the lamb
grazed in ripe pastures
and eagles perched, friendly,
on the shoulders of lazy cliffs—
and Germans tamed eagles,
and lions bowed to Britons,
and a rooster's comb shaped
the French crest.

But now savages have stolen
Herakles' holy club,
and the ungrateful black earth is dry,
as once long ago.
I'll kindle fire
with a wooden stick,
and the wild beasts I've wakened
will vanish in the hollow night!

Rooster, and lion, and dark-brown
eagle, and friendly bear:
we'll build a cage for war,
we'll treat the beasts well,
but I'll sing time's wine—
the fountain of Italy's words—
and I'll sing Russian flax, and German
flax, in their ancient Aryan cradle.

Italy: are you too lazy
to bother Rome's chariots?

You flew over the fence
when that tame bird cackled.
But neighbor, you too, be calm, please:
the eagle's in a foul mood.
A big rock like that
may not fit your sling.

And with the animals locked
in their menagerie, we'll rest, and rest,
and the Volga will deepen,
and the Rhine will grow brighter,
and men, wise with experience,
will regularly honor strangers
like demigods, honor them with loud dancing
on the shores of great rivers.

January 1916

---

# 84

The polyphonic chord of girls' voices
sings differently, in every loving
church—and in the Uspensky's stone arches
I see something like eyebrows, bent high.

And wonderfully high, on a rampart
held up by archangels, I watched the city;
from inside its walls I felt eaten away
by grief for a Russian name and for Russian beauty.

How strange that we dream of a garden
where pigeons soar in the dark, hot blue,
and a nun sings ancient Slavic chants,
and this tender Cathedral is in Moscow, but is Florence.

And Moscow's five-domed cathedrals,
Russian-souled, Italian-souled,

make me think of Eos, Goddess of Dawn,
but with a Russian name, and wearing a fur-coat.

                                                    1916

---

# 85

We were driving down from Sparrow
Hills to the familiar little church, driving
through enormous Moscow on a low sleigh
piled thin with a fatal straw.

And children play knucklebones, in Uglich,
and there's the smell of baking bread,
I'm not wearing a hat, here on these streets, they're
driving me to the chapel where three candles glitter.

Not three candles, but three meetings—
God Himself blessed one.
Never a fourth, no, and Rome is far off—
and He never loved Rome.

The sleigh fell into black pits, into black bumps,
people came home from a celebration.
Thin *muzhiks,* vicious peasant women,
shifting from foot to foot, in front of the gates.

Black, in the distance, with flocks of birds.
My roped-together hands are numb.
I'm the Tsar's son, I'm growing numb, and
they're burning the red straw.

                                                    1916

## 86
## A Last Straw

1

Little straw, lying awake in your enormous bed
and waiting for the ceiling to slide down,
the exalted ceiling, the pompous ceiling, to fall
calm, ponderous—oh how sad—on your delicate eyelids,

Oh ringing, oh dry little straw, you've soaked up
death and become still more loving,
my sweet little dead straw, you've snapped—
not Salomé in the raw, just a tiny dead straw.

Sleeplessness makes things heavier,
the silence is too intense, things concentrate,
pillows shine barely white in the mirror,
a round whirlpool reflects the bed.

No, not my little straw, in solemn satin,
in that huge room over the black Neva;
there are twelve moons singing the hour of death,
pale-blue ice streams in the air.

Mighty, magnificent December blows its breath,
as if the ponderous Neva flowed in the room.
No, not my straw—it's Ligeia, dying—
Oh beatific words, I've learned, I know you, now.


2

Blessèd words, I've learned, I know you, now—
Lenore, Straw, Ligeia, Seraphita.
Ponderous Neva flowing in the room,
light-blue blood running out of granite.

Mighty, magnificent December gleams over the Neva.
There are twelve moons singing the hour of death.

No, not my little straw, in solemn satin,
tasting a slow agony of peace.

December's Ligeia runs in my blood,
she whose belovèd sleeps in a tomb,
but that straw, maybe old Salomé,
she's dead of pity, and she'll stay dead.

            1916

## 87

"My lovely cameo, I lost it
somewhere along the Neva, who knows
where. I miss that beautiful Roman
lady," you told me, half crying.

My beautiful Georgian lady, why
ruffle dust on a holy tomb?
Another fluffy snowflake
melts on an eyelash fan.

You bent your gentle neck.
No more cameo; no more Roman lady, alas!
I pity that dark-skinned Tinotina,
girlish Rome on the Neva's shores . . .

            1916

## 88

I'm cold. Transparent spring
dresses Petropolis in green fuzz, but
like jellyfish the Neva's waves

make me vaguely sick.
Along the northern shore
fire-fly cars go running,
steel beetles and dragonflies,
golden star-needles, twinkling—
but no star can ever kill
the sea-wave's heavy emerald.

                                                            1916

---

## 89

We'll die in transparent Petropolis,
where Proserpina is queen.
Every sigh sucks in death's air,
every hour is our hour to die.
Sea-goddess, terrible Athena,
put away your great stone helmet.
We'll die in transparent Petropolis,
where Proserpina is queen, not you.

                                                            1916

---

## 90

No believers in the resurrection
we walked in the graveyard.
—This ground, this reminds me, you know,
of those hills, look

. . . . .

. . . . .

where Russia ends, snap, like so,
just above a hollow black sea.

A broad meadow runs down from
the cloister slope.
I really didn't want to go south,
away from the open spaces,
but how could I stay
in a dark forsaken wooden village
with such a wispy nun—
trouble, trouble there, for sure.

I kiss her tanned elbow
and one white bit of forehead.
I know where it's white, under
the heavy gold hair.
I kiss her hand, where a single white stripe
still shows, because she wore a bracelet.
Flaming summertime
makes these miracles.

How quickly you turned nicely brown
and came to your poor Saviour,
you kissed and kissed and kissed—
but in Moscow you were proud.
For us, then, only the name remains—
a wonderful sound, it will last us a while.
Go on, take the sand
I'm pouring from hand to hand.

1916

---

91

Nothing can be done for this night
but it's still day where you are.
A black sun rises
at Jerusalem's gates.

A yellow sun is worse, worse—
oh hushaby, hushaby—

Jews were burying my mother
in a bright temple.

Jews without grace,
Jews without priests,
saying their service over her ashes
in a bright temple.

And Jewish voices
rang across her body.
I woke in my cradle,
lit by the glow of a black sun.

                                                            1916

---

## 92

Golden honey ran so slow, out of the
bottle, ran so long, that the waitress could tell us:
"Here in miserable Taurida, where fate has brought us
all, we're never bored." She looked over her shoulder.

They serve Bacchus everywhere, as if the world
were all watchmen and dogs. Walk, you'll see no one.
Days roll like heavy barrels:
voices deep in the hut—you don't understand, you don't answer.

We walked in a huge brown garden, after tea.
Dark blinds like eyelashes drop on windows.
We strolled past white columns, to see the grapes,
where airy glass runs down sleepy hills.

I said: Vines live like ancient battles
where curl-headed horsemen fight curl-ordered wars.
Stony Taurida has learned Greece's lesson—
and here are the noble, rusted acres, in rows.

Well, silence sits in the white room like a spinning wheel.
A vinegar smell, a paint smell, and fresh wine from the cellar.

The Greek house, remember: the woman everyone loved—
not Helen—the other one—who spun and wove, on and on?

Oh golden fleece, golden fleece, where are you?
All voyage long the heavy sea-waves boomed,
and then, leaving his ship, all sea-worn, canvas-stretched,
Odysseus came home, full of space and time.

1917

---

## 93

The asphodels' transparent
grey spring is a long way off.
Sand is rustling, really,
waves are breaking white.
But here, like Persephoné, my soul
enters the sphere of no-weight
and there are no beautiful tanned
arms in the kingdom of the dead.

Why trust a boat
with a funeral urn's weight,
why make holidays of black roses
over amethyst water?
My soul pulls there,
past Meganom's misty cape,
where the black sail will come
from, after the funeral!

Quick black clouds run by,
unlit,
and under this windy moon
flocks of black roses go flying.
And behind the cypress-stern
the bird of death and mourning-tears
drags itself,
a huge flag of memory.

And the fan of buried years
opens, rustling, toward the amulet,
where, once, with a dark shuddering,
it buried itself in the sand:
my soul pulls there,
past Meganom's misty cape,
where the black sail will sail
from, after the funeral!

1917

## 94
## The Decembrist

"Consider the pagan senate:
causes never die!"
He pulled on his Turkish pipe, wound himself
into his robe; next to him they sat playing chess.

He traded an ambitious dream
for a hut in wild Siberia,
and that *chic* pipe at his poisonous lips—lips that
told the sad truth.

German oaks rattled—the first time;
Europe wept in its traps.
Black chariots reared up,
racing triumphant curves.

Blue punch burned in glasses, once.
The broad burble of a samovar
blended with the soft voice
of its Rhine sweetheart, the freedom-fond guitar.

"Sweet liberty rouses citizens'
voices, living voices!"
But blind heaven wants no sacrifice:
work and good faith work better.

It's all confused. Who should be told
that it's all mixed up, it's growing cold,
and anyway it's good to keep saying
Russia . . . Lethe . . . Lorelei.

1917

---

# 95
# To Cassandra

Time blossomed and I did not reach for
your lips, Cassandra, your eyes, Cassandra,
but in December—oh what a solemn vigil
—memory torments us!

In December of 1917
we lost everything, and love too:
this one robbed himself,
that one was robbed by the people . . .

But if life is a necessary madness,
and a masted forest is tall homes—then
run, armless victory,
icy plague!

A square, and armored cars, and
I see a man, frightening
wolves with burning logs:
Freedom, Equality, Order!

Cassandra, sweet-singing Cassandra,
you're moaning, burning—Why
did Alexander's sun hang, a hundred years ago,
shining on everyone?

In that crazy capital on the Neva,
some Scythian holiday,

some sickening loud ball,
they'll rip the kerchief off that lovely head . . .

December 1917

---

## 96

The organ's high-arched forest never droned,
that night. They sang us Schubert—their own
cradle. The windmill hummed, and in the hurricane
songs blue-eyed drunken music laughed.

The world of old songs—maybe brown, maybe green,
but eternally young, a world where the forest king's
reckless fury shakes roaring
crowns on nightingale lime-trees.

And that song, wild like black wine, terrible,
is what the night sings:
a *doppelgänger,* a hollow ghost, an imitation
staring, stupidly, through a cold window!

1917

---

## 97

The way you speak is miraculous,
like the hot whistling of vultures.
Or should I say: the bright sense
of silken summer lightning?

"What? What?"—A heavy head.
"Uh? Uh?"—I'm calling you!

And somewhere, distant, faintly:
I live on this earth, too.

They can say: Love flies, but
Death has a hundred hundred more wings;
the soul fights on,
our lips fly to her.

And there's so much air, so much silk
and wind in your whisper,
and like blind men in the long night
we drink a sunless brew.

1917

## 98

Grasshopper clock, singing,
fever rustling,
dry stove, stirring?
Red silk burning.

Mice gnawing at life's
thin foundation,
a swallow, and my daughter, too,
who's untied my little canoe.

Rain mumbling on the roof?
Black silk burning—
But the cherry tree will hear and
down under the sea: Goodbye.

Because death is innocent
and nothing can be done,
in nightingale fevers
the heart stays warm.

1917

## 99

When we slowly go mad,
out on streets, in quiet cells,
cruel winter will give us
some iced, some pure Rhine-wine.

Hard frost offering us
Valhalla's white wine in a silver
bucket, and we remember
the bright image of northern man.

But northern poets are rough,
they never play, or laugh,
and northern soldiers relish
amber, and fires, and feasts.

Southern air, the magic of alien
skies, haunts their dreams, only their dreams
—But stubborn women
say no, won't go.

1917

## 100

FOR A. V. KARTASHEV

A young Levite on morning watch
he stood with the priests, and stayed.
Judaic night thickened over him
and in the darkness they built the ruined temple, and wept.

He said: Heaven's yellow is uneasy.
It's night on the Euphrates: priests, run!
And the elders thought: Whose fault is it? Not ours.
This yellow-black light is Israel's joy.

He stood with us on the shore when we swaddled
the Sabbath in holy flax and holding high
a heavy seven-candled torch, lit
Jerusalem's night and the children of non-existence.

*1917*

---

101

A light drifting terribly high,
glittering brighter than a star:
Oh transparent star, drifting light,
your brother, Petropolis, is dying.

At that terrible height earth-dreams
burn, and a green star glitters.
Oh star, if sky and water are your brothers,
your brother, Petropolis, is dying.

At that terrible height a monstrous ship
spreads huge wings, and flies—
Oh green star, your ruined and beautiful
brother, Petropolis, is dying.

Transparent Spring cracks, above the black Neva,
And immortality melts, melts.
Oh star, if you are Petropolis,
your brother, Petropolis, is dying.

*1918*

---

102

When Moscow's feverish forum dies
into silence, in the dark night,

and theaters' wide yawns
empty crowds in the streets,

An exuberant night funeral
flows down shining boulevards,
gloomy-gay mobs poured
from some divine depth.

The rabble, excited by the games,
comes burying its night-time sun,
comes home from midnight feasts
to the hollow beating of hooves.

And Herculaneum, buried by Vesuvius, rises
again, a sleeping city in the moonglow,
hovels and huts in the market,
mighty doric columns.

                                                1918

---

## 103
## Freedom's Twilight

Glorify, brothers, freedom's twilight—
the great crepuscular year.
A massive forest of traps
dropped in the boiling waters of the night.
Oh sun, judge, people, you rise
out of hollow god-forsaken years.

Glorify the terrible burden
our Leader assumes, with tears.
Glorify the dark burden of power,
its unbearable weight.
Anyone with a heart can hear
Time's ship sinking. Anyone. Can. Must.

We've tied flocks of swallows
into fighting legions—they've blocked
the sun. Nature twitters,

chirps, stirs, still alive.
The sun is invisible, through dense twilight,
through the traps, and the earth is sailing.

Okay, let's try: a huge clumsy
creaking swing of the rudder.
The earth is swimming. Courage, men!
Cutting the ocean as if we were plowing, even
in Lethe's cold hard frost we'll remember
how earth was worth ten heavens, to us.

                                                       Moscow, May 1918

---

## 104
## Tristia

In night's bare-headed laments
I've learned the science of farewells.
Oxen chew, you wait, you wait,
the city's last hour of watching, waiting,
and I honor the ritual of a rooster night
when tear-red eyes stared at the distance
and took up a load of portable sorrow,
and a woman's weeping mixed with the Muses' songs.

Who can know, when farewells are spoken,
what separation will bring us,
what cock-crows promise,
when fires burn in the city,
or why, at the dawn of some new life,
an ox chews lazily in the hall
and a rooster, herald of new lives,
flaps his wings on the city wall?

I like this routine of spinning:
shuttle scurries, spindle hums,
look, like swansdown, coming to meet you,
a barefooted Delia, running.

Oh the thin, thin foundation of existence,
the poverty-struck language of joy!
Everything's been told before, everything will happen again,
and all that's sweet is the instant of recognition.

So be it: a tiny transparent figure
lies in a clean clay dish,
stretched like a squirrel skin,
and a girl stares, bending over the wax.
Telling fortunes about Greek Erebus: not for us.
Wax is to women as bronze to a man.
Battles work out our fate, only battles,
but they can die, if they want to, while casting fortunes.

1918

## 105

On a rocky spur of Olympus
the Muses led the first round dance
so the blind peasant poets, swarming like bees,
would give us ionic honey.
And a tall cold breeze blew
from a girl's high forehead
so our distant grandchildren's grandchildren could see
Greece's tender coffins.

Spring runs through the meadows of Hellas,
Sappho is wearing her gay-colored boots,
and cicadas bang tiny hammers, forging
a gossamer ring.
A strong carpenter built a tall house,
hens have been throttled for the wedding,
the clumsy cobbler
stretched five ox-hides, for shoes.

The turtle-lyre moves slowly,
a heavy slow toeless crawl,

lying free in sunny Epirus,
warming its golden belly, quiet.
Well, who wants to pet *her,*
turn her over as she sleeps?
Is she dreaming of Terpander?
Sensing swooping dry fingers?

Oaks drink from cold lily-glasses,
bareheaded grass hums,
blue-flowers blossom and wasps laugh.
Oh sacred islands, where are you,
islands where bread's not broken,
where there's only honey, and wine, and milk,
where no creaking labor shadows the sky,
where wheels are light, and easy to turn.

1919

## 106

What steepness in a crystal pool!
Siennese mountains intercede for us,
prickly, insane cliff-cathedrals
hanging in mid-air, in wool, in silence.

Down the hanging ladder of prophets and kings
comes an organ, fortress of the Holy Spirit,
sheepdogs' brisk barking and decent fierceness,
shepherds' sheepskins, judges' staffs.

That's the earth, immobile, and she and I drink
Christianity's cold mountain air,
steep Credo, psalm-singer's quick break,
rags and keys of apostolic churches.

What cable could carry
crystal high notes, in this fortified ether?

Like the song of Palestine, from the wonder-struck
empty spaces of these Christian hills, grace descends.

>                                              1919

---

## 107

Oh the air, drunk with sedition,
here in the Kremlin's black square!
Mutineers rocking a shaky peace,
poplars anxiously reeking.

Old wax faces, in cathedrals,
dense forest of bells;
perhaps a tongueless robber
climbed into stone rafters.

And in sealed-up cathedrals
it's cool, it's dark,
the way Russian wine
plays in delicate clay casks.

The Uspensky, wonderfully rounded,
amazement of the arcs of paradise,
and the green Blagoveschensky
that seems ready to coo like a dove.

And the Archángelsky, and the Cathedral of the Resurrection,
translucent as your palm—
hidden enthusiasm burning everywhere,
secret fire in stone pitchers . . .

>                                         1919/1920

## 108

Heaviness and Tenderness, sisters, marked
the same. Bees and wasps suck heavy roses.
Man dies, warm sand cools, and yesterday's
sun is carried off on a black stretcher.

Oh heavy honeycombs, tender nets,
lifting a rock is easier than saying your name!
The only problem left in my world:
a golden problem: getting rid of time's load.

I drink turbid air like dark water.
Time is plowed up, roses are dirt.
Tender heavy roses go round in a slow whirlpool
and turn to double wreaths, heavy, tender.

*Koktebel, March 1920*

---

## 109

Leah, back where you came from,
back to that blending bosom,
because you wanted yellow twilight,
not Ilium's gold sun.

No one will stop you, go
to your Father, in the obscure, toneless night,
go and let an incestuous
daughter droop her head on his breast.

But a fateful change
works in you, will happen in you:
you will be Leah—not Helen—
not because in your blood

Royal blood streams heavier
than any other—

No, you'll love a Jew and vanish
in him—and that, my dear, will be that.

                                                                1920

---

## 110

Venice's barren gloomy life
is perfectly clear. I see it
staring in its faintly blue mirror, its cracked
blue mirror, with a cold blue smile.

Delicate air-skin. Fine. Blue veins, visible.
White snow. Green brocade.
Everyone on a cypress stretcher, extracted,
sleepy, out of warm cloaks.

And candles burn, burn, in baskets,
As if a pigeon had entered the ark.
On the battlefield a man is dying,
In the useless political meeting a man is dying.

Love and fear are inexorable,
Saturn's ring is heavier than platinum!
An executioner's block hung with black velvet,
a beautiful face.

Heavy Venetian drapery,
mirrors in cypress frames.
Cut-glass air. Mountains of cracked blue
glass melt in bedrooms.

But a rose in my hand, a tiny bottle—
oh green Adriatic, forgive me!
Then why so silent, my Venetian lady? Tell me
an escape from this holiday death!

A black Vesper gleams in the mirror.
It all goes by. Truth is dark.

A man's born. A pearl dies.
And Susanna can only wait for the elders.

1920

## III
# Theodosia

High hills all around you
you run down the mountain like a herd of sheep,
sparkling in dry transparent air
with rose-pink-white stones.
Turkish flags burn in port, like poppies,
bandits' sailboats rock,
thin reed masts, crystal wave-muscles,
and tiny rowboats on ropes.

Everyone sings the Apple Song, cries the
Apple Song, high and low, morning and night.
Wind blows off the golden seeds—
vanished—forever.
But in little alleys, at twilight, crude
musicians scrape and saw, bending
to their work, clustered in little bands,
unwinding unbelievable variations.

Oh tiny hook-nosed nomads!
Oh gay Mediterranean zoo!
Turks in towels, strutting
like roosters at little hotels.
Dogs in paddy-wagons,
dust drifting down streets,
and deep in the Furies of the marketplace
the huge battleship cook, cool, calm.

They have science, where we're going, science
in abundance, and craftsmen of *shaslik*, artisans of mutton pastry;
a tailor's signboard
tells us what Man is.

A man's long coat—an urge without a head,
a barber's flying violin
and the hypnotic iron of heavenly
washerwomen—a smile, heavy, hard.

Aging girls with bangs
consider odd clothes,
admirals in stiff cocked hats
remember Scheherezade and her dream.
Transparent distance. Some grapes.
And always, always a fresh wind.
Smyrna's not far, Baghdad's not far,
but it's a hard voyage and the stars are all the same, everywhere.

1920

## 112

When Psyché visits the shadows, in that half-
transparent forest where Persephoné went before her,
a blind swallow throws itself at her feet
with Stygian tenderness and a green branch.

A crowd of ghosts hurries to greet
the new refugee, the new friend, weeping and crying
and wringing their weak hands,
bewildered, timid, hopeful.

One holds up a mirror, another a jar of perfume—
the soul being female, fond of small pleasures—
and like a fine drizzle dry
complaints sprinkle the leafless forest.

And confused by the soft tumult, not knowing where to begin,
the soul sees but does not know the transparent trees;
she breathes on the mirror, it takes her a long time
to hand over her copper crossing-penny.

1920

## 113

What had I wanted to say? I forgot.
The blind swallow flies back to Pluto's palace
on amputated wings, and plays with transparent souls.
Night songs sing in unconsciousness.

But no birds sing. Flowering evergreens aren't in flower.
Night's horses have transparent manes.
An empty canoe drifts in the dry river.
The grasshoppers' password is: be unconscious.

Growing, slowly, like a tent, a temple,
now throwing itself to the side, suddenly, like mad
Antigoné, now like a dead swallow throwing itself
at your feet with Stygian tenderness and a green branch.

Oh, if I could give back the shame of sensate
fingers, the shameful joy of knowing.
Niobes' tears terrify me,
and the fog, the ringing, the gaping opening.

And men can love, men can know,
even sound pours itself into their fingers,
but I forgot what I want to say
and the unbodied thought goes back to the palace of ghosts.

That transparent thought keeps repeating the wrong thing,
keeps fluttering like a swallow, my friend, Antigoné . . .
and echoes of Stygian ringing
burn on her lips, black like ice.

                                        November 1920

---

## 114

The phantasmal stage barely flickers,
faint choirs of spectres,
the Tragic Muse shuttering her windows

with sudden silk,
coaches standing like a gypsy camp,
black, in the courtyard where frost crackles
and everything is shaggy—people, things,
and hot snow crunches.

Bit by bit servants unpile
bear-skin coats.
A butterfly flits through the noise,
a rose is wrapped in furs.
Modish bright circles, fly-people,
the theater's light glow,
and earth-pot lamps blink in the street
and heavy steam comes pouring out.

Coachmen breathless with shouting,
darkness snorting, breathing.
My dove, my Euridice, don't mind
our fierce cold winter.
To me Russian is even sweeter
than Italian sung,
it babbles, mysterious,
with the spring of alien harps.

A battered sheepskin reeking of smoke,
streets drifted black with snow,
Immortal spring comes flying to us
from a holy musical horizon,
to keep the song sung forever.
—You'll go back to your green meadows,
the live swallow falls
into burning snow.

1920

---

## 115

I dream of hunchbacked Tiflis,
sazandaries moan,

people crowd the bridge,
a capital all carpet,
and down below the Kura rolls and blows.

Wine shops above the river,
*dukhans* with rice and boiled lamb,
and a red-faced shopman
with glasses in his hands
and a glass for you, too.

Good to drink thick
*kakhetin,* wine in a wine-cellar—
drink where it's cool, drink in peace,
drink all you want, two of you,
no, never drink alone.

Ask for Teliani
and there's always someone to drink with, even
in the smallest *dukhan*.
Tiflis will start to float in fog,
you and the dukhan will start to float, too.

A man can be very old
and a lamb very young,
and under a lean new moon
rose-colored wine-steam will stream up,
mixing with *shaslik* smoke . . .

1920

## 116

Take some sun and a little honey
out of my hand, to make you happy,
the way Persephoné's bees said we should.

Unfastened boats can't be untied,
shadows wearing furs can't be overheard,
in a life thick as a forest, fear can't be beaten.

All we have left is kisses,
shaggy like new-born bees
that die when they leave the hive.

Rustling in the labyrinth night, in the transparent thickets,
they live in the dense forest of Siberia,
and they eat—time, blueflowers, mint.

So go ahead, take my crazy happiness
present, a dull dry necklace
of dead bees, which have turned honey back into sun.

November 1920

---

## 117

There, there, the Eucharist carried out like a golden sun,
suspended in air: a gorgeous moment
in which only Greek must ring:
it takes the world in its hands, like a simple apple.

Festive height of the service,
light under the round dome, July,
and outside time we sigh, chests full, over
that modest meadow where time does not run.

And like eternal noon the Eucharist endures—
all partake, are blessed, play, sing,
and there where everyone can see the holy vessel
flows with unending joy.

1920

We'll meet in Petersburg
as if we'd buried the sun there,
and for the first time we'll say
the blessèd senseless word.
In the black velvet of Soviet night,
in the velvet of universal emptiness,
women's eyes sing on, belovèd eyes, blessèd women,
immortal flowers bloom on.

The capital, arched like a wild cat;
a patrol on the bridge:
only angry motors rush by in the haze,
shouting like cuckoos.
I need no night pass,
I'm not afraid of sentries:
and I'll pray, in this Soviet night,
for the blessèd senseless word.

A faint rustle, half deliberate,
and a girl's startled "Oh!"—
and a huge heap of immortal roses
in Venus' arms.
We sit at a campfire, bored, warming
our hands, maybe centuries will pass,
maybe blessèd women's belovèd hands
will gather the thin ash.

There are rows of red velvet seats, somewhere,
luxuriant *chiffoniers* of theatre boxes;
officers' clock-work dolls; but
nothing for black souls, for low hypocrites . . .
Well, maybe blow out our candles
in the black velvet of universal emptiness;
blessèd women, steep shoulders sing on,
and you'll never notice the night-time sun.

25 November 1920

## 119

Because I did not know how to keep your hands,
because I betrayed your salty, tender lips,
I have to wait for dawn here in this dense city.
How I hate ancient log walls and their weeping.

Greeks are fitting out a horse, in the darkness,
gnawing its walls with jagged saws,
nothing can stop the blood's dry noise,
and for you there is no name, no sound, no molded copy.

How could I expect you to return, how did I dare!
Why did I pull myself away from you so soon!
It's still dark, the cock hasn't crowed,
hot axes haven't cut into wood.

Resin extrudes from walls, like transparent tears,
the city feels its wooden ribs,
but blood gushed down ladders and fought on walls,
and three times they dreamed of a seductive ghost.

And where is Troy, lovely Troy? The royal palace, the women's
house? Priam's tall starling house is waiting
for destruction, arrows falling like dry wooden rain,
arrows growing in the ground like a nut-grove.

The last star's arrow-point goes out, painlessly,
morning will be here to knock on the window, a gray swallow,
and like an ox roused from its straw, the slow day
moves about on streets rough from long sleep.

December 1920

---

## 120

I'm sorry it's winter,
you can't hear mosquitoes in the house.

But you remind me, you,
of frivolous summer straw.

Dragonflies whirling in dark blue,
fashion spinning like a swallow:
a tiny basket on your head
or a pompous ode?

I've no advice to give
and excuses are useless,
but the taste of whipped cream
is eternal, also the smell of orange peel.

You explain everything, instantly, emptily,
but nothing gets damaged, it doesn't
matter, the most delicate of minds
fits neatly on the outside.

You whip at an egg yolk
with an angry spoon.
It turns white, breaks with exhaustion,
but you keep on beating, beating.

And really, it's not your fault.
Why such serious judgments, everything inside-
out? You were made for these comic
squabbles, you were, yes.

Everything teases, in you, everything sings,
like an Italian roulade.
Your cherry-small mouth
asks for dry grapes.

Don't try to be smartest,
your're completely caprice, completely
this minute—and the shadow of your tiny
bonnet is—a Venetian masquerade mask.

                                December 1920

## 121

When the city moon walks in wide streets,
and the dense city slowly glows in its honor,
and night thickens, heavy with sadness and bronze,
and singing wax surrenders to rough time,

And cuckoos weep on their stone towers,
and a pale woman, a harvester, goes down to the world of the dead
and gently ripples the huge knitting needles of shadows,
and throws them on the wooden floor, like straw . . .

1920

---

## 122

Like everyone else
I want to serve you,
to tell fortunes with lips
dried by jealousy.
Words don't quench
this dried-out skin
and without you the thick air
is empty again.

I'm not jealous, now,
but I want you,
I bring myself like
a sacrifice to the executioner.
I won't call you happiness,
I won't call you love:
they've drained my blood and filled me
from some wild man's veins.

A moment, just one,
and I'll tell you:
what I find in you

is not joy, but torment.
And like a criminal to his crime
I'm drawn to your
confused, bitten,
cherry-tender mouth.

Quick, come back to me:
without you
I'm afraid, I've never
felt you more powerfully,
and everything I want I see
without dreaming.
I'm not jealous, now,
but I'm calling you.

1920

---

## 123

I broke into the shadows' round dance, in the gentle
meadow, with a musical name,
but everything melted, all my misty
memory had left was a fading echo.

Maybe, I thought, the name was: seraphim,
and I avoided that lightweight body,
but a day went by, and another, and I fused
and dissolved in the tender shadow.

And again the apple tree drops its wild fruit,
and the secret shape opens in front of me
and curses itself, and spouts blasphemy,
and swallows jealousy's coals.

And happiness rolls like a golden hoop,
rolling to someone else's will,
and you chase light-footed spring,
cutting the air with your hands.

And it's all arranged, we never
break the magic circle.
The firm hills of our virgin earth
lie swaddled tight, tight.

                                                    1920

---

## 124

Under the arches of gray-haired silence
I love roaming requiems and public prayers
and the moving obligatory rites
of funerals at Saint Isaac's Cathedral.

I love the priest's slow step,
the open display of Christ's shroud
and, in a shabby fish-net, the Galilean
darkness of Lent.

Old Testament smoke on warm altars
and the priest's helpless orphaned cry,
royal meekness: pure snow on shoulders
and purple mantles gone wild.

Eternal Saint Sophia, eternal Saint Peter, cathedral
granaries of air, of light,
storehouses of ecumenical goods,
threshing barns for the New Testament.

In these heavy years, the spirit is not pulled
to you, but misfortune's wolf-tracks
are what is dragged along these gloomy wide steps,
and we will never betray them:

Because the slave no longer afraid of fear
is free, and there's more than by the measure
stored in cool granaries, in deep bins:
the seeds of full, deep faith.

1921

*Poems* (1928)

The third subdivision, entitled "Poems, 1921-1925"

## 125
## Concert at a Railway Station

I can't breathe, the sky is full of worms,
no stars speak,
but God knows there's music up there,
the station trembles as Eternity's daughters sing,
violin air ripped apart by train whistles,
then coming together, blending.

A huge park. The station's glass ball.
An iron world, bewitched all over again.
Railway cars run quickly, solemnly by, to
where harmony revels in a foggy Elysium.
A peacock cries, the piano's low rumble—
it's too late. I'm afraid. This is a dream.

And as I walk into the station's glass forest
the violin-system is out of tune: confusion and tears.
The night choir makes a savage start,
I smell roses rotting in hothouses
where my own shadow spent a night,
under glass skies, with wandering crowds.

And I feel the iron world, covered in music,
in foam, trembling like a beggar.
I push on the hallway's glass walls;
hot steam blinds the violin's eyes.
And where are you going? A final music
for us, at a belovèd shadow's funeral.

1921

---

## 126

In the courtyard, washing up, night,
a sky rich with coarse stars.

Starlight like salt on an axe-head,
the full barrel frosting with ice.

The gates: locked, and stern,
frank, open soil all around—
no foundation anywhere, I think,
purer than the truth of fresh canvas.

Like salt, a star melts in the barrel,
ice-cold water gone blacker,
and death tidier, misery saltier,
and soil more truthful, more frightening.

1921

## 127

Some people have winter, some have Asian *arak* and blue-eyed punch,
some have wine sweet with cinnamon,
some get salty orders from brutal stars
and bring them to their smoky huts.

Warm chicken dung,
a stupid sheep's warmth:
I'd trade everything for life—I need so much
that a match-glow could warm me.

Look: a clay pot in my hand, that's all,
and the stars' chirping tickles my feeble ear,
but you can't help loving yellow
grass and warm loam, under these stinking feathers.

Stroke fur, quietly, stir straw;
wrapped in rags, starving, like an apple tree in winter;
reaching stupid tenderness to a stranger,
fumbling in the emptiness, patient, waiting.

Let conspirators rush across snow
like sheep, let the brittle snow-crust crunch.

Some have winter—wormwood, bitter smoke—to sleep in.
Some have the sharp salt of solemn injustice.

Oh, if I could lift a lantern on a long stick,
a dog in front of me, and walk under salty stars,
a rooster in the pot, to a fortune-teller's yard—
but the white white snow eats at my eyes until they hurt.

1922

## 128

Rose-foam of exhaustion on his soft lips
the bull paws, violent, at green waves,
snorting, angry at the strange oars—lady-killer not used to
his load, and working hard, hard.

A dolphin's wheel jumps out, here, there,
and then a prickly sea-urchin.
And Europa's delicate hands—take it, take it all. Bull,
could you find a better yoke?

Bitter, Europa hears the heavy splashing,
the fat sea all around her starting to boil.
See: she's frightened of the waves' high oily sheen,
she'd like to slide off the rough slopes, the high slopes.

Oh, she'd rather hear real oarlocks' creak,
see a flat deck, a flock of sheep,
fish flashing behind the tall stern—
And the oarless rower swims on with her, on and on!

1922

## 129

My scalp goes cold,
I can't admit it, not just like that—
Time is cutting me down, me,
the way it mowed off your heel.

Life tries to recover but
sound melts, bit by bit,
there's always something missing
and never enough time to remember.

But it was better before, it was: Blood,
maybe you can't compare
how you rustled, then, and
how you rustle, now.

Sure, there's always a price
when these lips move,
and the top of that tree swings, creaks,
and it has to be cut down, it does.

1922

## 130

How yeast-dough rises,
handsome,
how thrifty housewife-souls
rave in the heat—

As if doughy Cathedrals
rose out of cherubim tables,
domes filled with
spherical fever.

Time, regal shepherd's helper,
tries to coax out a magical surplus—

coax or caress or force—tries to
trap the small round bread of the word.

And the stale stepson of the ages
finds his proper place—in the
make-weight bit bakers add,
to fatten dried-out loaves.

1922

---

## 131

I can't remember just when
this song began—
do thieves rustle to this song,
and mosquito princes ring?

I'd like to chat
about nothing again, this once,
to scrape a match, to push night
with my shoulder and wake it;

To tip the air a little, like a stuffy
haystack, wearying as a cap;
to shake out a sack
sewn tight with caraway—

So the bond of rose-colored blood, the ring
of these dry grasses, bound together
and stolen, could be
found across a century, a hayloft, a dream.

1922

## 132

I climbed a narrow ladder,
up a disheveled haystack.
I breathed milk-stars' haydust,
I breathed the clotted hair of space.

And I thought: why wake
swarming oblong phonemes,
why, in all this endless squabble, try
to trap some marvelous Aeolian pitch?

Seven stars in the Bear's dipper,
five senses on earth, five good senses.
Darkness swells, rings,
and grows, and rings, again.

A huge unharnessed cart
sticks out across the universe,
the haystack's ancient chaos will start
to sing, to turn to powder.

We're not rubbing our own fish-scales,
we're singing against the grain of the world's
fur, tuning our lyre as though in a rush
to cover ourselves in shaggy fleece.

The haymaker brings back finches,
fallen from their nest.
I'll run from these burning rows,
back where my own sounds grow,

So rose-colored blood and the dry-handed
ring of these grasses would break their bond
and say farewell, one of them, now, secure, unafraid,
the other gone into an esoteric dream.

1922

## 133

The wind brought us comfort
and suddenly in the blue
we sensed dragonflies' Assyrian wings,
zig-zagged, elbow-cranked darkness.

And a thunderstorm like war darkened
low-hung clouds,
the webbed membrane of a mica forest
filled with six-footed flying bodies.

One corner of the sky is blind
and in noon's high bliss
one fatal star is always flickering,
like some hint out of clotted night.

And then fighting up on crippled
fish-scale wings, the Angel of Death
lifts one tall hand
and pulls down the conquered sky.

1922

---

## 134
## Moscow Drizzle

. . . Him: He hands out, oh so
niggard, this sparrow chill, gives
us a little, clusters of trees a little,
drops a little on street-vendors' cherry-trays.

And then, in the darkness, something boils:
the faint fuss of tea leaves,
as if an aerial ant-hill
were feasting in dark-green shrubs,

And a vineyard of fresh drops
has begun to stir in the grass.
As if a hotbed for cold
had opened in web-footed Moscow.

                                                                            1922

---

## 135
## My Time

My time, my savage beast, who
will be able to glance in your eyes
and using his blood as glue
paste up the backbones of a pair of centuries?
Blood the builder gushes
from earth-things' throats,
but lice living behind the spine
tremble as new days dawn.

While there's life in his lungs, a creature
carries his backbone behind him,
and waves play on
that invisible column.
And earth-time is tender
like a child's bones.
And life's head goes on the block
again, a sacrificial lamb.

To tear this time into freedom,
to begin a new world, we
need a flute to tie up
the joints of knotty days.
Our time rocks the waves
of men's anguish,
and in the grass an adder breathes
the age's golden measure.

And buds will swell with moisture,
again, green shoots splash out,
but oh my beautiful pitiful time
your backbone's broken.
You stare behind you with a senseless
smile, cruel, weak,
like a wounded animal
staring back at his paw-tracks.

1923

## 136
## Whoever Finds a Horseshoe

We see a forest and say:
There's a sea-going wood,
rose-colored pines free of
shaggy burdens right to their tops—they ought to
be creaking in a storm, their
lonely umbrella tips
in a white rage of treeless air. But fitted
square to the deck, they'd stand the salt wind's heel.

And sailors
Unconquerably hungry for space,
dragging delicate chronometers over damp ruts,
measure the earth's pull against
the seas' rough face.

And breathing the fragrance
of resinous tears, oozing from a ship's planks,
feasting our eyes on riveted
boards shaped into bulkheads,
not by the Bethlehem carpenter, but the other one
(Father of voyages, and the sailor's friend),
we say:

They stood on the uncomfortable ground
too, as on a donkey's spine,
their tips forgetting their roots,
stood on famous mountains,
rustled under sweet rainwater,
forever offering heaven, which never accepts,
their noble load for a pinch of salt.

How to begin, with what?
Everything chirps and rocks.
The air quivers with comparisons.
No word is better than another word,
the earth honks with metaphor,
and light carts
of bright bird flocks, straining, thick,
break apart,
like snorting circus horses.

Whoever sets names in a song is triple-blessed;
songs decorated with names
live the longest—
marked off by a headband
that cures frenzy, a stupefying scent,
strong, too strong, perhaps a man's presence,
perhaps some powerful animal's fur,
or only the breath of mint, rubbed between palms.
The air can be dark like water, and everything swims like fish,
pushing fins against the dense, resilient sphere,
faintly heated, shaking the crystal
where wheels and horses spin,
and the damp black soil of Neyera, plowed every night
with pitchforks, tridents, hoes, and plows.
Air kneaded thick as earth—
you can't leave it, and it's hard to get in.
A rustle runs through the trees, like a child's ball;
childen play knucklebones with dead animals' spines
Our time's brittle chronology runs out.
Thank you for what we have had:
I was wrong, I lost the way, my count went bad.
Our time rang like a golden globe, cast
hollow, held by no one,
and answering, to any touch, "Yes," and "No."
The way a child answers:

"I'll give you the apple," or "I won't give you the apple."
And as he speaks his face perfectly mirrors his voice.

The sound's still ringing, though what made it has gone.
A horse in the dust, snorting a lather,
but the steep bend of his neck
remembers running with legs flung out—
not just four of them
but as many as the stones in the road,
all renewed in four shifts
in proportion as hot hooves pushed off the ground.

So
whoever finds a horseshoe
blows off the dust
and rubs it with wool, and it shines,
and then
he hangs it over his door
to rest,
never again to strike sparks out of flint.

Human lips with nothing left to say
keep the shape of the last word spoken,
and arms keep the feeling of weight
though the jug splashed half empty, carrying it home.

What I'm saying, now, is not being said by me,
it's dug from the ground, like grains of petrified wheat.

Some
   coins show lions,
some
   show a head;
flat cakes of copper, gold, bronze,
lie in the ground, all equal.
Their time tried to bite them through, here are the teeth-marks.

Time cuts me down like a clipped coin
and I'm no longer sufficient unto myself.

Moscow, 1923

## 137
## A Slate Ode

Star with star—a mighty juncture,
that stony road out of Lermontov's song,
the language of flint and air,
flint and water, horseshoes and flaming rings,
a milky slate drawing
on soft cloud-shale—
not worlds' apprenticeship
but the delirium of a half-sleeping sheep.

Under a warm fur cap we sleep
standing, in the thick rich night.
A cave-spring babbles, running under wooden braces,
burbles like a chain, foaming faintly orating.
Here fear writes, and earth-fault writes, they
write with a milk-heavy stick,
and rough drafts ripen here, spun
by apprentices of running water.

Steep goat cities;
a stratum of mighty flints;
and still another cloud-ridge—
sheep churches, sheep-villages!
preached to by vertical slopes,
taught by water, corroded by time—
and air's transparent forest,
long since sated with them all.

The gay-colored day swept out, disgraced,
like a dead hornet alongside the hives.
And that black bitch hawk, night, carries
burning chalk, feeds slate-pencils.
It rubs day's drawings
off the inconoclast slab, and like
some fledgling shakes phantoms,
gone transparent, off its arm!

Fruit coming to a boil. Grapes ripening.
Day raging, as days rage.

And the gentle knucklebone game,
and vicious sheep-dogs in mid-day furs;
and hungry water flows,
like rubbish out of glacial heights—
green icons inside out—
spinning, turning like animals at play,

And crawls to me, like a spider, and
every juncture is splashed by the moon,
and on the dumb-struck slopes
I hear slate whining.
Memory, can it be your voices,
teaching, quarrying the night,
tossing slate-pencils to the forest,
tearing them out of the beaks of birds?

Only its voice will show us
what was scratching, fighting, over there,
and we'll aim the dry slate-pencil
where the voice tells us.
Burning chalk, night, I quarry you
for a single firm moment I can record.
I give up noise for the singing of arrows,
I gave up harmony for the angry flight of steppe-birds.

And who am I? No honest mason,
no roofer, no sailor:
I'm a two-souled double-dealer,
night's friend, hunter-guide-day shooter.
Blessèd is he who named flint
a student of running-water.
Blessèd is he who knotted ropes, and nailed them
into hard ground, for climbing mountains.

And now I study the diary
of a slate summer's scratches,
the language of flint and air,
a stratum of darkness, a stratum of light,
and I want to get my fingers into
that stony road out of Lermontov's song,

as into an ulcer, closing a juncture,
flint and water, horseshoes and flaming rings.

                                                                    1923

---

## 138

I know the language of cobblestones better than the language of doves,
stones are—doves, here, houses are dove-cotes,
and the horseshoes' story flows along the echoing cobblestone roads
of this great-grandmother of cities like a bright little river.
Crowds of children, here, beggars of history,
frightened herds of Paris sparrows
hurriedly pecking up leaden groat-crumbs,
peas scattered by a Phrygian grandmother,
and forgotten currents float through the air,
and a wicker basket survives, in memory,
and cramped houses—a row of milk-teeth—
like siblings standing on senile gums.

Months had nicknames, here, like kittens,
and loving lion cubs had milk and blood,
but when they grow up—for two years, maybe,
the big head sticks on their shoulders.
Oh the big-headed ones—they'd raise their hands
and swear an oath, there on the sand, and play with it like an apple.
It's hard for me to tell it: I saw nothing,
but I'll say it, yes: I remember one big-head
raising his paw, like a fiery rose,
and, just like a child, showing everyone a splinter,
but no one listened, coachmen laughed,
and children nibbled apples to the song of a street-organ,
they were pasting up posters, and setting traps,
and singing little songs, and roasting chestnuts,
and down the bright street, as through a straight cutting
in a forest, horses flew out of thick leaves.

                                                                    1923

## 139

Like a tiny body, with a tiny wing,
the heavy liquid turned with the sun
and a kindling glass
caught, and burned, there on the Empyrean heights.

Mosquito-like, an exquisitely trivial trifle
in the sky whined and rang,
a sky-splinter torturing itself, muted, with
squid-bugs singing:

"Don't forget me, punish me,
but name me, give me a name:
I'll feel better—oh understand me,
there in that full deep blueness."

*1923*

---

## 140
## January 1, 1924

Whoever kisses time's exhausted head
will remember like a son, later,
how time fell asleep
in the wheat snowdrift, outside the window.
Whoever lifts our time's sick eyelids—
two great drowsy apples—
will hear forever the sudden roar of the rivers
of deaf and god-forsaken and fake, fake old times.

The lord and master, time, has two drowsy
apples and a fine clay mouth,
but as his aging son trembles he'll kiss
his hand in farewell, and press it, and die.
Every day life breathes a little
harder—I know it—a touch more and they'll cut

that little song of clay wrongs,
they'll seal lips with tin.

Oh clay life! Oh you dying time!
I'm afraid that no one can know you
without that helpless smile,
mark, emblem of the man who has lost
himself. The pain, the pain—hunting lost words,
lifting sick eyelids,
and with lime in your blood, gathering night grasses
for an alien tribe.

Our time. Lime in the sick son's blood
hardens. Moscow sleeps like a wooden box,
and there's nowhere to run from our lord and master, time . . .
Snow smells like apples, as it used to smell, once.
I want to run through my door.
Where? The streets are dark, outside,
and as if they were spreading salt on the cobblestones
I see my conscience, white, there in front of me.

Down narrow alleys, bird-houses, straw-boards on roofs,
having bundled myself together, somehow, for a quick trip,
simple rider wrapped in fish-furs, ready,
trying to fasten the sleigh-robe.
A street runs by, another,
and the frosty sleigh crunches like an apple,
the tight buttonhole is stubborn,
it keeps falling out of my hands.

What an iron clatter night makes,
ringing along Moscow's streets.
Now the smack of frozen fish, now steam from
rose-colored tea rooms—beating like silver fish-scales.
Moscow—again Moscow. And I tell her, "Greetings.
Don't be too harsh, there's nothing the matter, by now;
as it was in the old days, I bow to the brotherhood
of frost, of justice according to the fox."

Pharmaceutical raspberries burn in snow,
and somewhere a typewriter clicks, clacks;
the cab-man's back, and a foot of new snow:
What else do you want? You're safe, there'll be no murder.

Here's winter, beautiful winter, and the goat sky
spills out stars, it burns like milk,
and the sleigh-robe rubs and clinks its horsehair
on frozen runners.

And little alleys, smoking like oil-stoves,
gulp down snow, raspberries, ice,
they peel off everything like a Soviet sonatina,
remembering 1920.
Could I ever betray a writer's wonderful oath—
betray vows marvelous to the point of tears—
there's frost smelling like apples again—betray them
to disgraceful gossip?

Who else can you kill? Who else make famous?
What kind of lies will you invent?
There's the typewriter: quick, rip out a key—
there's a fishbone in there,
and the sick son's blood will flood over
with melted lime, and blessèd laughter will spray out . . .
But the typewriter's plain sonatina—that's only
the shadow of those mighty ones and all their mighty music.

1924

## 141

I was never anyone's contemporary, no,
that kind of honor's not right for me.
Oh how I detest this person with my name
who wasn't me, who was somebody else.

The lord and master, time, has two drowsy apples
and a fine clay mouth,
but as his aging son trembles he'll kiss
his hand in farewell, and press it, and die.

I used to lift pain-sick eyelids, time and I,
two great drowsy apples,

and roaring rivers used to tell me
how people were succeeding, suing for their rights.

A hundred years ago there was a rickety folding
bed, white with pillows,
and a clay body, stretched out, strange—
the end of a century's first drunkenness.

With all the squeaking, creaking world-boots
what a lightweight bed.
All right, so what: if we can't design
a new time, let's spend a hundred years here.

And in some hot room, some desert-nomad-tent,
a century lies dying—but later
two drowsy apples on a horny wafer
shine, glow with feathery fire,

                                                    1924

---

## 142

Greetings, greetings, square-windowed
low houses—greetings, mild Petersburg winter.

And there, sticking out like fish ribs, unfrozen rinks,
and in half-blind hallways a scattering of skates.

And how long ago, potters with red glazes, floating down canals,
selling honest goods at granite stairways?

High galoshes walking, grey galoshes near arcades of shops,
and the orange-peel peels itself.

And roasted coffee in little bags, straight out of the cold,
and an electric mill grinding golden mocha.

Oh chocolate, oh brick, oh low houses,
greetings, greetings, mild Petersburg winter.

And grand-pianoed reception rooms, easy-chair seats,
doctors treating you to piles of old picture-magazines.

After a steam-bath, an opera, it doesn't matter,
final trolly-car warmth all muddled, unintelligible.

1925

---

## 143

No lies: tonight
I was walking from some strange little station,
waist-high in melting snow.
I look—a peasant hut. I'm in the hall,
monks drink tea with salt,
a gypsy woman fooling about.

Again and again, sitting on her bed,
she jerks up an eyebrow,
and her talk was pitiful:
sitting till dawn
she'd say: "Give me something,
a shawl at least, anything, a small small shawl."

The past stays past,
oak tables, small salt-cellars, a knife,
and instead of bread a pregnant hedge-hog.
They wanted to sing—they couldn't—
they wanted to get up—and flew like an arc
through the window, into the courtyard.

And half an hour goes by
and horses chew, lazy,
at black oats,
and at dawn gates creak
and horses are harnessed in the yard
and your hands get warm, slowly.

The canvas twilight grows thinner.
Anyway, boredom spills out
chalk diluted with water, even if
for no good reason, and through its transparent canvas
a milky day looks in the window
and a tubercular hawk gleams, for a moment.

1925

## 144

I'll run around in the dark street's gypsy camp,
behind a branch of bird-cherry on a black coach with springs,
chasing a hood of snow, the eternal, the mill-wheel turning . . .

All I remember is the chestnut hair that never fired,
smoking, bitter—no, ant-like sour;
my lips retain an amber dryness.

Even air seems hazel to me, in those moments,
and the eyes' inner ring is fringed with bright braid,
and what I know of pink apple-skin . . .

But the cab runners creaked on,
prickly stars stared through the matting,
hooves beat over frozen keys, beat in shifts.

And all the light there is—is in the prickly, starry untruth,
and life floats by like foam on a theatrical hood,
and there's no one to tell: "From the dark street's gypsy camp . . ."

1925

# Poems Uncollected and Unpublished Before the Strouve Edition

## 145

My slow dream, my every-minute dream, is
an invisible, magical forest
where some dim rustle skims
like the marvelous rustle of silk veils.

In misty meetings and mad arguments,
at the crossroad of astonished eyes,
an invisible, unknowable rustle flashed
like ashes, and died.

And as mist falls on faces
and words die on lips,
a frightened bird—really? a dream?—kicks
restlessly in bushes growing dark with night.

1908

## 146

Loathsome toads jump into
bushy grass, here.
Except for death, I'd never
know I was living.

Earthly life, earthly beauty,
why should you bother with me?
But she, she reminded me who
I am, and who I dream of.

1909

## 147

A violet Gobelin tapestry thins down
to the fineness of decay.

Skies descend to us where we
are, on water, in forests.

Some indecisive hand
sketched out these clouds,

And wistful eyes meet
their blurry patterns.

I stand, quiet, unhappy,
I—creator of my worlds,

Where skies are artificial
and crystal dew sleeps.

                                        1909

---

## 148

The screams of predatory birds
float under storm clouds;
time has turned more than
enough fiery pages.

Creatures live in sacred fear,
each soul performing,
like swallows before a storm,
an indescribable flight.

Silver clouds, when, when
will the sun melt you down,

and when will the high sky grow light
and silence spread her wings?

1909

## 149

Where the river's noisy glass
fights to break free
curling foam chills
like a swan's wing.

Oh time, don't torture with envy
him who has frozen in time.
Chance lifts us like foam,
joins us like lace.

1909

## 150

Over the altar of smoking waves
the gentle sea-god brings his sacrifice.

The hollow sea boils like wine,
above the sea the sun quivers like an eagle.

And fog drifts across the sea,
and the drum of silence rings,

And the sky with its blue heart
takes the sea's white smoke as its son.

And the ocean is wider, when it sleeps,
and its majestic rumble is more restrained.

And in the sky—portentous, heavy—
as if cast in metal: an eagle.

1909

## 151

TO ANNA AKHMATOVA

Today you seemed to me
a Black Angel in snow,
and I can't keep this secret to myself:
God's seal is on you.
So strange a seal—
Heaven-granted—
that you seem supposed to stand
in a church, in a niche.
May it be that love not of this earth
and love of this earth will mix,
may it be that storm-blood
will not run into your cheeks,
and magnificent marble will set off
all the deceptions of these rags,
all the nakedness of your softest flesh,
but not your blushing cheeks.

1910

## 152

When mosaic grasses droop
and the echoing church is empty,
in darkness, like a cunning snake,
I drag myself to the foot of the Cross.

And I drink monastic tenderness
from rapt hearts,
like the hopelessness of the cypress
at inexorable heights.

I love the saints' bent eyebrows,
the color in their faces,
the spots of gold and blood
on wax statue bodies.

Maybe it's only the illusion of flesh
lying to us, in our dreams,
showing through these rags
and breathing in fatal passions.

                                                               Lugano, 1910

## 153

TO ANNA AKHMATOVA

You want to be wound like a toy
but your spring's out of order.
No one will walk within cannon range
without poems in his hands.

                                                                1911

## 154

A poor artist, I've long been in love
with loneliness, with poverty.
To boil my coffee on an alcohol flame
I bought me a cheap little tripod.

                                                                1911

## 155

The new moon is high
and clear in the sky.
Horseshoes come trying
roads' hard ground.

A deep breath—
like scooping up
light blue sky
with a silver ladle.

I'll wear this heavy
wreath of joy;
the blacksmith
works at his happy forge.

1911

## 156

I know how to free
my soul from the world
outside: I hear my blood singing,
boiling, and quickly I'm drunk.

And the basic links
in matter organic to me
combine, again, in a chain
somewhere on the edge of languor.

Our essences are weighed,
out in the impartial ether—
star-weights tossed onto
suddenly quivering scales.

And the ecstasy of life
is the triumph of the end—
the body remembering
its immutable homeland.

1911

## 157

Caress of spring, babbling;
current of a thousand streams.
A carriage slipped by,
light as a moth.

I smiled at spring,
glanced behind me, secretly:
a woman in smooth gloves,
driving—as if asleep.

Running away,
dressed in mourning silk,
her thin veil
—black, too . . .

1911

## 158

I could not win, there was nothing I could do
against earth-imprisonment's dark bonds,

and the heavy armor of contempt
fetters me from head to foot.

Now and then my double is tender
with me, pursues me
as me—he too is inevitable,
pressed courteously up against me.

Because I hold some obscure *dénouement,* hidden, inchoate,
I challenge myself to a tournament;
I rip off my mask and, contemptuous,
cherish the world.

I'm not worthy of my grief, and
my final day-dream is
the fatal, brief boom of holes eating
into my patterned shield.

1911

## 159
## The Street-organ

Street-organ—plaintive songs,
rubbish of viscous arias—
like a disfigured apparition
harrassing autumn's canopy.

For the song to rock stagnant waters'
indolence, to stir it for an instant,
dress your sentimental
gush in foggy music.

What an ordinary day!
Inspiration's impossible—
there's a needle in my brain, I wander like a shadow.

I'd welcome the knife-grinder's
flint like a deliverance—
I'm a tramp—what I love is motion.

June 1912

## 160

When the clock on the giant cathedral
shows eight,
in our half-sleep we carry
your image, alien city.

Serving girls argue with merchants,
baskets in hand,
pigeons coo in the marketplace,
flap blue-gray wings.

Loaves of bread, silver-scaled
fish, fruit, potatoes, onions,
peasants—blocks of rock
and dark lively colors.

And in the gay fog's net
a tender flock, bunched,
as if the early-morning square
were a living tent-temple of trade.

1912

## 161

Autumn twilight—rusty iron—
creaks, sings, corrodes the flesh . . .

What is temptation, and all the riches of Croesus,
against the blade, Lord, of Your anguish?

I'm drained as if by a dancing snake,
and I tremble, yearning, in front of her.
I don't want the windings of my soul,
I want neither reason nor the Muse.

It's enough to unwind the tortuous
thread of sly negations;
complaints and confessions have no harmonious language,
my cup is heavy, my cup is shallow.

Why breathe? A sick boa-constrictor
dances on stiff rocks, coiling, curling;
it swings, encircles itself, and
falls, suddenly tired.

And for what? On the eve of torture,
shaken by vision, amazed by singing,
I listen like a prisoner, but without fear,
to iron's whine and the wind's dark moan.

1912

---

162

Hiding in myself like a snake,
writhing around myself like ivy,
I rise over myself—

I want myself, fly to myself,
flap dark wings
over water,

And like a frightened eagle
come home, I find my nest
gone, fallen into an abyss—

I'll wash myself with lightning fire,
I'll conjure solemn thunder
and vanish in a cold cloud!

1912

## 163

Rabble asleep. Square gaping; an arch.
Bronze door flooded with moon.
Here harlequin sighed for glory,
here the beast wore out a tortured Alexander.

Bells chime, shadows of emperors and kings . . .
Oh Russia, on rock, on blood,
bless me with the burden, at least, of
sharing your final punishment!

1913

## 164
## Self-portrait

There's a wingèd hint in the head
as it rises. But the long coat is clumsy.
A whole unbroken cache of movement
in the eyes closing, the hands' peace.

So that's who's supposed to fly, to sing,
to overpower innate shyness
with innate rhythm
and the flaming malleability of the word.

1913

# 165

Hunters lured you, trapped you:
stag, forests will weep for you!
Oh sun, take my black cloak
but leave me my living power!

1913

# 166
## Sports

The ruddy-cheeked captain chucked the huge ball
and the mob loved him.
Progeny of thick-skinned football:
croquet on ice, polo on horses.

Jumps and lunges bloom among
the young, as once they bloomed,
and Oxford and Cambridge, two river
schools, meet in lightweight linen!

But the only real sportsman, the true athlete,
rips the sad imprisonment of existence:
he knows a world where happiness breathes, foams . . .

And the tiny mallets of children's croquet,
and our tiny northern towns,
and that gift of the gods—magnificent tennis!

1913

## 167
## Football Again

Heavy morning-fog fades,
day walks in barefooted,
and little boys play football
in the military school-yard.

A poisoned bodyguard . . .
football's thick-skinned god
broke down, disfigured, beheaded
in unequal battle.

And light as a heavyweight
a boxer beat off blows . . .
Oh unguarded curtain,
defenceless tent! . . .

The crowd must have bunched like this
when, tormentingly alive,
the goblet undrunk, the vacant
head rolled to their feet.

Ineffably hypocritical:
That, like that, Judith? You and his other enemies,
feet kicking the warm corpse
of Holofernes, mocking, jeering!

1913

## 168

Gap patter:
Oh weekday prose—the dance of savages!
I size it up, again,
from a low knoll.

Some tastes are honest,
and an enterprising sailor
grabs up beads,
colored glass, and tobacco.

I love to trade. Feathers flash,
a rain of naive exclamation.
The leader sneaks a glance at the little
keg, shining with hypocrisy.

Hurry, throw them rings and pipes,
take fur and gold and poison
and return, conscience clean,
to your frigate, rowing a lifeboat.

June 1913

---

## 169

I haven't much money,
I'm not popular in pubs,
and maidservants weave their brooms,
hacking angrily at slivers.

I dirtied my hands with soot,
there's lampblack on my lashes,
I make my own mirages
and keep everyone from working.

Blue scullery girls,
virtuous servants!
And even on the hardest of bunks
honesty spreads out paradise.

The basket's heavy with wash,
the butcher strokes his knife like his sex, tells jokes,

and wine pours redder and redder
till dawn, in the masters' crystal cups.

*June 1913*

---

170

A bronze bell down the lane,
French talk, tender glances—
and behind the forbidden grating
the garden gradually empties.

What can you do, in the city, in June?
The street lights stay dark . . .
I want to hurry, I want to leave
on a yacht, a Finnish schooner.

The Neva—is like a swollen vein . . .
riding before red-cheeked morning roses bloom,
piled high with dishevelled grass,
a haycart drags itself along the asphalt.

And there's a worker's hut,
and tar crackles and cooks—
gypsy-fate has brought
the drayman back to Siberia . . .

And next, with an endless petition
all about justice and truth,
black on a granite bench:
a young suicide.

*June 1913*

## 171
## The Egyptian:
## Inscription on a Rock of the
## Eighteenth–Nineteenth Dynasty

I escaped harsh reproach,
I attained honors;
my knees trembled
like a reed, from happiness.

And they threw medals
large as the moon
into the courtyard, off a high balcony,
straight into the skirts of my long robe.

What I did was magnificent,
and I did it!
My new post is lucrative,
it makes life good.

And expecting the gleam of happiness
I danced a refined and elegant
dance in the king's presence,
and not for nothing.

Birds fly in the air.
Poor men walk on foot.
Rotten dry roads
aren't fit for noblemen.

And taking my presents with me,
and a bale of my medals,
I'll sail south on a wooden
barge, as my station deserves.

1913

## 172
## The Egyptian [Poem 2]

I built a house of prosperity,
made all of wood, not a piece of granite,
and the king's courtiers inspected it,
it has vineyards, and flowers, and a reservoir.

To lead air into my comfortable home
I removed three walls of the storeroom,
and I chose these corner palms myself,
unerringly, trees straight as spears.

Who can describe an official's income!
Important people are immortal!
Where's my steward? Is the tomb ready?
To save time, I listen to a written report.

A dwarfed maidservant will grind
grain with a heavy millstone;
the priests will have their tax, on time;
they've written a report on the bread and linen.

A dog's on the floor, in the dining-room,
and a strong arm-chair stands on its lion-paws.
I breathe the sweet smell of roasted geese—
solid pledge of joy beyond the grave.

1913

---

## 173

Let the clock wheeze and strike in the stuffy room,
with tufts of gray cotton and phials of acid—
giant footsteps with the hinges removed—
and in misty memory, phantoms will come alive.

And the feverish patient, crucified by boredom,
his skinny fingers twisting a bit of cloth,
squeezes his handkerchief like a winged talisman
and stares, loathing them, at the circle of minutes . . .

That was September, weathervanes were whirling,
shutters were banging—but the wild playing
of giants and children seemed a prophecy,
and the delicate body would rise, easily,
fall, heavily: a live carousel in that gay
household, revolting without music!

                                                    1913

---

## 174
## American Bar

No girls in the bar, yet,
the barman is rude, sullen;
I almost see the American's acrid mind
in his strong cigar.

The bar-counter shines with red lacquer,
a siphon teases, excites anyone
who doesn't know the buffet sign,
who's not too sure of the labels.

A heap of golden bananas,
offered in case of need.
A waxen saleslady,
imperturbable—like the moon.

We'll be faintly depressed, at first,
ask for coffee and curaçao.
Then our fortune will wheel
half-face around!

Later, talking not-too-loud,
I climb the revolving stool,

wearing my hat; I stir
ice with a straw, listen to the hum, the buzz . . .

The owner's thrifty eye, yellower than gold,
never insults a day-dreamer . . .
We're annoyed at the sunlight,
at slow-spinning orbits!

*1913*

---

## 175

You walked through fog.
On your cheeks: delicate rouge.
A day, shining cold, sick.
I wander useless, free . . .
Malicious autumn tells fortunes on us,
threatens with ripe fruit,
talks mountain peaks with mountain peaks,
kisses our eyes with spiderwebs.
How life's anxious dance has stiffened!
How your high color plays on everything!
How the gaping wound of bright days
shines transparent through the fog.

*1914*

---

## 176
## Poles!

Poles! Your mad gunners
make no sense to me!
Are ravens to kill eagles with their pecking?
Should the Vistula learn to flow backwards?

Is snow no longer to cover over
feather-grass, in winter?
Or should Poland lean on
a Hapsburg crutch?
You, Slavonic comet,
your age-old wandering
has scattered foreign fire,
turned partner to alien worlds!

                                                    1914

---

## 177

I cheered up, in the end,
tasted perfection of spirit,
tested my bliss
and settled down like a tsar,
having sensed glory behind my shoulders
when the high priest was in the temple
and a dove flew to the altar . . .

                                                    1914

---

## 178

Euripides' old men ran
like sheep, in a wretched crowd.
I walk a snake-like path,
dark offense in my heart.

But that's not far off, not far off:
I'll shake off grief

the way a boy, at night,
shakes sand from his shoes.

						1914

## 179

A German helmet—sacred trophy—
hangs over the fireplace in your guest-room.
Touch it, light as lambskin,
bronze, spiked, pierced through with air.

Not everyone fights in Poland,
sees the enemy with his own eyes
and, hearing cannonballs chorus,
tears proud gear from an enemy head.

						1914

## 180
## Fragment

What prophetic Cassandra
predicted your disaster?
Oh Russia of Alexander,
may you be blessed even in hell!

A fatal handshake
on a rickety river raft
. . . . .

						1915

## 181
## Rheims and Cologne

. . . But there's a cathedral in old Cologne, too,
unfinished, beautiful,
with at least one unbiased priest
and wonderfully preserved forests of high arches—

Shaken by a monstrous alarm-bell,
and in that threatening hour, when darkness thickens,
German bells sing:
"Your Rheims brother, your Rheims brother, what have you done to him?"

1915

---

## 182

Unquenchable words . . .
Judea stood still as stone.
His head drooping, drooping,
heavier every moment.
Soldiers guarded
the body as it grew cold;
the head hung on its thin, strange stem
like a halo.
And He ruled, and drooped,
like a lily in its whirlpool,
and the depths, where stems drown,
celebrated its law.

1915

## 183

Faint smoke melted in frosty air,
and I, tormented by sad freedom,
want to rise in a cold, quiet hymn
and vanish forever, but what I'll do, I know,
is walk this snowy street at this exact night hour.
Dogs bark, the West's not snuffed quite out,
and people come in my direction.
Don't talk to me! What could I say?

1915

## 184

Indignation of a senile lyre . . .
Rome's injustice lives on,
and dogs howl, and there are poor Tartars
in god-forsaken villages, up in stony Crimea . . .

Oh Caesar, Caesar! Can you hear sheep
bleating and the moment of vague waves?
Moon, why pour out light for nothing,
you pitiful nothing without Rome?

But not the moon watching over the Capitol at night,
lighting up a forest of cold columns—
No, only a country moon—that's all—
a moon, sweetheart of hungry dogs!

October 1915

## 185

TO ANNA AKHMATOVA

A face twisted
by some kind of senile smile.
Really, are gypsy women too
meant to feel all Dante's torments?

1915

## 186

The wet nurse counselled
killing Hippolytus—
Sorrow hangs like bitter smoke,
charcoal corroding your eyes.
. . . . . .
. . . . . .
. . . . . .
. . . . . .
Noble, lawless
Phaedra buried the sun—
In the king's hearth-fire
boring ashes go mad again!
But the golden-curled luminary
recovers, recovers.
Love: malicious lies, wise truth,
it's all the same to you.

1915/1916

## 187
## Madrigal

No, leave the magic frigate where it is:
the room's flooded with tobacco blue—
and they find a water-nymph guilty—
the one in seaweed, with green eyes!

She's never smoked before, of course,
ashes scorched her lips;
she never noticed her dress smoldering,
green silk, and ashes on the floor . . .

So sailors in emerald coolness
found no Turkish pipes, no Russian pipes;
but learning to breathe land air, dry
and bitter, well, they find even that hard!

*1916*

## 188

No street lamps for us, only the candles
of slender Alexandrian poplars.
You pulled the black fur off your breast
and put it on my shoulders.
The Neva's grandeur upset you,
and you gave me your wonderful fur.

*1916*

## 189
## The Palace Square

The imperial palace,
chariots with motors—
In the capital's black whirlpool
an angel prays, perched high on the Alexander Column.
Pedestrians vanish
in the dark arch, like swimmers,
and on the square wooden paving-blocks
splash, hollow, like water.
Only there, where the sky is lit,
a black-yellow rag, peevish,
as if the bile of a two-headed eagle
streamed in the air.

March 1917

## 190

The earth still grieves
for an earlier country, too early—
We all stand in the black line
along the Kremlin's black square.

1917

## 191

How the poplars smell! We're drunk,
the earth is coming to an end—
But we trouble-makers aren't out on the
Kremlin's black square to make trouble.

Wax-faced cathedrals
sleep, and Ivan the Great, accustomed
to rob as he pleases, stands silent,
straight and savage like a gallows.

                                                        1917

---

## 192

When October's favorite was making us
a brutal, angry yoke,
and armored killer-cars sprang up,
and low-browed machine-gunners—

"Crucify Kerensky!" the soldier cried,
and a vicious rabble applauded:
Pilate said we could hang our hearts on bayonets,
and our hearts stopped beating!

And then, for a moment, a reproachful shadow
along the red horseshoe of these houses,
and I almost hear, in dreary October,
"Get him, get him, Peter's pup!"

Blazing with the subtlest anger
you walked through civil storms and fierce masks,
fearless, free,
wherever Psyché led you.

And if this rapturous people weaves
golden wreaths for others, well,
to bless *you,* Russia itself will walk
lightly down to far-off hell.

                                       November 1917

## 193

Who knows, maybe my candle won't last,
and right in broad daylight I'll drop into night,
and breathe scattered poppy seeds
and wear a black mitre on my head:

Like the dilatory patriarch, in ruined Moscow,
unconsecrated world on my head,
racked with argument, blind, blind
like Tikhon—protégé of the last church-council.

1918

## 194
## The Telephone

Midnight friend of funerals
in this savage, frightening world, you,
in your tall strict
suicide's cabinet—telephone!

Black asphalt seas
dug up by angry hooves,
and soon the sun: soon the mad
reckless rooster will crow.

And then oaken Valhalla
and an old, a joyful dream;
fate decreeing, night deciding—
and the telephone wakes.

Heavy curtains drain the air,
dark on the theater-square.
A bell—and spheres spin:
suicide, it's all settled.

Life resonates, and where can we run,
escape this stony box?
Shut up, damn you!
It blossoms from the ocean floor: Forgive me! Goodbye!

And only a voice, a bird-voice
flies to the joyful dream.
You—deliverance, summer-lightning
of suicide—telephone!

*1918*

## 195
## Actor and Worker

Here on the yacht-club's steady landing,
tall masts, life-rings,
near a southern sea, under a southern sky,
a fragrant wood framework goes up!

Raising walls is the game, here:
isn't work play?
What delight to walk down
fresh-laid planks!

Actor-shipowner on the deck of the world!
Actor's house-on-waves!
No lyre ever feared
heavy hammers in a brother's hands!

What artists say, workers say too:
"Our truth is the same, truly the same!"
A single spirit lives in carpenter
and in poet-drinker-of-holy-wine!

My thanks! We worked together
night and day, our house is done!

Workers hide the future's high
tenderness under a mask of severity!

Gay shavings smelling of the sea,
the ship's ready—*bon voyage!*
Sail toward dawns as they come,
actor, worker, there's no resting!

                                                    1922

---

## 196

A star flames out the window,
icon-lamp fire blinks.
The way it is, I guess, the way it has to be,
that delight fades into bitterness,
escapes who knows where.
A peaceful light over the cradle
and a lullaby coming from somewhere maybe outside you.
And snow and stars, and fox tracks,
and a young gold moon
that knows no days, no years.

It hurts, it's painful to frighten
that familiar curve off your eyebrows,
to take your hand, as ever, in my hands.
Forgive me the earthly pain
and never forget, never, the earthly joy.
A star in the window, an icon-lamp in the corner,
and the gentle tracks of the quiet cradle.
Morning: a table, a stool.
The way it is, I guess, the way it has to be, no other
happiness, no other needed.

                                                    1923

## 197
# But a Sky Pregnant with the Future . . .

War's dissonance, again,
on the world's ancient table-lands,
and propeller blades gleam
like tapir's sharp-chiselled bones.
Wing and death are one,
flown down from algebraic orgies,
remembering the dimensions
of other ebony toys, the dark
enemy-night, the enemy's
breeding-ground of short fin-footed creatures,
and gravity's young strength:
power for the few starts that way . . .

So get ready to live in time,
no wolf, no tapir,
but a sky pregnant with the future,
with well-fed ether-wheat.
And the conquerors made their rounds
of summer's cemeteries, today,
breaking dragonfly wings,
murdering with tiny hammers.

Let's be like Bach's grandchildren
and listen to the thunder's sermon,
and in the east, in the west,
let's put on our organ-wings!
Let's throw storm-apples on the table
for earth-people to relish
and let's set out a cloud
on a glass plate, there in the middle of the food.

Let's cover everything with a
bright new tablecloth of silk space,
let's talk, let's be happy,
let's serve each other.
When we come to trial, in the circular court
of peace, blood will freeze
at dawn. A huge worker-bee
buzzes in the deep, pregnant future.

And for you, flying in this hard motionless time,
whipped by war, as they struggle for power—for you
mammals' honor, anyway,
fin-footed conscience, anyway.
And sadder for us, bitterer for us
that people-birds are worse than bird-birds,
and that willy-nilly we'd rather trust
carrion vultures, high black hawks.
War's cold palms
are like a cap of mountain cold—
year-in, year-out, heat, summer—
on mankind's high forehead.
And you, deep, well-fed,
grown heavy with blueness,
like many-eyed fish-scales,
the alpha and omega of storms—
from generation to generation they hand you down,
always lofty, always new, this
strange, browless
wonder.

1923

## 198

Life fell like summer lightning,
like an eyelash in a water-glass;
it had lied itself out at the root—
it's no one's fault, don't misunderstand me . . .

You want some night apple?
a fresh thick hot-honey-and-spice drink?
If you like I'll take off my felt boots
and pick you up, like a bit of fluff?

An angel in a bright spiderweb,
wearing a gold sheepskin,
lantern-light
up to his tall shoulder.

Maybe a cat jumps,
turns into a jackrabbit,
quilts the road, suddenly,
and disappears . . .

How her raspberry-lips quivered,
how she fed her son tea,
talked at random,
not to the point, irrelevant . . .

How she stumbled and stammered,
lied her way out, smiled
so that her clumsy beauty
blazed out.

Past the palace's dark poison-flowers,
past the garden's white boiling foam,
there's a land behind-the-eyelashes:
you'll be my wife, there.

We'll take dry boots
and gold sheepskin coats,
we'll take each other by the hand
and go down that same street.

No looking back—no fences to climb—
going toward radiant landmarks—
from dawn and to dawn,
full street-lamp molds.

January 1925

---

## 199

Oh was my aunt ever rich.
A real palace of china and silver,
assorted little nothings—and furniture!
*Louis quatorze,* rococo—I can't remember it all.
And in the hall, with all the other stuff,

a plaster Beethoven on a big bronze piano.
She really dug Beethoven, my aunt.
I came to see her, once,
and that stubborn old lady, proud as hell,
stood in front of Beethoven and cooed, in that hollow
voice: "My dear, do you see? Marat, sculpted by Mirabeau!"
"Ah come on, aunt! What are you talking about?"
But stale old age is a little deaf to instruction:
"That, that," she says, "is a study of the famous Marat,
sculpted, I believe, by Mirabeau."

Reader, she was just plain wrong, you know she was!

1926

---

## 200

TO ANNA AKHMATOVA

Bees get used to the bee-keeper,
that's the way bees are.
But I've been counting Akhmatova's stings
for twenty-three years, now!

1930

---

## 201

Don't tell anybody,
forget everything you saw—
a bird, an old woman, a jail,
anything . . .

Or else, the minute you unlock
your lips, when dawn comes
you'll start to shake
like a fine-firred pine tree.

And you'll remember a wasp at the summer cottage,
a children's pencil-case,
or forest blueberries
you never picked.

          Tiflis, October 1930

---

## 202

Pretty scary, eh,
my big-mouthed friend!

Ach, how this tobacco crumbles, you
dry-shelled bug, you fairy's nut-cracker—my stupid little friend!

And yet you could have whistled away your life, like a crow,
chewed it up with a nut-cake . . .

But it doesn't look like it, does it? No way at all.

          Tiflis, October 1930

---

## 203–215
## Armenia

i   [203]

People here see work
like a six-winged terrible bull,
and pre-winter roses bloom
swollen with venous blood.

ii   [204]

Rock the rose of Hafiz, cradle
your little ones gently, nurse,

breathing with the eight-sided shoulders
of a *muzhik's* ox-shaped church.

Painted with raucous ocher
you're all far beyond the hill,
and what's here is a little picture
in a saucer filled with water.


iii  [205]

You wanted colors, suddenly—
and a drawing lion grabbed
pencils from the pencil-case
with his paw.

Country of musk-shop fires
and dead plains, ripe for the potter,
you suffered red-bearded Moslem
captains among your stones and clay.

Far from tridents and anchors,
where a dull dried-out mainland slept,
you saw all the lovers of life,
all the torture-loving lords.

And women walk by, simple
as children's drawings,
their lion-like beauty
not making my blood leap.

How I love your ominous tongue,
your young graves
where the letters are a blacksmith's pincers
and every word is an iron parenthesis . . .

                              26 October–16 November 1930


iv  [206]

Agh, I'm blind, my poor ear is deaf,
all I can see is red and hoarse ocher.

And—who knows why—I've dreamed Armenian mornings;
I think—I'll go see how the tomtit's making out, in Erivan,

How bakers bend down, playing blind man's buff with bread,
how they pull out flat-bubbled bread, and wet thin pastry
  skins . . .

Oh Erivan, Erivan! Did a bird draw you,
or a lion paint you, like a child, out of a colored pencil-case?

Oh Erivan, Erivan! You're not a city—you're a roasted nut,
I love the crooked turns in your big-mouthed streets.

I've fingered my muddled life, like the *mullah* his dirty Koran,
I've anesthetized my time, I've spilled none of my smoking blood.

Oh Erivan, Erivan, now I need nothing, nothing,
not even your frozen grapes!

21 October 1930

v   [207]

Wrapping up your mouth like a moist rose,
holding eight-sided honeycombs in your hands,
you spent whole mornings standing
at the edge of the world, swallowing tears.

And you turned from the bearded cities
of the east, in shame and sorrow;
and there you are on a musk-shop bed
and they're lifting off the death-mask.

25 October 1930

vi   [208]

Tie a shawl around your arm and bury it
in the kingly sweetbriar,
down to the very center of its celluloid thorns,
boldly, until you hear crackling.

No scissors, but we'll have roses.
But don't let them shed all at once—
rose-pink sweepings—muslin—Solomon's petals—
useless even for sherbert,
no fragrance, no oil.


vii [209]

Country of screaming stones—
    Armenia, Armenia!
Calling hoarse mountains to war—
    Armenia, Armenia!

Flying endlessly toward Asia's silver trumpets—
    Armenia, Armenia!
Throwing showers of the sun's Persian gold—
    Armenia, Armenia!


viii [210]

Ruins—no—but poachers cutting a mighty compass forest,
oak-anchor stumps of a wild, fabled Christianity;
bolts of stony cloth, as if plundered from some pagan shop,
grapes like pigeon eggs, ram's-horn curls,
and sulky eagles with owls' wings, never profaned by Byzantium.


ix [211]

Cold, for roses in the snow:
    three yards of snow on Lake Sevan,
    mountain fishermen pulling out a painted blue sleigh,
    whiskered snouts of well-fed trout
    playing policemen
    on the lime lake-bottom.

But in Erivan and in Echmiadzin
    an enormous mountain drank up all the air;
    if the mountain could be tempted by an ocarina
    or tamed by a flute
    maybe snow would melt in her mouth.

Snow, snow, snow on rice paper,
   the mountain floats to my lips.
   I'm cold. I'm happy . . .


x  [212]

Clattering on purple granite
a peasant's pony stumbles,
climbing the bald buttress
of ringing State rock.


And behind her, with bundles of cheese,
barely catching breath, run Kurdistanis
who have reconciled God and the Devil,
having given half to each . . .

                              Tiflis, 24 December 1930


xi  [213]

What luxury in this wretched village—
water's rippling-haired music!
What? what? thread? a noise? a Warning?
Get thee behind me! Is it ever far to bad luck?
And in the labyrinth of wet choir-practice
a stuffy darkness chirrs,
as if a water-nymph had come
to visit an underground watch-maker.

                              Tiflis, 24 November 1930


xii  [214]

Myopic Armenian sky
I'll never see you,
I'll never squint up
at Ararat's traveling tent, never again,
and never open a hollow potters' book,
in a library of clay authors,

book of a beautiful country,
book by which the world's first people studied.

xiii [215]

Azure and clay, clay and azure,
what else could you want? Hurry, squint
like a myopic shah over a turquoise ring,
read these ringing clay-books, this bookish ground,
this rotten stinking book, this expensive clay
over which we suffer as with music, as with words.

                    Tiflis, 16 September–5 November 1930

---

216

Thorny words on the Plain of Ararat—
Armenian words like wildcats—
predatory tongue of mud-walled cities—
speech of starving bricks!

And the shah's myopic sky—
turquoise, born-blind—
can never decipher the brick-hollow book
of clay baked with black blood.

                    Tiflis, October 1930

---

217

I love this hard-living people—
counting years like centuries—

giving birth, sleeping,
screaming, nailed to the earth.

Everything sounds fine
in your frontier ear—
Yellow jaundice, yellow jaundice, yellow jaundice!
In this damned mustard backwoods!

                                                              Tiflis, October 1930

---

## 218

Armenian words are wildcats—
harrassing, scratching my ear—
If I could only lie down on that humpbacked bed—
Oh fever, oh pestilence, oh plague!

Glow-worms fall from the ceiling,
flies crawl on the sticky sheet,
and cranes and storks march by, in regiments,
along the yellow plain.

A terrified bureaucrat—face like a mattress—
no one on earth more pitiful, absurd—
here on business—oh fuck your mother!—
and he can't get horses to ride inland.

Shit to you, they say,
get lost, disappear—forever, no breath of you left—
you fat-ass clerk, you till-robber,
you barracks soldier, you has-been.

And a familiar "Hah!" in the doorway—
"Is it you, old chap?" What a taunting jeer!
How long do we have to run to our graves
like village girls hunting mushrooms . . .

Once we were men; we're only non-men, now,
and what we're in for—what rank is this?—

is a fatal sting in the chest
and a bunch of Erzerum grapes.

                                              Tiflis, November 1930

## 219

On the police blotter:
night swallowed a lot of prickly fish—
stars sing—clerk-birds
write and write their little reports.

They may want and want to wink, but
they end up submitting a statement,
and they'll always renew your permit
for twinkling, for writing, and for putrefaction.

                                                   October 1930

## 220

People howl like animals, now,
and animals practical-joke like people . . .
A marvelous clerk, needing horses—but how to
get them—sent on an official mission to a prison wheelbarrow—
and here he touched his lips to a cup of black plague—
here, in a sour pub, on the road to Erzerum . . .

                                          Tiflis, November 1930

## 221
# Leningrad

I came back to my city, familiar to the point of tears,
to the point of veins under the skin, to the point of a child's swollen glands.

All right, you came back—all right, get busy and gulp in
the fish-oil of Leningrad river lamps!

Hurry up, remember this December day,
sinister tar mixed with egg-yolk.

Petersburg! I don't want to die, not yet:
you have all my telephone numbers.

Petersburg! I still have the addresses
for finding dead men's voices.

I live on a black back staircase, and a bell ripped from
its meat kicks and stabs at my forehead.

And all night long I wait for my dear guests,
clanking the iron chains on my door.

Leningrad, December 1930

---

## 222

I was only childishly tied to the mighty world,
afraid of oysters, cautious with policemen,
and not a grain of my soul owes it a thing,
though I tormented myself; we all do.

I never stood under a bank's Egyptian portico,
in a beaver mitre, scowling with stupid
importance, and no gypsy danced for me over
the lemon Neva, never, to the crackle of hundred-ruble notes.

Sensing executions, I ran from rebellion's howl,
ran to Black Sea Nereids—
and how much torment and grief I took
from Europe's tender women, from the beauties of those times.

And why has this city these ancient rights
over my thoughts, my feelings?
It's more insolent after fires than frosts,
touchy, damned, empty, and young!

Maybe it's because, on a child's picture, I saw
Lady Godiva with her ginger mane let down,
maybe that's why I still say to myself, secretly,
goodbye, Lady Godiva . . . Godiva, I don't remember, I don't . . .

January 1931

## 223

Lord: help me to live through this night.
I'm in fear of my life, I'm afraid for Your servant.
Living in Petersburg is like sleeping in a coffin.

January 1931

## 224

Let's sit in the kitchen a while,
the white kerosene has a sweet smell.

A sharp knife, a round loaf . . .
If you like, pump up the stove,

Or else get some rope
and tie up the basket, before dawn comes,

And we can take a taxi to the station,
where no one can find us.

          Leningrad, January 1931

---

## 225

After midnight the heart steals
a forbidden silence right out of your hands,
it lives quietly, it's an expert practical joker—
love it—love it not—there's nothing else like it.

Love it—love it not, but know it, just once, and you'll never
catch it . . . so why shake like an abandoned child?
After midnight the heart feasts,
chewing a little of its silvery mouse.

          Moscow, March 1931

---

## 226

I'll tell you with final
frankness:
it's all raving, sherry-brandy,
angel mine!

Where beauty shone
for the Greeks,
for me shame yawns out of
black holes.

The Greeks heisted Helen
across the waves,
well, but for me it's salt foam
washing across my lips!

Emptiness will smear
across my lips,
and a kick in the stomach will teach me
to be poor.

Oh really? Is that so? Blow or blowhard,
who cares?
Angel Mary, drink, drink,
drink!

I'll tell you with final
frankness:
it's all raving, sherry-brandy,
angel mine!

                         Moscow, Zoological Museum, March 1931

---

## 227

For the future's roaring courage,
for that lofty, exalted generation,
I gave up a cup at the feasts of my fathers,
and my happiness, and my honor.

The Time's wolfhound leaps on my shoulders,
but I'm no wolf by blood;
you'd better shove me, like some cap,
up Siberia's fur sleeves—

So no one will see the coward, the weak insignificant
dirt, nor the bloody bones in the wheel—
so blue foxes can shine for me, there, all night
long, glow in their primeval beauty.

Lead me into the night, where arctic Yenisey runs,
and pines reach to the stars,
because I'm no wolf by blood
and only my equal can kill me.

*17–28 March 1931*

---

## 228

A Jewish musiker,
Alex Herzovitch,
wound his Schubert around and around
like diamonds.

Morning to night, happy, oh happy,
he ground out that same old
sonata, ground it by rote, ground it
to a crunch.

Well Alex Herzovitch,
it's dark on the street . . .
Stop it, my Alex Scherzo-vitch,
who's listening, who cares, why bother? . . .

Let some *bella ragazza*
chase her Schubert from a tiny
sleigh, flying
on crackling snow.

For us, with our dove of music,
death's no very big deal,
we die, we hang on a peg
like a crow-skin coat.

It's all wound up, wound up, my
Alex Rare-tsevitch . . .

Stop it, Alex Scherzo-vitch,
who's listening, who cares, why bother . . .

> 27 March 1931

---

## 229

My eyelashes sting. There's a tear sticking
to my heart. I feel what's coming, but no fear. A storm's
coming. Some funny fellow pushes me to forget
something. It's stifling, and still I'm dying to live.

He lifts his head from the boards, he hears a banging,
looks wildly around, still half-sleep-filled—
That's how the man in stripes sings his coarse song
when dawn rises, just another stripe, up over the jail.

> Moscow, March 1931

---

## 230

It's night out there. Pompous fraud.
*Après moi*—let the deluge come.
And then? Townspeople snoring,
crowding in the cloakroom:

A masquerade ball. Our time is a wolfhound.
So grit your teeth:
hat in your hands, hat in your sleeve—
and God have mercy!

> Moscow, March 1931

## 231

Holding a smoking stick I enter
the hut where six-fingered falsehood lies:
"Let me see you, damn it—
I'll be sleeping in a pine-board box!"

But she gives me salted mushrooms,
takes the pot out under her bed
and serves me a nice hot soup
of children's belly-buttons.

"Maybe," she says, "maybe I'll give you more . . ."
Well, I stopped breathing—was I sorry I came?—
I ran for the door—no good!—she grabbed
my shoulder, she's dragging me back.

She lives in the backwoods, it's dull, she's got moss
and lice, half a tiny bedroom, half a jail.
—What the hell, she's all right, she's all right!
Listen, old buddy, I'm just the same myself.

Moscow, 4 April 1931

---

## 232

No, I can't hide from that stupid mess,
down behind cabman-Moscow's back—
I'm a streetcar-cherry in this terrible time—
and God knows why I'm alive.

Us, we'll run Track A, Track B,
and see who'll die faster.
But she—now she narrows like a sparrow,
now she swells like a pie, and

She barely makes it out of a hollow—threatening—
Well, okay, but not for me, no thanks,

I haven't heat enough to circle
this whole whore-curve of Moscow.

*April 1931*

---

## 233

I drink to soldiers' star-flowers, to everything I was blamed for:
to lush furcoats, to asthma, to Petersburg days and their bile,
to pine-trees' music, to petrol in Elysian Fields,
to roses in Rolls-Royces, to Paris-paintings.
I drink to Biscay waves, to pitchers of Alpine cream,
to arrogant red-haired English girls, to quinine from colonies.
I drink: to which? I still don't know, wine
from the Pope's cellars, or a lovely Asti *spumante* . . .

*11 April 1931*

---

## 234
## The Grand Piano

A huge hall breathing limp,
like Parliament chewing the Opposition—
Montagne isn't after the Girondists
and the shock-troops are wilting.

Insulted and insulter,
a grand-Goliath muted,
sound-lover, soul-bearer,
Mirabeau of music laws.

My hands—hammers?
Ten fingers—a little herd of horses!

And Meister Hendrik, a flying hunchback-horse,
jumps up, shakes his tail-coat.

He turns the pages of something
different from waltzes and preludes—
waves of inner rightness flow,
overflow, all through him.

To make the world roomier,
to keep the world complex,
don't rub sweet earth-pear
root into the keys.

To keep the gin-sonata oozing
like tar out of backbones,
there's the Nuremberg mainspring:
It straightens dead men out.

16 April 1931

---

235

TO ANNA AKHMATOVA

Preserve my words for their after-taste of misery and smoke,
for the resins of circular patience, the honest tar of labor.
The way water in Novgorod wells must be honey-black
so by Christmas you can see, reflected, a star with seven fins . . .

And in payment, father, friend, rough helper,
I—unacknowledged brother, renegade in the people-family—
I promise to build such thick log-walls
that Tartars could lower princes in them like buckets.

If only these old executioners' blocks loved me! The way they play
croquet in the garden, like aiming at Death himself,

oh I'd walk the rest of my life in an iron shirt, for that, and
for executions like Peter's, I'd hunt a huge axe-handle in the woods.

Khemelnitsky Street, 3 May 1931

---

## 236
## Canzonet

Will I really see tomorrow—
my heart beats on the left; pour, glory—see
you, bankers of mountain slopes,
you, mighty shareholders of rocks.

Now a professor's eye, an eagle's—
Egyptologists, numismatists—
gloomy-crested birds
with tough meat and wide breast-bones.

And now Zeus, with a cabinet-maker's
golden fingers, carefully screws in
expensive, remarkable onion-bulb windows—
a psalmsinger gave them to the wiseman.

He stares into fine Zeiss binoculars—
King David's choice present—
notices all wrinkles in the rock,
sees pines, and villages, like nits.

I'll give up the land of milk and honey
to clog fate's eyes with seeing,
I'll say *shalom* to the head of the Jews
for his raspberry kindness.

Unshaven mountain-land, still unclear.
Bristle of half-grown trees in clumps.
And the green valley, fresh like clean
fables, so green that my mouth almost puckers.

I love military binoculars,
adding usury to eye-sight—
Only two colors have never faded:
yellow, which is envy, and red, which is impatience.

26 May 1931

---

## 237–246
## Fragments from Discarded Poems

**237**

In the century's thirty-first year
I came back—no, read: I was forcibly
brought back to Buddhist Moscow,
but still I saw Ararat, before that,
Ararat, rich with Biblical tablecloths,
and I spent two hundred days in the land of the Sabbath,
which they call Armenia.
When you're thirsty they have water, there,
that flows from the Kurdish spring of Arzni—
good, prickly, dry,
and the most truthful of waters.


**238**

I love Moscow's laws, really,
I've stopped missing Arzni water—
Moscow has bird-cherry trees, and telephones,
and . . .


**239**

If you want to live, suddenly, you stare
at Buddhist-blue milk, and you smile,
your eyes follow a Turkish drum

as it hurries by on a red hearse,
galloping back from a funeral,
and you meet a cart loaded with pillows
and you say: home, geese-swans, home!


240

I'm not a child, now.

You, oh grave,
don't dare instruct a hunchback—shut up!
I speak for everyone, powerfully, for
the palate to become the sky, for lips to
crack like rose-colored clay.

Moscow, 6 June 1931

241

The bear-tongue turns tonelessly, obscure,
in its mouth-cave. As it has been from the psalmsinger
to Lenin: for the palate to become the sky, for
lips to crack like rose-colored clay,
again, again. . . .


242

I don't write with the sunset's tobacco-blood,
shop-girls don't rap with tiny abacus-bones—
a hot, twisted mouth
is indigant and says, "No. . . ."


243

Moscow, wood sidewalks, golden sweet-cherry trees,
a truck panting at the gates,
and down streets, toward palaces and lakes,
all the ordinary people, automatic ledger-entries, came
   walking. . . .

## 244

. . . and working monks walked
forward, like naughty children.
Blue foxes, palaces, lakes—
only one voice singing, imperious . . .

. . . but hearing that voice, I'll make myself into an
axe, and anyway, I can finish this song, I can . . .

## 245

Quiet! Nothing, never, nohow, to no one—
In that huge fire, there there, time stands singing . . .

## 246

Ssh! I believe nothing, by now—
I'm a pedestrian like you, just like you,
but my shame returns to me
in your twisted, threatening mouth.

                                                            1931

## 247

Enough sulking! Shove those papers away,
I'm possessed by a glorious demon, today,
it's like maître François had scrubbed my skull
with shampoo, straight to the roots.

I'm still not dead: I bet I'm not,
I'll bet my head I'm a jockey
who can give them something to think
about, still, out on the trotting track.

I won't forget: this is the century's thirty-first
beautiful year, blooming in the cherry trees,
the rain worms have grown up,
all Moscow is sailing in little boats.

Don't worry. Impatience—is luxury,
I'll pick up speed as I go, a little
at a time—we'll hit the path with a cold
step—I've kept my distance.

Moscow, 7 June 1931

---

# 248
# The Carriage-Driver

Up a high mountain
in Mussulman land
we were carousing with death—
it was terrifying, like a dream.

We'd found a carriage-driver,
baked through like a raisin,
like the devil's day-laborer,
morose, monosyllabic.

First an Arab's guttural yell,
then a senseless "what what what?"
He cherished his face
like a rose, or maybe a toad.

Hiding his horrible nose
in a leather-tanning mask,
he drove the pony somewhere, drove him
to the point of terminal hoarseness.

And then bumps, lurches,
and there was no way down—

carriages began to whirl, carriages,
inns . . .

I came to. "Friend, stop!"
I remembered, damn it—
he's the plague-chairman, he's
lost, and his horses too.

He drives in his noseless slowness,
seeing him sweetens the soul,
and the sour-sweet earth
spins like a carousel.

And so, in upland Karadagiy,
in that predatory place, Shusha,
I tasted terrors
that the soul knows too well.

Forty thousand dead windows
stare from all directions, there,
and labor's heartless cocoon
lies buried on the mountain.

And naked houses show rose-colored,
shameless, there,
and above them flickers
the sky's dark-blue plague.

June 1931

---

## 249

Like some huge people-thing,
making the earth sweat,
a multi-layered herd
swims head to head, steady,
floating like a dust-filled fleet.
Heifers with tender flanks

and scampering bull-calves,
and behind them—like ships—
buffalo cows, buffalo bulls,
and oxen-clergy.

Moscow, June 1931

---

## 250

What a summer! Young laborers'
glittering tartar spines,
with bright girl-scarfs tied to their backs,
mysterious, narrow shoulder-blades
and child-like collar bones. Greetings, greetings,
mighty unchristened vertebrae,
which will last us more than a century, more than two!

Moscow, July–August 1931

---

## 251

I'm still no patriarch, not quite,
I'm still only half-venerable, and
they still abuse me behind my back
with words out of street-car quarrels,
non-sensical, nothing:
"You so-and-so!"—Okay, sure, I'm sorry—
but there's nothing I'll do differently . . .

When you think what ties you to the world
you stop believing it: it's nonsense, it's
a midnight key to someone's apartment, it's
a silver dime in your pocket
and a negative from some crook's film . . .

At every hysterical ring
I rush to the telephone like a puppy—
all I hear is Polish, *Dzenkuye, pane!*
—a sweet scolding at long distance,
or maybe a broken promise.

You keep thinking: what's there to like
among all these pop-guns and firecrackers—
you'll boil over the edge—and then, see, all that's left,
then, is fuss, and noise and no jobs—
"Get yourself a light over there, will you?"

So I'll smile, first bitter, then shy, I'll huff and puff
and leave, walk out with my blond walking-stick
swinging—I listen to sonatas in alleyways,
lick my lips at food-vendors,
turn the pages of books in massive gateways,
and I'm not alive, and yet I'm alive, anyway.

I'll go to sparrows and to reporters,
I'll go to street photographers,
and in just five minutes they'll pull
my picture out of a little pail, with a little shovel,
there under the cone of that violet Shakh mountain.

Or maybe I'll take off on errands
into steamy stuffy cellars,
where clean, honest Chinese
snatch small dough-balls with wooden sticks,
play savage games of cards
and drink vodka, like swallows from far-off Yangtze.

I love the starling-streetcars, starting and stopping,
and the asphalt's Astrakhan caviar
covered with straw matting,
making me think of Italian baskets,
and steel ostrich-feathers
where they're building the Lenin Housing Project.

I walk into museums' marvelous thieves-dens,
where deathless Rembrandts goggle on walls,
shining with the brilliance of Cordova leather;
I'm stunned by Titian's horned mitres

and gay multi-colored Tintorettos
with a thousand garish parrots . . .

And how much I want to make things move in me,
to get the talk going, to tell the truth,
to send sour sorrow to a demon, to the devil, off into the fog,
to take someone's hand: "Come with me,"
I'd say to him, "we're going the same way . . ."

Moscow, July–September 1931

---

# 252

TO S.A.K.

The bath-house-cotton-mills,
and the broadest green gardens:
day-world talking-room, on the Moscow River,
with crests of rest, and culture, and water.

This weak-chested, procrastinating river,
these dull, not-dull *chalva* hills, these
navigable stamps and postcards
that carry us quickly along.

The Oka turns an eye-lid out
and there's a breeze on the Moscow.
The little Kliazma turns up an eyelash
and a duck swims on the Yauza.

It smells of post-office glue, on the Moscow River,
they play Schubert in megaphone bell-mouths.
The water's on pins, the air's more delicate
than frog skins of balloons.

April 1932

## 253

Oh how we love to play hypocrisy
and how easily we forget
that as children we're closer to death
than any adult.

A sleepy child
still sucks up injury like tea from a saucer,
but who can I be huffy with, now,
I'm alone on every path.

Animals shed, fishes play
in the water's deep swoon—
and if only I could keep from looking as
people's passions wind, as people suffer.

April 1932

---

## 254
## Lamarck

An old man, once, shy as a boy,
a timid, clumsy patriarch . . .
dueling for Nature's honor?
Fiery Lamarck, of course!

If everything living is only a brief mark
for a day time takes back,
I'll sit on the last step
of Lamarck's mobile ladder.

I'll lower myself to snails and mollusks and crabs,
I'll rustle by lizards and snakes,
I'll go down those firm gangways, over wide ravines,
and shrink, and vanish like Proteus.

I'll wear a horny robe,
I'll say no to warm blood,
I'll be over-grown with suckers and I'll sting
deep in the ocean's foam, like a tendril.

We passed ranks of insects
with ripe liqueur-glass eyes.
He said: "Nature is all ruptures,
nothing can see—you're seeing for the last time."

He said: "Enough harmony—
you loved Mozart in vain:
a spider's deafness is setting in, and here
the trapdoor is stronger than we are."

And Nature stepped back away from us—
as if we were superfluous,
and the longitudinal brain she inserted
in the dark sheath was like a sword.

And she forgot the drawbridge,
it came down too late
for those with green graves,
red breathing, and supple laughter . . .

                                    7–9 May 1932

---

## 255

When Russian gold-pieces
went rolling to far-off Korea,
I'd run into the green-house,
sucking a caramel in my cheek.

It was a time of liquid laughter
and thyroid glands,
time of Taras Bulba
and of storms approaching.

Willfulness, hubris,
trip of the Trojan horse,
and an embassy of ether, and sun, and
fire above the heap of logs.

Out in the courtyard the air was greasy
like a caterpillar, from burning logs,
and hurrah for Petropavlovsk, hurrah for
Tsusima, out on the fire-wood mountain.

We walked to the young tsarevitch
and—God have mercy!—
went uphill, in tall boots,
to fetch chloroform . . .

I've outlived that youth,
my path is broad—
I have different dreams, different families,
but it's impossible not to steal.

11–13 May 1932

---

## 256
## Novellino

Remember how Dante
had the runners
race in honor of spring,
in their green faith?

Morocco boots
over dark-velvet meadows,
they showed parti-colored along the hills
like poppies on a path.

Enough of these wind-bags,
these Florentine tramps:
liars, all desperate liars,
assassins.

They prayed to God, dead drunk,
while bells rang,
they gave gift falcons
to the Sultan.

Ah, the steel thugs
who walked the streets in half-shoulder
green camisoles: time
has melted their candle;

They learned to live without shame,
they learned to live with the plague,
they learned to serve every possible
master, all at the same time.

And who can tell of their wives,
wearing wanton long gowns,
spending days, like dreams, in
fascinating work:

They melted wax, they wound
silk, instructed parrots, and seeing
the sense in it, allowed scoundrels
into their bedrooms.

Moscow, 22 May 1932

---

## 257
## [A Variant of 256]

Remember the runners
around Verona, forced to
unwind a strip
of green cloth?

But one will outrun
them all—he who runs away,

out of Dante's book, leading arguments
around and around in a circle.

Begun Moscow, May 1932;<br>
Completed Voronezh, September 1935

## 258
## Impressionism

The painter painted us
lilac's deep swoon,
he put sonorous steps of color
on canvas, like scabs.

He understood oil's thickness—
its clotted summer
warmed by lilac brain,
dilated to an oppressive heat.

But the shadow, the shadow's more violet all
the time—a bow, a whip, it goes out
like a match. You'll say: the cooks
are cooking fat pigeons.

A swing can be guessed at,
veils are never painted down
to the end. And in this sunny disorder
a bee manages to tidy his house.

Moscow, 23 May 1932

## 259

Give Tyutchev a dragon-fly:
can you guess why—

and Venevitinov—a rose.
Well, and a ring? No one, no one!

Baratynsky's shoes
irritate time's dust,
he carries cloud-pillowcases
without lace frills.

And then, tyrant
Lermontov—tormentor.
And always ill with its short
breath: Fet's fat pencil.

And then there's Khomiakov's
beard, God-preserved, forever
sticking out from a nail
in Jerusalem's gates.

           Moscow, May 1932

---

# 260
# Midnight in Moscow

Midnight in Moscow. A sumptuous Buddhist summer.
Streets split off in narrow steel boots, with a fine drumming.

Avenue-rings blissful with black smallpox;
Moscow's never quiet, even at night.
When peace runs out from under
hooves, you'll say: over there, somewhere, where they shoot at targets,
two clowns have settled in—Bim and Bom,
and they're busy with racks and little hammers.
a lip harmonica, first,
now a child's toy piano—
do-re-mi-fa,
sol-fa-mi-re-do . . .

Time was, when I was younger, I'd go out
in a glued-up rubber coat

and walk the boulevards' wide paws,
where a tiny gypsy-girl's matchstick legs
knocked in her long skirt, and a chained bear
strolled—Nature's eternal Menshevik.
And it smelled of cherry-laurels, it overflowed . . . Ah,
where are you going? There are no more laurels, there are no more
 cherries . . .

The kitchen clock bottle-weight,
I'll tighten it, it's fast.
How uneven time is—but all
the same, I love catching its tail:
you can't blame it for running, after
all, and anyway it's a bit of a practical joker.

Get thee behind me! No favors, no whining! *Stop* it!
No whimpering!
Middle-class intellectuals tramped their heat-cracked boots—
for that? For me to betray them, now?
We'll die like foot-soldiers,
not glorifying Theft, or Flattery, or Lies!

We have a spiderwork of honest old plaid—
drape it over me like a flag, when I die.
Drink, old friend, to our mutual barley grief—
bottoms up! . . .

Crowds out of dark moviehouses,
dead, depressed, as if after
chloroform. How venous, how terribly
venous, how desperate for oxygen!

You ought to know, I'm a contemporary, me too,
a man of the Moscowseamstress Era.
See my coat puckering,
see how I can strut, and talk!
Just try and rip me out of this time!—
You'll wring your own neck, I'm telling you!

I speak as this time speaks—but is its soul
really wound out of hemp, is it really
our own bastard,
like a wrinkled little beast in a Tibetan temple—

will it scratch, then climb into a zinc tub—
again, again, show us how it looks, Marya Ivanna!

Maybe it's insulting—okay, but get this:
there's a whoring after labor, too, and it's in our blood.

It's growing light. Gardens hum like a green telegraph.
Raphael comes to visit Rembrandt.
He's in Moscow with Mozart, loves him madly—
for a hazel eye, for a sparrow's drunkenness.

And some pneumatic mail-tube,
some aspic of Black Sea jellyfish,
seems to float the air from house
to house, like a conveyor,
like student-loafers in May . . .

May–June 1932

---

## 261
## Batyushkov

Like an idler with a magic walking stick,
loving Batyushkov lives with me—
he strides down alleys to Zamostye,
smells a rose, and sings Zaphne.

I bowed to him, apparently never
believing we'd parted;
with a feverish envy I squeezed his cold hand
in its light glove.

He grinned. "Thank you," I said,
and embarrassed, confused, found no words:
no one owns the winding curve of these sounds,
no one has heard this talking-noise of waves . . .

He brought us, he, tongue-tied,
our torment, our wealth—

the noise of poetry-making, brotherhood's bell,
harmony of flooding tears.

And he who'd mourned Tasso, he answered me:
"I'm not accustomed to honor;
the grape-meat of verse just
accidentally refreshed my tongue."

Okay, then, lift your startled eyebrows,
your city-dweller and friend of city-dwellers—
Pour eternal dreams, like test-tubes of blood,
from one glass to another.

Moscow, 18 June 1932

---

## 262–264
## Poems on Russian Poetry

### 262

Sit down, Derzhavin, make yourself comfortable—
you're slyer than a fox, friend,
and the Tartar *khoumis* you sipped
hasn't gone sour
yet. Give Iazykov a bottle,
shove him a glass—
I love his smirk,
that throbbing vein of drunkenness,
and the incandescence of his poems.

### 263

Thunder lives by its rolling—
why should it care about us?
With tiny sips, along the rolling
peals, it relishes muscat
on the tongue, the taste, the color . . .

Drops gallop down,
hailstones skip in a crowd . . .
a city-smell, a deluge-smell—
no, jasmine—no, dill—
no, oak-bark.

Noise! Shaking!
Moscow and the people who live around
Moscow began to shake
like fig-tree leaves.
Thunder rolls its cart
down the wood road,
and the cloudburst struts
with a long river-lash.

And the earth seems to slope, for a moment,
to stoop, obsequious,
and clouds march out
in soft executioner's boots.

Drops gallop down,
hailstones skip in a crowd
sweating like slaves, clattering like horses
and the gossiping of trees.

264

TO S.A.K.

I've come to love the forest,
beautiful, wild—oak is the ace,
maple leaves—are red pepper,
blue-black needles—are hedgehogs.

Pistachio voices fall silent
on milk, there,
and when you want to click your tongue
there's no truth in it.

Thin little people live there,
all in acorn caps—

and squirrels whirl their blood-white
eyeballs in terrible wheels.

And sorrel, and bird's-udder,
the peacock disorder of needles—
grandeur, naïveté, foolishness,
and egg-shell darkness.

Sheep-devils jab with swords,
the big-nosed in three-cornered hats,
hangmen sit on coals, with samovars,
and read books.

And then mushrooms blow like waves
in a harness of thin rain, and
rise from the forest-edge
like—this . . . and later . . .

And unlucky freaks
play cards, there—
Horses snort, the cards are marked—
Who'll win? Breakdown begins . . .

And trees—brother against brother—
rise, revolt: hurry, understand:
how coarse they are, how tasteless,
and Jesus Christ, how handsome . . .

Moscow, 3–7 July 1932

## 265

Today we can sneak a picture
of the robber-Kremlin: we dipped one finger
in the Moscow River. Delightful,
these pistachio dove-cotes—
pour them millet, at least—oats, at least!
And who's an ignoramus? Ivan the Great—

an ancient bell-tower
just standing on, just standing, blockhead
of blockheads, from God only knows
what century. Send him abroad to study. Oh not by a long
   shot . . . Shameful.

River Moscow in four-chimneyed smoke,
the whole opened-up city in front of us—
bather-factories, and there, beyond the river,
gardens. Just the way
you throw back the rosewood
top of an enormous concert grand,
and get into the resonant guts.
White Guards, did you see it?
Did you get to hear Moscow's grand piano? Boom-Boom-Roar!

Time: like everything else, I think
you're—a bastard . . . Like a little kid,
following grown-ups into wrinkled water,
I seem to be walking into the future,
and I think I'll never live to see it.

I won't march with the Young Communists
in a white-chalked stadium.
I won't jump up at dawn,
waked by motorcycles calling;
I won't run into glass palaces, on chicken-little-legs,
not those witches' huts, not even like a shadow.

Every day it's harder to breathe,
and yet I can't be patient—
Men's hearts, and horses' hearts, and only these,
are born to delight in running . . .

But Faust's demon—dry, and young for his age—
throws himself at the old man's rib
again, seduces him into renting a rowboat
by the hour, or flapping off to Sparrow Hills,
or whipping around Moscow on the streetcar . . .
she hasn't got time: she's a nursemaid, today—

rushing around with forty thousand cradles,
she's all alone, there's woolen yarn strung on her hands.

*Summer 1932*

---

## 266
## To German

FOR B. S. KUZIN

Ruining myself, contradicting myself,
like a moth and a tiny midnight flame,
I wish I could leave Russian,
for all I eternally owe it.

We praise without flattery, sometimes,
and we've point-blank friendship, without strict forms—
so now let's learn seriousness, and honor,
from an alien family to the West.

Storms are good for you, poetry!
I remember a German officer,
roses on his sword-hilt,
Ceres on his lips.

Burghers yawned, in Frankfurt,
no one had heard about Goethe,
they wrote hymns, horses pranced,
danced in the same place, like alphabet-letters.

Tell me, friends, what Valhalla
we sat in, cracking nuts,
what freedom we knew,
what landmarks you reared for me.

And we ran into our graves—down steps,
unafraid—like running off the pages of a first-

class, brand-new, literary almanac—
like running to a pub for a mug of Mosel-wine.

Alien words—like an envelope, for me—
and long before I had the courage, and was born,
I was a letter, I was a grape-line.
I was the book you dream of, now.

I slept, faceless, mindless, and I
was friendship, wakened by a gun.
*Nachtigal*-God, let me be as Pylades friend of
Orestes was, or rip out my tongue—I won't need it.

Oh *Nachtigal*-God, they still enlist me
in new plagues, in seven-year battles.
Sound has gone narrow, words hiss, mutiny,
but you're alive, with you I'm peaceful.

8–12 August 1932

---

# 267
# To Ariosto

Nicest, cleverest of all Italians,
amiable Ariosto has gone a bit hoarse.
He delights in counting fish
and peppers the seas with wicked nonsense.

Like a musician playing on ten cymbals,
untiring at snapping his narrative thread,
he leads here, there, not knowing himself what comes next,
a tangled story of knightly scandals.

Cicada-speech is a charming blend
of Pushkin's sadness with Mediterranean pride.
It toys with Orlando, it pipes through its hat,
and it shudders, transformed, utterly transformed.

And it says to the sea: Sound!—but no thought.
And to the girl on the cliff: Lie there!—but no blanket.
Tell us more, please—there's not enough of you, while
blood's in our veins, and sound's in our ears . . .

Oh soul-less lizard city!
Give us more of these men,
callous Ferrara . . . And again, again, from the beginning, while
blood's in our veins, quick, tell us the story . . .

It's cold in Europe. In Italy it's dark.
Power is disgusting, like a barber's hands.
And yet he calls himself noble, more slyly than ever,
and smiles, through the open window,

At a lamb on the hill, at a monk on a donkey,
at the Duke's soldiers, faintly cracked in the head
from too much wine, from garlic and plague, and he smiles
at the child sleeping under a net of blue flies.

I love his furious leisure—
a senseless tongue, a salt-sweet tongue,
delightful double-identical-rhymes, bivalve pearls
I'm afraid to pry apart with a knife.

Maybe, gentle Ariosto, a century will pass,
and we'll pour your blue-sky and our Black-Sea
in a single broad brotherly blueness.
We've been there, too. We've drunk honey-wine there, we have, we have.

*Old Crimea, 4–6 May 1933*

---

## 268
## Ariosto [A Variant of 267]

It's cold in Europe. In Italy it's dark.
Power's disgusting, like a barber's hands.
Oh if only I could throw open, soon, soon,
that wide window on the Adriatic!

Bees buzz above the musk rose,
on the southern steppes at noon: muscle-bound grasshoppers,
heavy shoes on the wingèd horse,
sandglass yellow, gold.

Cicada-speech is a charming blend
of Pushkin's sadness with Mediterranean pride.
Like clinging, sticky ivy it lies
like a man, playing games with Orlando.

Sandglass yellow and gold,
a muscle-bound grasshopper on the southern steppes,
and a broad-shouldered liar flies straight to the moon . . .

Gentle Ariosto, ambassadorial fox,
flowering fern, sail-maker, soap-plant,
up on the moon you heard yellow birds,
and out in the courtyard the fish got good advice.

Oh soul-less lizard city!
Callous Ferrara bore such sons from a witch
and a judge joined, then kept them on a chain—
and the sun of a red-haired mind rose from a hidden corner.

The butcher's petty shop amazes us,
and the child sleeping under a net of blue flies.
And the lamb on the hill, and the monk on a donkey,
and the Duke's soldiers, faintly cracked in the head
from too much wine, from garlic and plague,
and we're surprised at some loss, fresh like the dawn.

> Begun Old Crimea, 4–6 May 1933;
> Completed Voronezh, 1936

---

# 269
# [ A Variant of 267 and 268 ]

Ariosto's friend, Petrarch's friend, Tasso's friend—
a senseless tongue, a salt-sweet tongue,

and delightful double-identical-rhymes—
I'm afraid to pry at bivalve pearls with a knife.

> Old Crimea, May 1933

---

## 270

Don't tempt alien tongues, try to forget them—
Anyway, can you chew through glass with your teeth!

Anyway, no strange name will save a dying body
and thinking, immortal mouth, at the moment of separation.

Oh how hard to honor alien screams—
an evil eagle-guard pounces on illegal enthusiasms.

And suppose Ariosto and Tasso, charming, fascinating,
are monsters with azure brains and moist-eyed fish-scales?

And to punish pride, incorrigible sound-lover,
there'll be a vinegar sponge for your traitor's lips.

> Old Crimea, May 1933

---

## 271

Cold Spring. Hungry Old Crimea,
just as under Wrangel—just as guilty.
Sheepdogs in the courtyard, patches on tattered rags,
the same gray stinging smoke, just as faint.

The scattered distance, just as lovely,
trees blooming a bit,
standing like just-landed strangers—and the pitiful
almond tree, still hung with yesterday's foolishness.

Nature doesn't know its own face,
and terrible shadows, frightening shadows—from the Ukraine,
    from Kuban . . .
like hungry peasants in felt shoes
guarding the gate, never touching the ring.

Old Crimea, May 1933

---

## 272

The room's as quiet as paper—
empty, nothing going on—
you can hear moisture gurgling
down pipes inside radiators.

My property's all in order,
my telephone's frozen like a frog,
my possessions have seen things before
and beg to get out in the street.

And the damned walls are thin,
and there's nowhere left to run to—
and I like an idiot am forced
to play tunes on a comb . . .

More outrageous, even, than the Komsomol cell,
more brazen than an official school-song,
this teaching executioners who have perched
on school benches how to chatter.

I read ration-books,
I catch at hemp speeches,
and I sing this good little Kulak
a threatening lullaby.

Some imitator, some
comber of collective-farm flax,
mixer of ink and blood,
deserves this sharp stick to sit on.

Some honest traitor,
washed clean in purges, like salt,
some supporter of a wife and children
will swat that moth to death . . .

Each hint hides such torturous
malice in itself
that it feels like Nekrasov's hammer
driving these nails.

It's been like an executioner's block
for seventy years, and more. Let's begin—
it's time, old man, slob,
to make some noise with your boots.

And instead of the pure, the blushing Hippocrene
a stream of ancient fear
will tear at the hack-work walls
of this vicious Moscow house.

                       Moscow, Furmanov Alley, November 1933

---

## 273

Tartars, Uzbeks, Samoyeds,
all the Ukrainians,
even the Volga Germans
are waiting for their translators.

And maybe this very minute
some Japanese is translating
me into Turkish
and has reached the depths of my soul.

                       1933

## 274

Our sacred young ones
have excellent songs in their blood:
like lullaby-little-baby-songs
attacking rich landowners.

And I observe myself
and sing about like this:
I rock the landowner-of-collective-farms,
I sing the good Kulak baby.

1933

---

## 275–285
## Octaves

### 275
I love seeing the canvas appear,
two, three, sometimes
four gasps
leading to a resolving sigh—
and sketching out open forms
in racing-boat-arcs,
space plays, half-awake—
a child unaware of the cradle.

Begun Moscow, November 1933;<br>Completed Voronezh, July 1935

### 276
[A Variant of 275]

I love seeing the canvas appear,
two, three, sometimes
four gasps
leading to a resolving sigh—
and I feel so good, and I feel such pain,

when the moment comes closer—
and suddenly an arc-like lengthening
can be heard in my mumbling.

                                                  Moscow, November 1933

## 277

Oh butterfly, Moslem girl,
wrapped in a slit shroud,
oh little life-girl, oh death-girl,
so big, so shining!
With a toothy great moustache
she buried her head in her shawl.
Oh shroud unfurled like a flag—
fold your wings—I'm afraid!

                                                  Moscow, November 1933

## 278

The sixth sense's tiny appendage,
a lizard's sincipital eye,
monasteries of snails and oysters,
flickering eyelash-voices.
How close, the unattainable!
You can't untie it, you can't see it—
like a note shoved in your hand:
Answer, answer at once.

                                                  Moscow, May 1933

## 279

Having conquered Nature's memorizing,
the hard blue eye penetrated to its law:
deep in the earth a rock lets itself be bent,
and a moan struggles out of the chest, like ore,
and a deaf under-development stretches out,
as on a horn-shaped road—

to comprehend the internal redundancy of open space
and the petal's guarantee, the dome's high pledge.

*Moscow, January 1934*

280

When you throw away the outline
and work at remembering
a period with no painful footnotes,
one unit of internal darkness—
and just of its own weight,
screwing up its eyes, it holds on, stands firm—
it's relating to paper as
a dome to the empty skies.

*Moscow, November 1933*

281

Schubert on the water, Mozart in birds' clatter,
and Goethe whistling on a winding path,
and Hamlet meditating with anxious steps,
all counted the crowd's pulse, all believed the crowd.
Maybe, before there were lips, there was a whisper,
and before there were trees there were leaves whirling,
and those to whom we dedicate this our experiment,
before the experiment, have accumulated eyes and noses and mouths.

*1933*

282

The maple's jagged paw
bathes in round corners,
and one can compose wall-drawings
of butterfly specks.
Some mosques are lively,
and I guessed it right off:

maybe, maybe *we*—are Saint Sophia, wise
with an infinity of eyes.

Moscow, November 1933–January 1934

283

Tell me, desert draftsman,
geometer of pouring sands,
can lines' lack of restraint
really be stronger than a blowing wind?
—His quivering Jewish
worry is none of my business—
he shapes a babbling experiment
and drinks the babble he makes.

1933

284

We drink the delusion of motives
from needled plague-cups,
our hooks touch magnitudes
tiny like an easy death.
And there, where the jackstraws fought,
there the child is silent—
a large universe sleeping in a cradle,
next to a small eternity.

Moscow, November 1933

285

And I walk out of space
into the rank garden of magnitudes,
and I pick an imaginary loyalty
and an awareness of motives.
And I read your primer, alone,
Infinity, all alone—

a wild handbook of remedies and herbs—pageless—
a book of logarithms with enormous roots.

>                                  Moscow, November 1933

---

# 286

We live, not feeling the ground under our feet,
no one hears us more than a dozen steps away,

And when there's enough for half a small chat—
ah, we remember the Kremlin mountaineer:

Thick fingers, fat like worms, greasy,
words solid as iron weights,

Huge cockroach whiskers laughing,
boot-tops beaming.

And all around him a rabble of thin-necked captains:
he toys with the sweat of half-men.

Some whistle, some meow, some snivel,
he's the only one looking, jabbing.

He forges decrees like horseshoes—decrees and decrees:
This one gets it in the balls, that one in the forehead, him right between the eyes.

Whenever he's got a victim, he glows like a broadchested
Georgian munching a raspberry.

>                                          November 1933

## 287

The way water runs out some high
crack in a mountain, taste-contradictory,
half-harsh, half-sweet, flowing two-faced—

So, to really die, a thousand times a day
I lose the everyday freedom
of sighing, the usual knowledge of the goal.

*Moscow, December 1933*

---

## 288

TO THE MEMORY OF ANDREY BIELY

Light-blue eyes, a burning forehead-bone—
world-anger, cleansing-anger lured you on.

And because you were given a marvelous power
it was written: he shall never be judged, he shall never be cursed.

They gave you a tiara—cap of God's fools—
turquoise teacher, tormentor, sovereign, fool.

Like a light Moscow-snow, a gold-bird hatching a mess,
wise-gibberish, half-understood, tangled, trivial.

Collector of space, new-certified fledgling,
writer, baby goldfinch, young student, little cap-bell . . .

First-born, skater, evicted by our time
into the frosty dust of a grammar still being written.

It is written, often: "Execution." But read it right and it says—
"Song." Maybe simplicity's a disease that can die?

Our straight-thinking is more than a child's pistol;
news saves people, not quires of paper.

Fat pencils swoop down on the dead man
like dragonflies landing in reeds, knowing nothing of water.

They held pages for their glorious descendants, standing on their knees—
they painted pictures and asked forgiveness from every line.

An icy bond forms between you and this country—
so lie there, growing younger, lie there, endlessly getting yourself straight.

And then the young won't have to ask you, Russians still to come—
How is it, there?—in the emptiness, the cleanliness?—asking you, orphan!

*Moscow, 10 January 1934*

---

# 289
# January 10, 1934

Two, three chance phrases haunt me—
I say them all day, over and over: my sorrow is greasy, succulent, obese,
oh God, how black, how blue-eyed
death's dragonflies, how black the sky!

What's happened to primogeniture? to nice regular habits?
Where's the flowing hawk at the bottom of your eyes?
What's happened to learning? Where's bitter silence?
And clear, straight people? And straight speech

Tangled like honest zigzags?
A skater into blue flames has them—
are they twisting iron fluff in a frozen thirst, clinking
wine-cups with a blue-hard river?

The voices of German wisemen,
the brilliant arguments of Russian first-born,
molecular models for three-tiered salts, all
came to him, half a century in half an hour.

And suddenly, there was Music, waiting in ambush,
no longer a hunting beast, pouring from violins,
not flowing for ears to hear, not coming to bring comfort—
flowing for muscles, for pounding foreheads,

Flowing for the tender mask, just-now stripped off,
for plaster fingers not holding a pen,
for swollen lips, for the consolidated caresses
of a coarse-grained good, a coarse-grained peace.

Fur coats breathed. Shoulder pressed on shoulder,
health's cinnabar boiled—sweat and blood—
dreams in a membrane of sleep, dreams of
pushing half-a-step forward.

An engraver stood in the crowd,
ready to transfer to true bronze
what the artist (who had charred the paper)
had earned the chance to imprint only by splitting hairs.

It's like hanging from my own eyelashes,
all of me ripening, stretching, and
until I drop off, I go on performing.
It's all we know, here, now.

January 1934

---

290
[A Variant of 289]

TO FAVORSKY

And a bearded engraver was in the crowd,
thoughtful friend of copper-pine-boards
glazed into a bent shining by three-layered oxide, all
radiant as truth rolls on through wax.

It's like hanging from my own eyelashes
in the crowd-winged air of pictures,

painted by the masters who cultivate arrangements
of sight and the ordering of the multiplicities in faces.

*Moscow, January 1934*

---

## 291
## [Another Variant of 289]

TO ANDREY BIELY

Confront the timid hasty soul
with the profound inner heart of things
and she runs down a tiny winding path,
but she does not see Death's wide way.

And he seems to have shunned death,
with a novice's glorious shyness, the
shyness of the first sound at a brilliant assembly,
a sound pouring—down into violin-bows' longitudinal forest,

Pouring backwards, still lazy, measuring itself
first against flax, then against fibre,
pouring down into silence—so silent it hardly believes itself—
out of nothing, a thread, the darkness—

Pouring for the tender mask, just-now stripped off,
for plaster fingers not holding a pen,
for swollen lips, for the consolidation caresses
of a coarse-grained good, a coarse-grained peace.

*Moscow, January 1934*

## 292

TO A. BIELY

Caucasus mountains shouted for him,
and the crowded, tender Alps—
His visionary foot climbed
steep choirs of ascent.

He endured the branching of European
thought, carried it like someone meant to carry it:
Rachel stared at the mirror of phenomena,
and Leah was singing and weaving a wreath.

*Moscow, January 1934*

## 293
## [ A Variant of 292 ]

TO A. BIELY

He conducted the Caucasus mountains, waved, and waving,
climbed paths on the cramped Alps, then
looking back, with nervous steps walked
across on an endless crowd's conversation—

A crowd of impressions, events, minds . . .
He endured the branching of European
thought, as if no one else could carry it:
Rachel staring at the mirror of phenomena,
Leah singing and weaving a wreath.

*Moscow, January 1934*

## 294

TO A. BIELY

Where did they bring him from? Who? Which one died?
Just where? I'd never thought of it, somehow . . .
Tell me: did they say some Gogol died?
Not Gogol, no, just a writer . . . a gold bird, a little Gogol.

The one who created that misty mess,
who tried to seem nimble, but a lightweight, all right.
Forgot something, never learning something,
organized a mess, stood twirling till the snow gave up.

Quiet as an oyster—you can't get near him
—there's a guard of honor.
Something hidden here—something strange:
———* made a mess, got it all wrong, and went to sleep.

Moscow, 10 January 1934

* Words missing from the manuscript.

---

## 295

You're a master of guilty glances,
proprietor of tiny shoulders—
dangerous male stubbornness is subdued,
words run to the water and are drowned.

Fish swim by, fins glowing,
spreading out gills. Here, take them—
feed them with the half-bread
of flesh, these soundless mouths.

We're not red goldfish,
this is just how we are, sisters all:

thin ribs in a warm body,
pointless wet brilliance of eyes.

An eyebrow-stroke opens dangerous roads.
And I like it, like some kidnapped Turk—why?
This tiny flying-red,
these lips' wretched half-moon.

Be calm my dear, my beautiful Turk,
I'll sew myself in a sack alongside you,
a hollow dark sack, swallowing your dark words,
I'll drink crooked one-eyed water, for you.

Mary, you help the dying.
You have to sleep, to tell death you're coming.
I stand on a strong threshold.
Go. Leave. Stay, just a little more . . .

Moscow, February 1934

## 296

Your narrow shoulders were meant to redden under
whips, redden under whips, burn in frost.

Your child-hands were meant to lift hot irons,
to lift hot irons and weave ropes.

Your tender feet were meant to walk bare over
glass, walk bare over glass and bloody sand.

Well, and I was meant to burn for you like a
black candle, burn like a black candle and never dare pray.

1934

297

Nereids, oh my sea-nymph Nereids,
tears are food and drink, to you—
For the daughters of Mediterranean insult
my compassion is itself insulting.

March 1935 [?]

---

298
Lady Violinist

They run after long-fingered Paganini
like a crowd of gypsies—
some like a herd of Czechs, some in a Polish ball,
some like a Hungarian *czardash*.

Female, haughty upstart
with tone as wide as the Yenisei River,
console me with your music—
Marina Mnishek's curls are on
your head, you Polack,
your bow is nervous, your violin's a hypochondriac.

Comfort me with horsey Chopin,
with sober Brahms—no, wait—
with animal-Paris, wild.
With sweaty, mealy carnivals, or
with fresh-brewed Vienna beer—

Nervous-prancing Vienna, in conductor's tail-coats
and Danube fireworks, horse-races,
or waltzes poured like wine
from grave to cradle.

So play till the aorta snaps,
play with that cat's-head in your mouth.

There used to be three devils—but you're the fourth,
the last blossoming wonderful devil!

> Voronezh, April–June 1935

## 299
## Black Earth

Too much fussed over, far too black, all under
care, strung-out like tufts of horse-mane, all air and attention,
spilling, crumbling, clotting in a choir—
wet lumps of my land, wet lumps of my will, my freedom.

So black that she's blue, in early plowing,
defenceless labor building itself in her—
a thousand hills of plowed-up rumor—
Thus: a circle without end, inside a circle, in a circle!

And yet the earth is—a mistake, the fat back-end
of a hatchet—begging's no good, nor lying at her feet:
she pricks up your ears with a rotting flute,
she freezes your ears with a morning clarinet.

How plows love the fat layers,
how steppes are silent, as April does its quick work.
Well, greetings, black earth, keep your eyes open, your heart
up—there's an eloquent black silence in just working.

> Voronezh, April 1935

## 300

Ear-flaps, my little ear-flap-whisperers,
sometime I'll think of Voronezh nights:

voices of undrunk wine
and midnight honking near Red Square . . .

Well, how's the metro? Shut up, hide it . . .
Don't ask how the buds are blooming . . .
But you, the Kremlin Clock striking,
you're the language of space, squeezed down to a dot.

Voronezh, April 1935

---

## 301

Let me go, Voronezh, make me go—
you'll drop me, you'll let me slip away,
you'll let me slide through your fingers—you'll pick me up—
Voronezh—vim and vigor, Voronezh, vigor and whim.

Voronezh, April 1935

---

## 302
## Shearing the Children

There's a lot of life left in us,
lots of Chinese dresses and butterfly
blouses, lots of web-footed stuff
walking Russian streets.

But our leading typewriter, caustic,
still takes his chestnut bribes,
and wise ripe locks of hair
fall on a clean napkin,

The world's still full of sweethearts and swallows, all kinds of good
birds. No comet's given us the plague, yet,

and sensible violet ink still writes,
still star-carrying, still wagging its tales.

Voronezh, April 1935

## 303

This street? This?
Mandelstam Street.
One hell of a name!—
Screw it this way, screw it that,
it never comes out straight.

He hadn't much linear
in him. His heart just wasn't
linear, and so this street—
really, this hole in the ground—
has this name, is known
by his name, this
Mandelstam.

Voronezh, April 1935

## 304

I live in an impressive kitchen-garden
—housekeeper Vanka could stroll around, here.
The wind blows free-of-charge, in our mill,
and brushwood roads run into the distance.

The half-iced edges of black steppe-nights, black-arable nights,
are bone-chilled, glass-pearled fires:
on the other side of the wall the surly boss
stalks in his Russian boots.

And the floor-boards curve themselves up
in this alien house where I cannot sleep,
the gravestone floor-boards of this house
where my own life means nothing much to me.

Voronezh, April 1935

## 305

I've died twice, but I have to live,
and the town's half-crazy with water.

How handsome he is, how happy, how high-cheek-boned,
how the plow likes the fat soil,

How the steppe is silent, at April's turning—
and the sky, the sky—is your Michelangelo!

Voronezh, 1935

## 306

Yes, I'm lying in the ground, I'm moving my lips,
but every schoolboy will memorize what I'm saying:

The ground is roundest on Red Square,
and her sloping choice grows hard,

The ground is roundest on Red Square, and somehow
her slope is free and easy,

Leaning back down to the rice fields
while the last slave on earth is alive.

Voronezh, May 1935

## 307

You've taken the seas, you've taken my running-start, my flying-start,
you've weighted my steps with the violent earth,
and for what? Brilliant, brilliant:
you've left the lips still moving.

*Voronezh, 1935*

---

## 308–310
## Kama River

### 308

How dark to the eye, on the Kama,
when towns stand on oak knees.

Burning, scalding spruce-groves run in the water, looking younger,
wearing spiderwebs—beard to beard.

Water leans heavy on a hundred oars, sweeping
up and down to Kazan, up and down to Cherdyn.

I sailed the river, there, with a curtain on my window,
a curtain on my window and my head on fire.

And my wife with me—not sleeping for five nights,
she never slept, for five nights—driving, driving with soldier after soldier
    after soldier.

*Voronezh, May 1935*

### 309
[A Variant of 308]

How dark to the eye, on the Kama,
when towns stand on oak knees.

Burning, scalding spruce-groves run in the water, getting younger,
wearing spiderwebs, beard to beard.

Water leans heavy on a hundred oars,
up and down to Kazan, up and down to Cherdyn.

This machinegun wood-flock moves
mighty with peasants, burned with underbrush.

And up the Tobol they shout: the Ob's on the float,
it's standing! The river's rising, the river's rising.

        Voronezh, May 1935

310

I was moving to the fir-east, I looked,
the deep Kama rushed at the buoy,

And I wish I could strip a mountain with fire,
but you barely have time to plant forests,

And I wish I could live right here—listen to me—
in these long-lived Ural Mountains, full of people,

And I wish I could somehow stand guard for
this reckless, glassy flatness, I in my long coat.

        Voronezh, May 1935

---

311

Speech from a damp sheet—
oh yes, yes, a sound-shepherd for fish—
and a picture came at me,
at everybody, at you.

Sneezing at crooked losses,
deathly cigarettes in their teeth,
the latest-model officers for the
steppe's yawning groin.

Buzzing of airplanes
burning to powder,
English horse-razor
on the admiral's cheeks.

Measure me, land, carve me over again,
marvelous fever of land hung onto me!—
Chapayev's rope drew tight—
help me, untie me, share me!

                                    Voronezh, May–June 1935

---

## 312
## Stanzas

1

I don't want to change my soul's last half-kopeck,
here in the middle of hothouse youngsters,
but one peasant joins a collective farm
and I go into the world, and the people they're good enough, they're good
    enough.

2

I like Red Army coats, long seam
down to the heels, simple sleeve, smooth sleeve,
cut like a Volga cloud,
so lying like a shovel on your back, on your chest,
it stays, not wasting itself on extra seams,
and it rolls up in the summer.

3

Some damned seam, some ridiculous fancy,
separates us. And listen:
I have to live, breathing and bolsheviking,
getting better-looking before I die,
ready to be here a while, to play with people a while.


4

Just think, in lovely Cherdyn
where it smells like the Ob, and the Tobol has a funnel-mouth,
I rushed around in a two-by-four mess—
I didn't stay to see slandering goats fight it out—
like a rooster in transparent summer darkness—
food and spit, and something else, and liars—
I shrugged off the woodpecker's knocking. A quick leap—and I'm in my mind.


5

And you, Moscow, my sister, you're a lightweight,
meeting your brother in an airplane,
before the first streetcar bell—
more delicate than the sea, more tangled than a lettuce—
made of wood, made of glass, made of milk.


6

My country talked to me,
spoiled me, scolded me, refused to read me,
but this ripened me she noticed, like an eye-witness—
she noticed—and suddenly lifting an optical lens
she turned a sunbeam on me and I burst into flames.


7

I have to live, breathing and bolsheviking,
to work at words, disobedient, not quite alone.

I hear Soviet machines tapping in the Arctic.
I remember everything—German brothers, their necks,
and how the gardener-executioner spent his spare time
with the Lorelei's lilac comb.


8

I've not been robbed, I've not been cracked,
I'm just too damned big—
like *The Tale of Igor's Men* my string is taut,
and after the asthma's over
my voice echoes the earth—a final weapon—
the black earth's dry moisture.

Voronezh, May–June 1935

---

313

The day had five heads. For a solid five twenty-four
hours, shrinking, I was proud of space, because it sprouted on yeast.
Sleep was older than hearing, hearing was older than sleep—all-in-one,
    keen, sensitive, tactful . . .
and highways came rushing after us, fast, fast, on a coachman's reins . . .

The day had five heads; dancing-mad
cavalry rode, and infantry, a black-topped mass walking:
aorta of might dilated in white nights—no, in knives—
the eye turned into pine-needle meat.

If I had just an inch of blue sea, just the-eye-of-a-needle's worth,
so that number two, time's convoyed number two, could get sailing along.
Crusty Russian fairy-tale! Wooden spoon—ho there!
Where are you, you three gentle fellows out of the GPU's iron gates?

Scholars in overcoats, packing pistols, the tribe of official Pushkin-keepers,
keep Pushkin's marvelous merchandise out of parasites' hands—

young dilettantes of white-toothed little verses,
oh if I had an inch of blue sea, the eye-of-a-needle's worth!

The train headed for the Urals. Chapayev galloped out of a
movie, jabbering, right into our open mouths—
riding behind a wooden stockade, on a sheet ribbon,
to die, to jump up on his horse!

Voronezh, June 1935

# 314

Can you praise a woman who's dead?
Alienated, strong . . .
some foreign love-power led her
to a forced, hot grave.

And round eyebrow-warblers left
the grave and flew to me,
saying they'd rested in a cold
Stockholm bed and were stronger, yes.

And your family prized great-grandfather's violin,
handsomer all the time from its narrow neck,
and you opened your little mouth,
laughing, like an Italian, becoming a Russian . . .

I cherish your heavy memory—
branch gone wild, bear-cub, *mignonne*—
But wind-mill wheels winter in snow
and the postman's tiny horn grows cold.

Voronezh, 3 June 1935–14 December 1936

## 315

Saint Isaacs froze on dead eyelashes,
and well-fed, lordly streets are blue—
the death of organ-grinders, and thick bear-fur, thick,
and someone else's logs in the fireplace.

The chief huntsman is driving merchandise out—
a tiny pack of branching lines—
Earth rushes along—a furnished ball—
and the mirror writhes, nasty, trying to know-it-all.

Along the staircase landings: argument, discord, mist—
breathing, breathing and singing—and Schubert
congealed, frozen in the fur-coat—
motion, motion, motion . . .

*Voronezh, June 1935*

---

## 316

Full-weight ingots of Roman nights,
the breasts that tempted young Goethe,

Maybe I need to answer, but I'm no beggar:
life outside the law has its reasons too.

*Voronezh, June 1935*

---

## 317

—No, it's not migraine, just give me the menthol pencil—
no languishing arty looks, no bright-colored space . . .

Life began in a trough, a burring wet whisper,
then burned like soft kerosene soot.

In a summer cottage, somewhere, later, bound in rough leather,
it flared up suddenly, an enormous lilac fire.

—No, it's not migraine, just give me the menthol pencil—
no languishing arty looks, no bright-colored space.

Then, squinting, agonized, through colored glasses, I see,
I see: sky menacing like a club, earth like a red-haired bald spot . . .

And then, and then—I can't remember—and then, it must have been
  broken,
It smells like tar, a little, and rotten train-oil, maybe, blubber-oil . . .

—No, it's not migraine, but space cold, sexless,
shredded cheese-cloth whining as it rips, the low rumble of carbolic
  guitars . . .

Voronezh, 23 April–July 1935

---

# 318

I'll perform a smoky ritual:
in this opal disgrace I see
a sea-summer's living strawberries—
double-sparked red quartz,
and the agate, ant-like brother—
But a simple soldier deep down from the maelstrom
means more, to me—a gray, wild
creature who pleases no one.

Voronezh, July 1935

### 319

A wave, running—a wave smashing a wave's spine,
leaping at the moon, a slave's anguished yearning,
a mercenary's forced abyss—
restless undulating capital—going
blind in one eye, rushing in circles, digging ditches in sand.

And crenellations of unbuilt walls sprout
in the twilight-cotton air,
and soldiers of suspicious sultans
tumble down foam stairways—smashed apart, sprayed,
while cold eunuchs carry poison.

Voronezh, July 1935

---

### 320

My borrowed dust should not go back
to the earth like a mealy white butterfly.
This thinking body
should turn to a street, to a nation—
this charred, vertebral body
that has realized its own length.

Exclamations of green pine-needles—
well-deep wreaths—
pulling life and precious time,
braced on mortal mountings,
hoops of red-flagged conifer—
round alphabetic wreaths.

Comrades of the last call, walking
to work in hard, harsh heaven,
silent infantry carrying
rifle-exclamations on shoulders.

And thousands of ack-ack guns—
hazel-eyed, blue-eyed—
and people, people, people in jagged mobs—
who's going to take their place?

Voronezh, 21 July 1935

---

321

Angry lamb in Raphael's canvas, smile—
canvas-universe-lips, but a changed universe, all changed . . .

Dissolve pearl-pain in reed-pipe's light air.
Ocean-salt eats into the velvet fringe, the dark dark dark
   blue . . .

Color of aerial theft, color of thickness of caves,
folds of stormy peace poured onto knees.

Thin-reed-groves, young on cliffs, drier than bread,
and delightful power sailing in the corners of the sky.

Voronezh, 9 January 1936

---

322

From the backs of houses, the backs of forests,
longer than freight trains,
come, buzz, honk, hoot, my helper
too, Sadko of factories and gardens.

Drone on, old man, breathe sweet,
like Novgorod-merchant Sadko, visiting
deep under the blue sea—

honk, honk the drone of Soviet cities
deep down in the depths of time.

Voronezh, 6–8 December 1936

## 323

I'll stare at the world some more,
amazed by children and snow,
but smiles are incorruptible, like roads,
disobedient, no one's servant.

Voronezh, 10–13 December 1936

## 324

Goldfinch, I'll tilt back my head:
let's stare at the world together.
Is this winter light, prickly like chaff,
harsh to your eyes too?

Tail like a boat—yellow-black feathers,
below the beak, poured into paint—
do you know, goldfinch, you, yes,
you, what a fop you are?

What an air, over that forehead:
black, red, yellow, white!
His eyes watch right and left—right and left!
But he won't look, he flew away.

Voronezh, December 1936

## 325
[ A Variant of 324 ]

Child-mouth chewing chaff,
smiles, chews,
and I'll tilt back my head like a fop
and see a goldfinch.

Tail like a boat, yellow-black feathers,
breastplate sewn red.
Yellow-black goldfinch, how much
of a fop are you, eh?

Voronezh, 1936

---

## 326
[ Another Variant of 324 ]

Child-mouth chewing chaff,
smiles, chews,
and I'll tilt back my head like a fop
and see a goldfinch—
hopping wild as bilberry-shot,
beady eyes watching—
Oh my likeness, I answer you:
Goldfinches shall live—that's my *ukaz*, there!

1936

---

## 327

A goldfinch suddenly shakes, like airy
fancy bread, shakes suddenly, large-hearted,

spite peppering a learned little cloak,
nightcap standing beautiful with black.

The plank is a slanderer, your perch is a slanderer,
the knitting-needle-spoke cage is a slanderer—
the world's all inside out,
and somewhere there's a forest university
for clever disobedient birds!

*Voronezh, December 1936*

---

## 328

It's not mine, it's not yours—it's theirs,
the power of grammatical links:
reeds sing, porous, with their air,
and human snail-lips, grateful,
pull their breath-weight up onto themselves.

They're nameless. Go into their gristle
and become heir to their kingdoms.
And wandering in their forks and windings
you'll paint, for people's living hearts,
all their delights, and all
that torments them, flooding, ebbing.

*Voronezh, 9–27 December 1936*

---

## 329

Today's a yellow-beaked virgin,
somehow: I can't figure it out—
And seaside gates stare
at me in anchors, in mists.

Battleships move along the faded
water, quiet, quiet,
and under the ice, canal
pencil-cases, narrow, are even blacker . . .

        Voronezh, 9–28 December 1936

---

## 330

An idol is idle, inside a mountain,
in careful, endless, guarded rooms,
fat necklaces dripping from his neck,
protecting sleep's flow, sleep's ebb.

When he was little, when he played with peacocks,
they fed him an Indian rainbow.
They fed him milk in rose-colored clays
and lots of red cochineal, lots.

A hypnotized bone, tied in a knot,
humanized knees, arms, shoulders—
he smiles his wide mouth,
thinks with his bone, feels with his forehead,
and tries to remember his human look.

        Voronezh, December 1936

---

## 331
## [ A Variant of 330 ]

An idol is idle, inside a mountain,
smiling like a baby with black plums,
fat necklaces dripping from his neck,
protecting sleep's flow, sleep's ebb.

When he was little, when he played with peacocks,
they fed him an Indian rainbow.
They fed him milk in rose-colored clays
and lots of red cochineal, lots.

Crossed strangely, tied in a knot
of shame and tenderness, of heartlessness and bone,
he smiles his wide mouth
and begins to live when guests arrive.

Voronezh, 1936

## 332

I'm at this time's heart—the road's not clear,
time takes goals away—
takes my staff's tired ash-tree,
takes the wretched bronze mold.

Voronezh, Winter 1936

## 333

And the gunshop foreman,
tailor of tombstones,
will tell me: Okay, old man,
we'll sew you up something . . .

Voronezh, 1936

## 334

You can peel off hibernation-
bristle with a Gillette—
let us remember
the half-Ukrainian summer.

You—eminent peaks,
shaggy-oak birthdays,
glory of Ruisdael paintings—
but for a start—just one bush
in the amber and meat of red clay!

The earth runs upward. It's good
to see clear strata,
to be master of an embraceable
seven-chambered simplicity.

Hills flying to some far-away
goal like light hay-ricks,
steppe-boulevard of roads
like a tent-chain in shady heat!
And willows ran to the fire,
and proud poplars stayed standing!
Rut of frosty smoke
over yellow stubble-camp.

And then the River Don, like a half-breed,
fine thin silver and awkward too,
heaps to half a dipper
and, flustered, is lost, like my soul
when night's burden lies itself
down on rough hard beds,
and tree-drunkards come out of the banks
and lift loud voices.

Voronezh, 15–27 December 1936

## 335

Pine-grove's law—
domestic ringing of viols and harps:
bare sinuous trunks,
but harps growing, viols
growing, as if Aeolus bent
trunks into harps
and then left them, sorry for roots,
sorry for trunks, sorry for all his work.
He woke the harps and viols
to sound in bark, turning brown.

*Voronezh, 16–18 December 1936*

## 336

I sense winter
like a tardy present:
and I love her initial
diffident sweep.

Her fright is beautiful,
like the beginning of terrible things:
even crows grow timid
seeing the whole woodless circle.

But the light-blue distinctness, that's
the most powerfully fragile:
rivers' half-round
forehead-ice, lulling, sleepless . . .

*Voronezh, 20–30 December 1936*

## 337

All my misfortune
comes from seeing
that usurious cat's eye—
grandson of stagnant greenery,
merchant of sea-grass.

There where immortal Koschey
guzzles flaming cabbage-soup—
there he waits for guests to happen,
there with talking stones—
moving rocks with his tongs,
nipping gold nails.

The cat in those sleeping rooms
isn't there for fun—
There's hidden mountain-treasure, tight-hidden mountain-
treasure, in his burning eyes.
And there are banquets of round sparks
in his imploring, begging,
ice-cold eyes.

                              Voronezh, 20–30 December 1936

---

## 338

A place in dark waters—
abysses of bread, buckets of thunder—
no natural resource for nobility—
an ocean's kernel . . .
I love this picture—
it looks like Africa—
light it up: no one can count
all the transparent holes . . .
Anna, and Rossosh, and Gremyachye—
I say their names over and over—

snow-white like eiderdown
out of the train window.

I whirled in *sovkhoz* meadows,
my mouth full of air,
the sunflower's terrible suns
revolving right into my eyes.
At night I drove into a Tambov of mittens,
blazing with snow,
I saw the Tsny—an everyday river—and its
white, white, white shroud.
I'll remember work-days in this familiar land
forever—
and I'll never forget the district
committee in Vorobyov.

Where am I? What's wrong?
Bare steppe, without winter:
Koltsov's step-mother—
Sure, sure: it's the goldfinches' native land.—Oh, sure.—
Consider the mute city,
ice-crusted,
only night's tea-kettle
talking to itself,
trains calling
in the thick sediment of steppe air—
and the Ukrainian sound
of their long-winded whistles.

Voronezh, December 1936

---

## 339
## [ A Variant of 338 ]

A full bucket of storms
going down into dark waters on a chain, moving out of
nobility's natural resources,
headed into the ocean's kernel.

It rocked, swayed,
cautious, threatening.
look: the sky's higher—
a new home, a house, a roof—
and out on the street, light, day! . . .

                                          Voronezh, 26 December 1936

## 340

Landmark-stakes of a distant convoy
through glass windows . . . a house, a real house . . .
It's warm, and it's frosty, and
so the river seems close.
And that, what sort of forest? Spruce?

—No, lilac!
—And a birch tree, there, over there?
—I can't be sure:
it's only the prose of aerial ink,
illegible, faint . . .

                                          Voronezh, 26 December 1936

## 341

Hillocks of human heads into the horizon,
and I am diminished—they won't notice me,
but I'll come back, resurrected in tender books and
children's games, saying: See? The sun is shining.

                                                              1936/1937

## 342
## Birth of a Smile

When children start to smile,
sweet and sour bifurcating,
smile-ends, seriously,
travel into ocean's anarchy.

Inexpressible wonderful sense,
corners of mouth playing in glory—
iridescent rainbow seam stitching itself
into eternal cognition of the real.

Continent lifting itself on paws, out of the water—
flow of snail-mouth coming closer—
an instant of Atlantis gushing in the eyes:
installation of reality into the possibilities of miracles.

Space losing color, losing taste,
continent lifting itself with a spine-ridge,
snail crawling out, smile shining,
rainbow tying the ends together,
and an instant of Atlantis gushes into both eyes.

*Voronezh, 9–11 December 1936–11 January 1937*

---

## 343

Near circular Koltsov
I'm ringed-in like a falcon,
and no messengers come,
and my house has no porch.

There's a blue pine forest
tied to my leg,
the horizon's thrown open
like a messenger with no message.

Nomad-hummocks on the steppe—
and lodging-for-the-night, and nights, and little nights
keep walking, walking, walking—
as if leading the blind . . .

          Voronezh, 1–9 January 1937

---

## 344

When magicians wind up
whispering bay horsehair, whispering
sorrel horsehair, there among
downcast branches,

The bleached-out, lazy epic
hero has no interest
in singing—the small, the
mighty wintering bullfinch!

I'll hurry under
the overhanging sky, under its
arching eyebrows, I'll hurry into a
lilac sleigh, and I'll sit down.

          Voronezh, 6–10 January 1937

---

## 345

Your eye's in a heavenly crust
turned to the distance, turned down;
parentheses defend
fine perceptive lashes.

Idolized, he'll live
in his native land, live long—
Amazed eye-whirlpool,
throw him after me!

He stares, cheerful, into
transient time—
bright, iridescent, incorporeal,
still pleading . . .

Voronezh, 9 January 1937

## 346

Precious world-yeast—
noise, tears, trouble—
like dents suddenly filled
with singing water,
thimbles under-the-hooves—
tracks of condensed running—
not handed out by lot:
to endure for centuries—no mica, no mica at all.

Road-splashes in little mirrors—
tired tracks
standing for a while
with no shroud, with no tombstone.
And what's mine has picked itself
up and gone, as if something else
had walked obliquely across it
and then echoed, echoed . . .

Voronezh, 12 January 1937

# 347
# [ A Variant of 346 ]

Precious world-yeast—
noise, tears, trouble—
rain-accents
of simmering misfortune,
sound-losses:
what ore can you dig them back out of?

Your beggared memory senses
copper water in
sodden dents: the very first time—
and you follow in their steps,
not cherishing yourself, unknown—
yourself blind man, yourself guide.

*Voronezh, 12–18 January 1937*

---

# 348
# [ Another Variant of 346 ]

Imp in wet fur hide, climbing up—
Okay, where are you headed? Where?
Into thimbles under-the-hooves,
into hurried tracks—
fleecing foliated air, kopeck
by kopeck, out of the villages.

Road-splashes in little mirrors—
hurried tracks
standing for a while
with no shroud, with no tombstone.
Sloping wheel-rumbles—
packed down, all there—and half as much trouble!

I'm bored—my straight
honest business is jabbering, oblique:
something has walked on over it,
laughed at it, and knocked it off its axle!

>                    Voronezh, 12–18 January 1937

---

## 349

I stare at the frost's face,
alone. He's going nowhere—I come from
nowhere, and the steppe's breathing marvel
keeps ironing itself, pleating itself, unwrinkled.

The sun squints in starched misery—
calm squinting, consoled squinting . . .
One forest is almost the same as any other forest . . .
and snow crunches in your eyes, sinless like fresh bread.

>                         Voronezh, 16 January 1937

---

## 350

And what do we do with these crushed plains,
the drawling hunger of this miracle?
Anyway, that openness we see
in them we see for ourselves, falling into sleep, we see—
and the question keeps growing—Where are they going? Where are they
    from?—
And isn't he crawling slowly along them,
him, the one we cry out at in our sleep—
him, the Judas of the future?

>                         Voronezh, 16 January 1937

# 351

Oh these slow short-winded open spaces—
I'm glutted, no more, no more!—
The horizon gets its breath, is thrown open—
oh, a bandage for my eyes, for both my eyes!

I could take the sand's flaky temper
better, on the Kama's jagged shores,
I'd hold onto her bashful sleeve, her
ripples, edges, pits.

I'd work with her, in harmony—for a century, for one single moment—
jealous of besieging rapids—
I'd listen to the fibrous motion of rings
under flowing forest-bark.

Voronezh, 16 January 1937

---

# 352

No comparisons: everyone alive is incomparable.
With sweet fright
I'd agree with the steppe's smooth equality, and
the sky's circle was like a sickness.

I'd turn to the servant-air,
waiting for news, for something,
and get ready to leave, and I'd drift down an arc
of journeys that never begin.

Wherever I've got more sky—I'll wander there, yes—
but this bright boredom won't let me leave
these young Voronezh hills, won't let me go
to those universal hills—there, clear, distinct, over in Tuscany . . .

Voronezh, 18 January 1937

## 353

How feminine-silver burns, having
fought the oxide, having fought the flux,
and quiet work silvers over
the iron plow, and the poet's voice.

Voronezh, 1937

---

## 354

I'm not dead, I'm not alone
while I'm still happy with my beggar-girl, delighting
in these great plains,
in twilight-shadow, in hunger, in snow-storms.

I live alone in beautiful poverty, in sumptuous
misery—peaceful, consoled—
blessèd days, blessèd nights,
and sinless sweet-singing labor.

Whoever's frightened by barking, and by his shadow, who's mowed
by the wind—he's really unlucky,
whoever's half-alive and begging
alms from shadows—he's really poor.

Voronezh, January 1937

---

## 355

I'm in a cobweb of light, today—
black-haired spider-thread, brown-haired spider-thread—
The people need light and blue air
and bread and Elbrus' volcanic snow.

And there's no one to talk to,
and I'm not even looking, now—
There aren't any transparent weeping stones
like that in the Crimea, or in the Urals either.

The people need poetry mysteriously their own,
always stirred awake by it,
bathing, washing in its breath—
its chestnut wave, flax-curled wave.

         Voronezh, 19 January 1937

---

## 356

Where's that bound-down, nailed-down moan,
where's Prometheus—helper of cliffs?
Where's the black-flying hawk—the yellow-eyed urge
of his claws, leaping from sullen eyebrows?

No, never again—tragedies don't come back—
but those approaching lips,
those lips lead me down into the essence
of Aeschylus the wood-loader, of Sophocles the wood-cutter.

He is echo—he is greeting, landmark—no, the plow: he is the plow.
Rock-air theater of growing time
standing—everyone wants to see everyone else—
see the new-born, the death-spreaders, and see the living.

        Voronezh, 19 January–14 February 1937

## 357

As if, somewhere, a heaven-stone wakes the earth—
a poem fell, a disgrace, not knowing its father;
creators accept the inexorable as it comes—
It is what it is—no one judges it.

*Voronezh, 20 January 1937*

---

## 358

I hear early ice, I hear it
rustling under bridges,
I remember bright intoxication
floating over our heads.

Singing from stale stairways, from streets
circled with the angular palaces
of his Florence, Dante's
tired lips
sang with more power.

That's how my shadow's eyes
gnaw at that granular granite, seeing
a row of cards, of logs at night, or maybe
a row of houses in the light.

Or my shadow twiddles
and yawns
or makes noise, here among people,
warming itself with their wine, their sky,

And feeds importunate swans
with dry, flat bread . . .

*Voronezh, 21–22 January 1937*

## 359

I love frosty breath,
the declarations of winter-steam:
me—oh that's me—and reality—that's reality!

A little boy, red like a lantern,
ruling his tiny child's
sled, runs sailing over water.

And I—peeved at the world, and with freedom—
I indulge the infection of little sleds
in silvery grappling-irons, in fringes—

I'd fall forever, lighter than a squirrel,
fall to the soft river, lighter than a squirrel—
half-a-sky in felt-boots, in felt-feet!

*Voronezh, 24 January 1937*

---

## 360

Where shall I go, this January?
This open city clings madly . . .
Am I drunk on locked doors, or what?—
I want to bellow: these locks, these clips, these clamps!

And the stockings of barking alleys,
and store-rooms in twisted streets, and corner-people
hiding, quick, quick, in their corners,
and running back out of their corners.

And in the warty darkness I slip
down a hole to the icy pumphouse,
I stumble, I eat dead air,
crows fly off, feverish.

And I gasp after them, beating
on some frozen wood basket:
—I want a reader! someone to talk to! a doctor!
Oh, on that thorny stairway—if I could have a real conversation!

                        Voronezh, end of January-February 1937

---

## 361

Our Time's mighty landmark
stands in all this bustle and running
in stations and streets
and begins to lift its eyebrows.

I learned, he learned, you learned—
now take us wherever you want:
into garrulous station-bushes
into expectations along a powerful river.

That station's far away, now,
that tank with its boiled water—
tin mug on a chain,
darkness clouding the eyes.

Finnish words went walking,
passengers came fighting,
the disapproval of those eyes
caressing me, out of the wall, drilling into me.

Our pilots and our harvesters,
and our comrade rivers, our comrade forests,
our comrade cities, they've all
got a lot coming, still hidden, now.

Impossible to remember what was—
lips are too hot, words are too stale—
the white curtain whipping,
the sounds of iron foliage.

And yet it was really quiet—
all there was was a ship on the river,
and buckwheat blooming behind the cedars,
and fish moving in the river-murmur.

And I walked into the Kremlin, and I
came to it—to its core—and I had no pass,
I'd ripped up the unbleached linen
of distance—I, heavy with my guilty head.

Voronezh, February 1937

---

## 362
## Poem on an Unknown Soldier

I

Let this air witness—
his long-range heart—
omnivorous, energetic in mud-huts—
ocean, substance with no window.

Are these stars informers?
They stare down all the time—why?—
into the judge's sentence, the witness' sentence,
into the ocean, substance with no window.

The rain remembers, cheerless sower,
anonymous manna,
how wooded crosses aimed at
the ocean, or at battlefields.

Cold, sick people will
kill, will endure, will
starve, and an unknown soldier
lies in his famous grave.

Puny swallow, teach me,
oh you have forgotten flight,

teach me to control this aerial grave
with no rudder, no wing.

And I'll give you a strict report, on behalf of
Lermontov, Mikhail,
the way the grave straightens
a hunchback, the way the aerial pit pulls you in.

Voronezh, 3 March 1937

2

These worlds threaten us
like moving grapes,
hang like stolen cities,
like golden tongue-slips, like slander—
berries of poisonous cold—
tents of extendible constellations—
golden oil of constellations.

3

Rapid-motion light: ground, crushed, smashed into a beam,
through decimal-marked ether,
starts a number, light made transparent
by bright pain and the moths of zeros.

And beyond the field of fields a new field
flies—like a three-cornered crane—
news flies down light-dusty roads—it feels
bright after yesterday's battle.

News flies down light-dusty roads—
I'm not Leipzig, I'm not Waterloo,
I'm not Armageddon. I'm—new—
I'll be the light of the world.

Austerlitz's tiny fire flickered out,
deep in a black-marble oyster—
Mediterranean swallows squint,
Egypt's pestilential sand sinks, sinks.

4

Arabian jumble, medley of
rapid-motion light ground into a beam—
and the beam stands on my retina
with its slanting soles.

Millions killed, cheap,
beating an emptiness-road,
and from earth fortresses:
Goodnight, all the best.

Trench-sky, incorruptible,
sky of great, of wholesale deaths,
in the darkness of my lips rush
after you—away from you—you, all-in-all.

Behind the shell-holes, behind the embankments
and the rock-slides, where he lingered,
dark—the sullen, pitted, humiliated
genius of inside-out graves.


5

Foot-soldiers die well
and night-choirs sing well
over Schweik's flattened smile,
over Don Quijoté's bird-lance,
over a knight's bird-flat feet.
And a cripple is a friend, there,
there'll be work for them both.
And a little family of crutches
knocks on our time's outskirts—
Hey, friends—it's the round earth!


6

Is that why the skull spreads
over the whole forehead—from one side to the other—
so troops can't help but flood
its lovely eye-sockets?

The skull develops out of life
and into the whole forehead—from one side to the other—
teasing itself with its pure seams,
clear, serene, like a knowing cathedral-dome,
foaming with thought, dreaming of itself—
cup of cups, homeland of homelands—
cap sewn with starry hems—
tiny cap of happiness—Shakespeare's father.


7

Ash-tree clarity, sycamore vigilance,
rushes faintly red into its house,
and as if with fainting fits enchants
both skies and their dim dull fire.

Our allies are only the redundant,
and up ahead—no traps, but measurements, and mistakes—
and fighting for the air of existence
is a glory unlike all other glories.

Is that why crates of charm
are stored in empty space—
for white stars to rush into their houses,
faintly red!—

And enchanting my consciousness
with this half-fainting existence do
I drink this broth? Do I have no choice? And here
under fire am I eating my own head?!

Gypsy step-mother of the star camp—night—
do you know what will be, present and future too?


8

Aortas fill with blood
and rows of little whispers sound:
—I was born in ninety-four,
—I was born in ninety-two . . .
And I clutch my worn old birth-year

in my fist, and there in that crowd, all of us
together, I whisper with bloodless mouth:
—I was born at night between
January second and January third in the ninety-first
untrustworthy year, and time
surrounds me with fire.

Voronezh, February–March 1937

---

# 363

He still remembers my worn-out shoes—
my soles' obliterated grandeur,
and I—remember him, discordant,
black-haired, up near Mount David.

Sly pistachio streets
renewed with chalk, with a touch of egg-white,
the balcony-slope, the horseshoe, the horse-balcony,
small oaks, plane-trees, slow elms.

And the feminine chain of letters, curly letters,
headier still in their envelope-shells of light,
and the clever clever city, running down into wooden piling,
and into summer, young for its age, but getting older.

Voronezh, 7–11 February 1937

---

# 364

Like Rembrandt, martyr of
chiaroscuro, I went deep into numb-growing time,
but my burning rib's sharpness
is not guarded by those watchmen,
or by this soldier: they're sleeping in the thunderstorm.

Will you forgive me, my magnificent brother,
master, father of blackgreen darkness—
But the falcon-feather eye
and the hot jewel-boxes in midnight's harem
senselessly excite
the tribe, troubled by twilight's wine-skins and furs.

Voronezh, 8 February 1937

---

## 365

I sing when my throat is damp, when my soul is dry,
and my eyes modestly moist, and my consciousness is not cunning.
Is wine healthy? Are wineskins healthy?
Is the heave in Colchis' blood
healthy? But the chest gets squeezed, with no tongue—
and it's not me singing—it's my breath—
and hearing is in a mountain scabbard, and the head is deaf.

An unselfish song praises itself,
delight for friends, black tar for enemies.

A one-eyed song sprouting out of moss,
one-voiced gift of the hunting way of life,
song sung on horseback, in high notes,
breath held free and open, honest, angry,
caring only about carrying young people
to a sinless wedding . . .

Voronezh, 8 February 1937

---

## 366

Bursts of round bays and rope and gristle-gravel and the dark-blue,
and slow sail prolonged by clouds—

I'm taken away from you, hardly knowing you:
Longer than organ fugues—bitter false-haired
sea-grass—smelling of old, old lies.
The head gets tipsy with iron tenderness,
rust gnaws the barely-sloping shore . . .
Why is there different sand under my head?
You—guttural Urals, broad-shouldered Volga-land,
or this level steppe-land—there's all the rights I have—
and, chest full, I still have to breathe them in.

Voronezh, 8 February 1937

---

## 367

Armed with the eyes of narrow wasps
sucking the earth's axis, the earth's axis,
I sense everything I've ever known,
and I know it by heart, I remember, uselessly.

And I don't paint, and I don't sing,
and I don't saw a black-voiced violin:
all I do is dig my fangs into life, I love
to envy mighty, cunning wasps.

Oh if the sting of air and summer warmth
could by-pass sleep
and death, sometime, and force me, too,
to hear the earth's axis, the earth's axis . . .

Voronezh, 8 February 1937

---

## 368

Eyes sharper than a whetted scythe—
cuckoo in each eye, drop of dew in each eye—

And just barely able, full-length, to learn
how to distinguish among the great lonely stars.

> Voronezh, 8–9 February 1937

## 369

Like bronze and wood—like Favorsky flying
in boarded-up air we're neighbors, time and I,
and this flaky fleet of sawed-off oaks
and copper sycamore leads us on, together.

But resin still oozes, angry, out of the rings—
and the heart is—is it, really?—just frightened
meat—I'm guilty, I own a heart—and hearts are part
of hours dilated on and on, into infinity.

Friends without number, sated with this one hour,
this hour of ferocious streets with happy eyes—
I'll look again, I'll consider again
this long street with its forest of banners.

> Voronezh, 9–11 February 1937

## 370

I'm down in a lion's ditch, under a fort,
going down, down, down
under the yeast-storm of these sounds—
stronger than lions, more powerful than Moses and his Five Books.

Your summons: how close, how close—
Before childbirth's commandments, and first-born's, which came before all
   commandments—

a string of ocean pearls
and Tahitian women's gentle baskets.

Approach, continent of punitive singing,
with the deep bottom-places of your voice!
The shy-sweet icon faces of all our daughters
is worth—less than your littlest finger, oh Ur-mother.

I still have time without end, time, all time,
and as a background organ
accompanies a woman's voice
I too accompany this universal rapture.

Voronezh, 12 February 1937

## 371

My sleep keeps me sleepy, here on the Don,
and also turtles running this way, that way,
quick-armor motion,
and strange carpets of human noise.
And clear words lead me into battle,
defending life, defending
country—a land where death will sleep like a day-time owl,
and Moscow-glass burns between cut-glass ribs.
Impregnable Kremlin words:
the defense of defense
and of armor and of eyebrows and of the head,
yes and the eyes—all cheerfully gathered. All.
And it listens, this land—and other lands listen—
beating, breaking, a battle rhythm:
—Slaves are not to be slaves, whores are not to be whores!
And so the choir sings, hand in hand, by the clock.

Voronezh, 13 February 1937

## 372

If our enemies took me
and no one would speak to me;
if they took everything, everything—
the right to breathe, to open doors,
to claim that existence will be, will be,
and that the people are judges and judge, they judge;
if they dared to chain me like an animal,
to throw my food on the floor—
it won't make me mute, I won't muffle pain,
I'll write what I'm allowed to write,
and when my nakedness rings like a bell,
and the home of hostile darkness wakes,
I'll yoke ten oxen to my voice
and move my hand like a plow, in the darkness,
and then, compressed in an ocean of brotherly eyes,
I'll fall with the weight of an entire harvest,
with the exactness of that oath, ripping into the distance,
and deep in the dark sentry-night
the earth's unskilled-laborer's eyes
will flare, and a flock of flaming years will flash by,
and like a blind thunderstorm, rustling out, will come—Lenin . . .
Yes, but that which will endure on this earth,
that which will destroy reason, which will ruin life, will be—Stalin.

Voronezh, 1937

---

## 373

France, have pity, be merciful,
give me a bit of land, and honeysuckle.

Some turtle-dove truths, some fables from your pygmy
vineyard-keepers, in their cheesecloth partitions.

In easy December your clipped air
is dusted with frost, pecuniary, vengeful,

But a violet even in prison—infinity can drive one mad!
whistles, oh ironic maker of street-songs, negligent, casual—

Where the crooked July street
boiled, washing away kings.

But there's a good king in Paris, now,
in Chartres, in Arles—good king Chaplin, good kind Charlie—

In an oceanic bowler, with absent-minded precision,
swaggering, on hinges, with the flower-girl.

      \*   \*   \*   \*   \*

There—there: a shawl petrifies, a rose on its
breast, in the two-towered perspiration of a spiderweb;
a shame that the airy-grateful carousel
swings around, breathing of the city—

Bend your neck, godless woman
with a goat's golden eyes,
tease piles of niggard roses
with crooked gutteral scissors.

          Voronezh, 3–7 March 1937

---

# 374

I saw a lake, standing, sheer,
fish playing with a cut-up rose
in a wheel (they'd built a fresh-sweet house),
a fox and a lion fighting in a canoe.

Diseases stared through three barking
doors—enemies of other undissected
arcs, and a gazelle ran over the violet arch
and the cliff sighed, suddenly, with towers.

An honest sandstone rose up, damp, rebellious,
and near the factory-city, cricket-loud,
an urchin ocean, swelled by a fresh river,
tossed cups of water at the clouds.

Voronezh, 4–7 March 1937

---

## 375

On a raspberry-gold game-board,
at the edge where mountains slide their chips,
extravagant and snow-bound mountains,
a haughty, sleepy sleigh-city pulled high,
half-city, half equestrian beach,
harnessed in red coals,
warm with yellow resin
fused into burned sugar.

Forget the winter-oils of paradise:
no ice-rink Flemish slope, here,
no merry crooked dwarves' pack
crowing in great-earned caps!—
Don't embarrass me with comparisons,
clip my little picture (which loves that far-off road)
the way smoke, running on stilts,
carries away a dry, live Maple-paw.

Voronezh, 6 March 1937

---

## 376

This is a rough copy—I'll whisper it,
it's not time, not time:
the sky's instinctive, unplanned playing
is achieved by sweat and experiment.

And here under purgatory's temporary
sky we forget, often, often,
that heaven's happy warehouse—
is an extendible, lifelong home.

Voronezh, 9 March 1937

---

# 377
# The Last Supper

Supper-sky adoring the wall—
wounded, scar-bright sky—
falling into her, flaring,
turned into thirteen heads.

And there: my night sky
and I under it like a child—
back cold, eyes aching,
trying to pluck a battering sky.

And every battering-ram blow
showers down eyeless stars—
new wounds for this same supper,
darkness of an unfinished fresco-mural.

Voronezh, 9 March 1937

---

# 378

I'm lost in heaven . . . Where shall I go?
You, near the sky, tell me.
Oh Dante's nine athletic discs,
it was easier for you to ring.

Life and I are inseparable—she's dreaming
of killing and then caressing,
so Florentine anguish might whip in my ears,
right in my eyes, into the eye-sockets.

Don't crown me, please,
with tender-sharp laurel—
chop my heart, please,
into ringing blue bits,

And having served my time, I'll die,
friend to everyone alive,
and heaven's answer will be heard, louder
and higher and wider, out of my chest.

        Voronezh, 9–19 March 1937

---

## 379
## [ A Variant of 378 ]

I'm lost in heaven . . . Where shall I go?
You, near the sky, tell me.
Oh Dante's nine athletic discs,
it was easier for you to ring,
to gasp, to turn black, to turn blue.

You, standing over me, if you're not
yesterday's, if you're good-for-something,
a bearer of wine-cups or a monkish wine-master,
give me strength to drink the whirling
tower's health, with no foam, the spinning
tower of this crazy hand-to-hand blue sky.

Dove-cotes, blacknesses, starling bird-pole-houses,
specimens of choicest, darkest blue,
yesterday's ice, high-sky ice!—spring-ice,

clouds—fighters for delight—
Quiet! They're leading a cloud by the bridle.

Voronezh, 9–19 March 1937

---

# 380

A speck of insanity?
Your conscience?
Life's knot, where we're known and tied
and untied into existence.

So honest spider-beams spinning
cathedrals of super-life crystals
onto ribs, gather them again
to a single bunch.

Grateful bundles of clean lines,
all collected by thin beams,
gathering together, sometime,
like guests with open faces.

But only here on earth, not in the sky,
like in a house filled with music—
just don't frighten them, don't wound them, please—
let us live to see that, let us live to see.

Forgive me this as I say it,
read it back to me, quietly, quietly.

Voronezh, 15 March 1937

---

# 381
# Rome

Where fountain-frogs croak
and splash until they cannot

sleep and, wide-awake, can only
weep with all their gullet-strength, their sea-shell strength, and
sprinkle the city with amphibious
water, city saying yes to the strong, oh yes.

Insolent antiquity, light, summer-blue,
flat-footed, with predatory
eyes—like an Angel's virgin
bridge flat-footed over yellow water . . .
Blue, absurd, ashen
in hideous excrescence of houses,
city sculpted by dome-swallows
out of alleys and winds—
now made a nursery of murder—and by
you, paid-up brown-bloods,
Italian blackshirts,
vicious little dogs of dead Caesars.

\* \* \* \* \*

Your orphans, Michelangelo,
wear rock, wear shame:
tear-damp night, and innocent,
light-footed David,
and the bed where motionless
Moses lies like a waterfall—
unrestrained power, a lion's measure—
stays hypnotically quiet, enslaved.

And puckered stairs open
into pouring, staircase rivers—
made by the slow Rome-man
so steps might sound like acts.
Not like lazy sea-sponges
for crippled sweet comfort.

The Forum's pits are dug out, again,
the gates swing open for Herod,
and the dictator's heavy rotten-sheep
chin hangs over Rome.

Voronezh, 16 March 1937

382

Wind and water, wanting their mutual friend
to preserve an inner sandstone,
scratched herons and beakers
into dawn's bottles,

There where Egypt's state shame
adorned itself with the best dog-meat
and provided the dead with multiple trivia,
there where pyramids jut up, minor insignificant nonsense.

And is that how it is with you, my blood favorite, is it oh
pleasantly sinful singer—
your teeth still audibly grinding,
plaintiff of care-free rights . . .

Having unreeled a ball of properties
for two weak-willed final testaments,
and having given away, in final farewell,
a squealing world as deep as a skull:

An insolent schoolboy and thieving angel
lived alongside the Gothic, a scandalous clown
who spit on spider-like rights,
namely the incomparable Villon, Master François—

A robber of heavenly clergy
and no shame to sit next to.
Just before the world ends
skylarks will ring . . .

Voronezh, 18 March 1937

---

383
A Greek Jug

Guilty debtor of long thirst,
wise pimp of wine and water—

goats dance on your flanks,
fruit ripens to flute-songs.

Pipes whistle, slander, grow angry
that trouble runs on your black-red
rim—and that no one, now, can take you
and set the trouble right.

*Voronezh, 21 March 1937*

## 384

Oh, how I want to be
what no one senses,
flying after a light-beam
to where there is no me.

But shine, shine bright in that circle—
for that's what happiness is—
and let a star teach you
what light means, what the world means.

But let me tell you,
I'm whispering, and whispering
I'm going to give you, my child,
to a light-beam.

All that makes it a beam,
all that makes it light,
is a swelling of whisper,
a warming of babble.

*Voronezh, 23 March 1937*

# 385

The dark-blue island is great with potters—
Crete, merry Crete, their gift has been baked
into resonant earth. Do you hear the underground
knocking of their dolphin fins?

It's easy to see that sea
in clay cheered by the kiln,
and the cold, cold power of the vessel
split into the sea, split into eye.

Give me back my own, blue island,
flying Crete, give me back my work,
and fill the kilned vessel
from the flowing goddess' breasts.

Oh that took place, that was sung, all dark-blue,
long before Odysseus,
before food and drink
were named mine, or not mine.

Then recover, star in an
ox-eyed sky, recover and emanate,
and you, flying-fish chance,
and you, water, eternal yea-sayer.

                                                          Voronezh, March 1937

---

# 386

Charlie Chaplin
      came out of the show,
Two boot-soles,
      a hare-lip,

Two bright peepers
      full of ink,
And God what wonderful
      astonished power.
Charlie Chaplin—
      a hare-lip,
Two boot-soles—
      ah a pitiful fate.
Somehow we all live unsuccessfully—
      strangers, strangers.
Tin horror
      on his face,
The head
      won't stay in place,
Soot-black struts,
      shoe-black minces,
And slowly, quietly, gently,
      Chaplin says:
"What am I known and loved
      and even famous for?"
And a great highway leads him
      to strangers, to strangers.
Oh Charlie Chaplin,
      step on it, Charlie,
Oh Chaplin, rabbit,
      fight your way into the role, shove, push.
Peel red-pulp Malta oranges,
      put on the roller-skates,
And your wife—
      a blind shadow—
And the alien distance tries
      to be original, and is strange.
And why does Chaplin
      have a tulip,
And why is the crowd
      so loving?
Because, because—
      this is Moscow, after all.
Charlie, Charlie—
      you have to take risks,
This is the wrong time to go sour.
Your bowler hat is that ocean, that same ocean,

And Moscow is so close you might fall in love
    with the sweet, sweet road.

Moscow, 1937

---

# 387

The "p," the "q" of a Greek flute—
as if gossip hadn't worn her down—
Uncarved, unconscious, she ripened
and she languished and she moved across ditches.

And who could desert her?
Clench your teeth, but she can't be shut up, from here
the tongue can't push on into words,
the lips can't knead her.

But the flutist can't reach peace—
he feels alone, he feels
he moulded his native sea
out of lilac clay, once.

He hurries toward thrift
with a ringing, ambitious whisper,
with the tramping of remembering lips,
grasping sounds—tidy—miserly.

Clods of clay in the sea's palms
we won't be able to repeat him,
and I, filled with the sea,
find my measure is my pestilence.

And I hate my own lips,
and murder is that very same root,
and I bend, I have no choice but to bend, to diminish
the flute's smooth driving force.

Voronezh, 7 April 1937

## 388

I touch this green to my lips,
this sticky oath of leaves,
this lying earth—
mother of snowdrops, of maples, of little oaks.

See how I go blind, grow strong,
obeying the meek roots,
all too splendid—yes?—for the eyes,
this thundering park.

And croaker-frogs, like balls of mercury,
join voices in a globe,
twigs turn to branches
and a milky fiction rises—steam.

Voronezh, 30 April 1937

---

## 389

Buds smell like a sticky oath,
and—there!—a star slips down—
Ah: a mother told her daughter
to take her time.

"Wait," the sky
whispered, but clear as day,
and the sloping rustle replied:
"All I want is a son!

"I'd take on a whole
new life,
a cradle rocking
with an easy foot.

"My wild blunt husband
would be gentle and tame—

It's terrifying, here without him in the smothering
world, just as the black book says."

Summer-lightning stammered,
winking in the middle of a sentence,
older brother frowned,
little sister stings.

A velvet big-winged wind
blew in the flute
so the boy would be great-headed
like the first two, one now great as two.

And thunder will ask his friends:
"Thunders! Have you heard
of pear-trees marrying
bird-cherries?"

And then bird-cries, out of the forest's
fresh lonelinesses—
matchmaker birds whistling
flattering homage to Natasha.

And such sticky oaths stick
to the lips that, by God,
the eyes come rushing
to die in the horses' clatter.

Rush her, rush her!
Serene Natasha,
for our happiness—marry,
for our health—marry.

Voronezh, 2 May 1937

## 390–392
# Rough Drafts from the Second Voronezh Notebook

### 390

And Natasha came. Where's she been?
She's eaten nothing, I'd guess, drunk nothing . . .
but there, black as night, her mother senses her:
her daughter smells of wine, smells of onions . . .

### 391

"Natasha, how do you write 'blockhead-hammer,' *balda?*"
"When you go to a *ball, da,* yes."
"And 'noon,' *polden,* and 'sex,' *pol?*" "Put them together,
by day, but not at night, it wouldn't be decent like that."

### 392

Oh this Lena, that Nora,
oh this abyss of Engineering Technical . . .
ether, zephyr, Eleonora—
the sweet and sour breath of two shrews.

*1937*

---

# 393

There's a pear-tree aiming at me, and a cherry-tree—
beating, beating at me with crumbly strength, and never missing.

Tassels and stars, stars and leaves—
what kind of double authority, there? Whose petals hold the truth?

This airy-white beating in the air—from petal-colors? from
heroic swings?—and the air being bludgeoned to death.

And the quarrelsome sweetness of this double scent—
struggling, stretching, blending—and then suddenly breaking off.

Voronezh, 4 May 1937

---

# 394

Limping slightly, against her will, pressing herself on the empty
earth with a sweet uneven walk,
she barely passes
a girl-friend, fast, and a boy born a year later.
The restrained freedom of a quickening
shortage pulls at her,
and the lucid surmise of her steps
seems to want to linger—
since this spring weather is the Ur-mother
of the arching grave, for us,
and it begins over and over and forever.

Some women are related to the damp earth
and their every step is a resonant sobbing,
a chanting to accompany the dead and to welcome
the newly resurrected: this is their task.
Criminal to ask them for caresses,
to leave them requires more strength than one has.
Today—an angel, and tomorrow—a grave-worm,
and the day after tomorrow—only an outline.
What was once a step becomes inaccessible;
flowers are immortal. The sky is whole.
And whatever will be—is only a promise.

Voronezh, 4 May 1937

## 395

Who hunts her husband, what wife
stalking the streets of Kiev—
dry waxen cheeks,
not a tear, not one.

Gypsies don't read beautiful palms,
there are no violins in the Park,
horses drop dead on Main Street,
the great lime-trees smell of death.

Soldiers took the last trolley
out of town, right to the edge,
and a damp overcoat shouted:
"We'll be back, do you hear! . . ."

Voronezh, May 1937

# Twenty-Two Poems

(Dated, on Internal Evidence, from 1909 to 1910) Unpublished During Mandelstam's Lifetime

i

Oh cheerful traveller,
who are you smiling at!
Why bless valleys
you've never seen?

No one will lead you
down slopes slowly going green,
no murmuring nightingale
will invite you on—when,

Wrapped in a thin cloak,
not warm, but nice,
you fly up like a humble beam
to heaven's commanding lights.

---

ii

Deferential silence
in the great twilight hall.
As empty crystal swells,
expecting wine,

Hopelessly offering lips
bloody in the light,
lips delicately opened
on chaste stems:

Look: we're drunk
on unpoured wine.
Is anything feebler than lilies,
sweeter, more loving than silence?

---

iii

What an autumn fades away
in lyres' cold modulations!
How tender, how unbearable
a gold-stringed priesthood!—

Singing in cathedral choirs
and in night-dark monasteries
and, scattering dust in urns,
sealing wine in great jars.

Like a motionless, windless
jar, everything settled to the bottom,
the spiritual—can be seen,
its outlines live, breathe.

---

iv

My hand releases
a silent spindle.
And then the spindle—
spun by itself, or by me—
whirls like an endless wave—a
spindle.

Everything's as dark as everything
else; everything in the world has been
interwoven by this hand of mine;
it's forever-turning, it's forever the same,
I was never meant to stop
what my hand held, and controlled—this
spindle.

---

v

Fresh-mown grain
lies in flat rows, even;
and thin fingers quiver,
pressed against fingers just like themselves.

---

vi

No talk of eternity—
I can't handle it.
But my eternal love, my eternal
liveliness, how keep from forgiving them?

I hear it growing, rolling
like a midnight wave.
But—come too close
and oh you'll be sorry.

I'm happy, sometimes, from far
away, hearing the quiet echo
of its huge foaming crash—
thinking about nice, unimportant things.

---

vii

Your gay tenderness
flusters me.
What good are sad words
when eyes
go burning like candles
in broad daylight?

In broad daylight—even that's
too far away—
a single tear,

remembering a meeting:
shoulders bending, and
tenderness raising them, faintly.

---

viii

Moonlight on the noiseless field-
mouse's house;
transparent trees
fanned by darkness;

When the mountain-ash curls
and uncurls its leaves, which will die,
and is jealous, fingering their
careful emerald polish, of:

Wanderers' wistful luck, of
children's tender luck . . .
And thousands of green fingers shake
on branch after branch after branch.

Cupid, sad, naked,
poised on a wet rock,
stands on one childish
foot, amazed

To find old age in the world.
Green moss, and wet rock—
and the heart's illicit heat—
are his infantile vengeance.

And a rough wind begins to blow
in naive valleys;
you can't close your martyred
long-suffering lips, not tight enough.

---

ix

If the winter morning is dark
your cold window
becomes an old panel.

Green ivy in front of the frame;
out beyond the icy glass,
silent trees under a slipcover—

Protected from wind,
woven tight with branches
and safe from all trouble.

The half-light glows.
Right in front of the window a last leaf
shudders, silky.

---

x

No one here. Nothing. The wind
blows on, weary of your absence.
The drink meant for your lips
stands steaming on the table.

To keep you from walking up
like a fortune-telling lady hermit—
to keep you from etching the window
with sleeping lips—

The long-suffering drink,
while it can still steam and smoke,
sketches frisky tendrils, playful, useless,
in the desert air.

---

xi

Autumn galaxies flare
in wise, obedient heights.
And there is no delight,
no bitterness in our worlds.

Everything makes monotonous sense,
enjoys absolute freedom:
Maybe nature embodies
a harmony of huge numbers?


But there's snow, now—and trees' nakedness
turns to mourning;
the sky's golden emptiness gaped,
last night, how uselessly—

And white, black, gold—
oh the saddest of consonances—
all echoed the inevitability
of definitive winter.

---

xii

Life-giving breath of my poems,
breath of prophesy,
what hearts do you touch—
what ears hear?

Or are you less inhabited than the songs
of seashells, singing in the sand,
their circle of beauty
never ever unlocked?

---

## xiii

The only path
is through your hand—
What other way
to my own sweet land?

Sailing to those sweet shores
if you'll help:
your hands at your lips,
don't take it away.

Thin fingers tremble;
a fragile body breathes:
a boat sliding across
silent chasms of ocean.

---

## xiv

What music for
my loving glorifications, for
waves of love
in my restless songs,

When hands
reach out,
there where sounds
and waves come from—

And twilight-fabrics
are run through with flesh—
in the white aureole
of your trembling?

## XV

Mourning trees, embroidered
like a pattern on the dark sky;
but you lift your eyes,*
struck with wonder, higher and higher.

The sky's icon-box is locked— †
You'll say: the hills' cold line
has knocked over time
and, just like night, rushed into light.

The dead trees' darkening lace
rips:
oh new moon, don't whittle down
your sickle, now so swiftly gone black!

* *A manuscript variant of line 3:* "oh why lift your eyes".
† *A manuscript variant of line 5:* "It's black, black overhead."

---

## XVI

A sole delight
for the heart, from this time on—
mysterious fountain,
fall, and fall, and go on falling.

Fly up like tall sheaves,
blow up, drop down
and let all your voices
stop—suddenly—at once.

But dress my whole soul
in a cloak of grand thought,
flickering like the damp
larch-tree's canopy.

xvii

When the bells' reproach
sweeps in from ancient towers
and the air itself is sick with rumbling,
and there are no prayers, no words—

I am annihilated, suppressed.
Wine is stronger, heavier,
it touches my heart's drunkenness—
and I'm parched again, unquenched.

I disown my holinesses,
I'll break my oaths—
and an ineffable wormwood
overflows my soul.

---

xviii

Frightening, to have my life behind me—
to jump back off the tree, like a leaf,
not to fall in love with anything,
to sink into oblivion like nameless rock,

And in the emptiness, as on a cross,
crucifying my living soul,
like Moses in the nothingness,
vanishing in a Sinai cloud.

And I keep watch on the threads
connecting me to living things,
and I collate the patterned smoke
of existence on a marble slab,

And through the net I try to see
warm birds shuddering,

and from decaying pages
I draw the dust of centuries.

---

## xix

I see a stone sky
over the waters' dim spiderweb.
The soul lives on, agonized, weary,
clutched by its loathsome Hell.

I understand this horror,
I comprehend this linkage:
the sky falls, yes, but not to the ground,
and simultaneously the sea splashes, but without foam.

Oh pale chimera wings
on the sand's coarse gold,
and the sail's gray triple-leafed flower—
crucified, like my anguish!

---

## xx

Tender evening, pompous twilight.
Roar after roar. Wave after wave.
And a damp wind in our face,
beating like a salty veil.

Everything extinguished. Everything interfering.
Waves getting drunk on the shore.
And a blind joy in us—
and our hearts grown heavy.

A dark chaos stunned us,
drunken air stupefied us,

an enormous choir lulled us:
flutes, and lutes, and drums . . .

---

## xxi

Evening bronze breaks
the haloes around words, kills them.
And the body demands thorns;
and faith—demands insane flowers.

To fall onto ancient gravestones
and call to a passionate God,
to know that senses and feelings merge
in prayer, one single unity of grace!

Glorification surges, floods—
and once again, waiting for the end,
with the wine of his divine blood—
hearts grow heavy:

And the temple, like a huge ship,
skims the abyss of ages.
And the spirit's homeless sail
is ready to taste winds, all winds.

---

## xxii

The heart is clothed, as if with a cloud,
and flesh pretends to be rock,
until the Lord reveals
what the poet's purpose is to be.

Some passion swoops down,
some heavy weight breathes, lives;

ghosts demand bodies,
and words belong to flesh.

Like women, things hunger for affection,
thirst for their sacred names,
but the poet, sunk in darkness,
hunts for secret signs.

He waits for the deepest of all signs,
ready for a song, ready for heroics:
mysteries of marriage breathe
in the simple linking of words.

# Two Later Unpublished Poems

Unlike the twenty-two preceding poems, these two poems (as printed in *Vestick* no. 98 [1970]) belong to Mandelstam's mature period. Whereas he clearly rejected the first twenty-two for publication, it is by no means clear that this is true of the last two. They are quite remarkable poems. The first belongs clearly to the Moscow cycle associated with Tsvetaeva (nos. 84, 85; see notes) and has some relation as well to the brief note Mandelstam wrote on Sukharevka, a Moscow landmark, published in *Ogonek*, no. 18 (29 July 1923), and republished in Mandelstam 2:133. The second poem, written in Koktebel, in the Crimea, in 1920, expresses Mandelstam's sense of the sterility and lack of issue of the situation. The Civil War was at its height, and A. Blok's famous poem, "The Twelve" was considered *the* poem of the revolution.—S. M.

## xxiii

It's all alien, for us, in this obscene metropolis,
with her dry, hard ground,
and Sukharevka, her raving grain market,
and the horrible look of her pirate Kremlin.

Dense, thick, she rules the world.
Millions of creaking oxcarts roll,
and she staggers abruptly down the road—and half a universe
crushes in the peasant-slut width of her streets.

Her fragrant churches, bees' nests
like wild honey dropped into forests—
and heavy bird-flocks migrate,
billowing sullen skies.

A sly fox, in business,
but faced with her prince—a miserable serf.
The great city-state's waters run muddy,
as they've always run, into dry gutters.

1916/1917

## xxiv

Where the night drops anchor
in lonely, hollow constellations,
dry October leaves,
lonely disciples of darkness,
where are you flying? Why drop
from the tree of life?
Bethlehem is queer, is strange to you,
you never saw the manger.

You've no descendants—none!
Your sexless anger runs you,
you'll descend into your painted, hollow
graves, childless,
and on the threshold of silence,
with Nature's frenzy all around,
the everlasting nations are fated
for the stars, but not for you, not for you.

                                        Koktebel, 1920.

# Notes

*by* SIDNEY MONAS

The notes are listed by numbers which correspond to the numbering not only to the poems in this English edition but also to those in the second edition of the Russian texts (Gleb Struve and Boris Filipoff, eds., *Sobranie sochinenii* [Washington, D.C., 1967]).

No. 14.  *Silentium.* The title, in Latin, is the same as that of a very famous poem by Fedor Tiutchev (1803–1873). Tiutchev's poem probably takes its title from a medieval book of monastic discipline and has to do with the vow of silence. The idea, in Tiutchev's poem, is that every effort to explain a thought, a feeling, a need, inevitably results in a distortion and therefore a betrayal. Mandelstam refers to a primitive and magical power of the word to be itself, to return to a primal creative force, prior to all "expression." For Mandelstam, language *contains* silence. There is here also some echo of Verlaine's *Art Poetique.*

No. 20.  "dark-lit lanterns." As much as "slow-stepping horses, "this suggests a funeral. Perhaps the first appearance of the "black sun" motif, associated with Judaism, Phaedre, Saint Petersburg, Pushkin. The funeral of a poet also suggests Pushkin, who was killed in a duel thought to have been provoked by figures highly regarded at Court, perhaps even by the Tsar himself. To avoid disturbances, Pushkin's body was sequestered and moved to its burial place at night.

No. 24.  The "black wind" echoes the "black sun" motif. The swallow is one of the *topoi* in Mandelstam's poetry—Procne, who had her tongue cut out for the sake of her sister Philomela, who was then turned into a nightingale as Procne was turned into a swallow. For Mandelstam the swallow is sometimes the gift of sacrifice, sometimes the gift of the word.

No. 31.  "Batiushkov's arrogance . . ." Konstantin N. Batiushkov (1787–1855), an older contemporary of Pushkin's, and a poet Mandelstam very much admired. A Latinist, student of Tasso and Petrarch, sojourner in Italy, translator of epigrams from the *Greek*

*Anthology*, Batiushkov, who had shown signs of melancholic depression earlier, went mad in 1821. Compare this poem with Pasternak's "About these Verses" [*pro eti stikhi*], *Stikhi i Poemy, 1912–1932* (Ann Arbor, 1961) in which he asks "what millennium is it out there?"

No. 35. "Tsarskoe Selo." Literally, "The Tsar's Village," a suburb of Saint Petersburg. It is now called Pushkino, because Pushkin went to school there at the famous "progressive" lyceum founded by Alexander I. Its main architectural monument is the superb Summer Palace, the work of Rastrelli. It is a town of beautifully designed parks, monuments, views, and landscapes, one of the best places to see the eloquent, lavish, beautiful, and rather melancholy Russian rococo, symbolic of that phase of Russian culture during which Saint Petersburg was the capital of the Russian Empire.

"Georgy Ivanov" (1894–1958). An Acmeist poet, friend of Mandelstam, died in emigration. He is the author of a dramatic but most unreliable book of memoirs, *Peterburgskie zimy* [Petersburg winters], first published in Paris in 1928.

No. 37. "The Lutheran." Another implicit reference to a poem of Tiutchev's—his well-known verses on the Lutheran service, emphasizing the eloquence of its simplicity. Whereas, here: "Who needs eloquence?"

No. 40. "Ulalume." The poem by Edgar Allan Poe.

No. 42. "N. Gumilev." Nikolai S. Gumilev (1886–1921), poet, critic, adventurer, Acmeist, the first husband of Anna Akhmatova. Besides Akhmatova, Mandelstam once said, Gumilev was the only person with whom he could carry on an imaginary conversation (see volume 1 of this series, *Selected Works of Nikolai S. Gumilev* [Albany: State University of New York Press, 1972]).

"the Admiralty." A building that forms one of the characteristic landmarks of Saint Petersburg. Its elongated needlelike spire, catching the sun with its covering of gold leaf, can be seen from almost any part of the city. As a building, it blends Western and Russian styles into something uniquely Petersburgian. Its original function emphasizes the function of the city as the greatest port of the Empire as well as its capital.

"Onegin's ancient boredom . . ." Reference is to Pushkin's Evgeny Onegin, who suffers from the English (Byronic) disease—"spleen"—called *khandra* in Russian.

"eccentric Evgeny." The very different hero of Pushkin's "The Bronze Horseman," in which Pushkin himself refers to the identity of their names.

No. 45. "created reality,/The Bronze Horseman . . ." The Bronze Horseman is the statue of Peter the Great by Falconet in the Senate Square in Saint Petersburg, commissioned by Catherine II. It became, through Pushkin's poem, "The Bronze Horseman," a symbol of the city, its purpose, and the cruel, grandiose vision of its founder. The city, created as an act of will, and at great cost, on a drained swamp, exposed to recurrent floods, had been built where only a couple of meager fishing villages had stood before.

No. 47. "a casual pedestrian." One of Mandelstam's many references to himself as pedestrian.

No. 48. "The Admiralty Tower." See no. 42.

No. 54. "Egypt, Joseph." Mandelstam's identification with Joseph in Egypt is more than a matter of the coincidence of names.

No. 56. "On the Aventine Hill . . ." In pre-Christian days, the Aventine was the strong point of the plebes, site of many temples; in Christian Rome, the site of numerous monasteries and nunneries.

No. 59. "Rachel . . ./An indignant Phaedra." Rachel (1821-1858), French actress, real name, Elisabeth Felix, daughter of poor Jewish peddlars. Her greatest triumph was in Racine's *Phèdre*. She was known especially for the passionate quality of her voice. The shawl, in Mandelstam, generally links Akhmatova to Phaedra.

No. 61. Reference is to the Kazan Cathedral in Saint Petersburg, and the columns that sweep out from it, modeled after the Bernini collonades of Saint Peter's. The architect, Andrei N. Vornikhin (1759-1814), was a serf of Count Stroganov, perhaps his illegitimate son.

No. 64. "Sumarokov." Alexander P. Sumarokov (1718-1777), Russian imitator of French neoclassical modes, in verse and in the theater.

"Ozerov." Vladislav A. Ozerov (1769–1816), author of *Fingal*, which D. S. Mirsky calls "a sentimental tragedy with choruses in an Ossianic setting." (See *A History of Russian Literature* [New York, 1949], p. 66).

No. 71. "Pope Benedict XV's Encyclical." Issued immediately after Benedict assumed the papacy in September 1914, an appeal for peace. Benedict's later appeals in 1915 and 1917 earned him a certain reputation, probably undeserved, of being pro-German.

"he who told me of Rome." Peter Chaadaev (1792–1856). See M. B. Zeldin, *Peter Yakovlevich Chaadaev* (Knoxville, 1969).

No. 79. "Chaldeans." Inhabitants of Chaldea, Babylonians. By implication someone practiced in astrology, astronomy, soothsaying, sorcery.

No. 80. Echoing Ovid's "Tristia."

No. 84. "Uspensky." One of the Kremlin churches built by Italian architects in the fifteenth century.

No. 85. "Sparrow Hills." Hills on the outskirts of Moscow, now called Lenin Hills, the present site of the new branch of Moscow State University, always known as an ideal spot from which to view the city of Moscow.

"Uglich." The town where the Tsar's son, or Tsarevich, had been incarcerated by the then regent, Boris Godunov. The Tsarevich was murdered there, in prison, precipitating the Time of Troubles when a "pretender" appeared at the head of an army, claiming to be the murdered Tsarevich.

"Never a fourth." Reference is to the doctrine of the Third Rome, a prominent feature of the new, raw Russian imperialist ideology of the sixteenth century. Moscow was the Third Rome (i.e., capital of the third world-empire) after Rome and Byzantium had fallen to the infidel. According to the doctrine, there would not be a fourth.

No. 86. The poem is entitled "Solòminka" in Russian, which means at the same time "little Salomé" (it is the diminutive, or pet name, for Salomé) and "little straw." The poem was written to a well-known Petersburg lioness, Salomé (or Solomei) Nikolaevna Andronnikova, with whom Mandelstam was in love. As Salomé Halpern, she lives today in London. The pun is important and plays throughout the poem. Solòminka, or "little straw," is placed in her own splendid bedroom overlooking the Neva in the company of some euphoniously named ladies: Lenore, Ligeia, Seraphita. Lenore is the heroine of a German ballad by Buerger but better known as a heroine of Edgar Allan Poe, over whose lost presence the narrator of "The Raven" broods. Ligeia is another Poe heroine in the story that has her name as title. Both these ladies have a presence in the mind of their lovers that gives them the power of resurrection, of returning to life after they have died. "*Serephita,*" writes Clarence Brown, "is the title of one of the philosophical novels of Balzac, published in 1835. . . . The great interest which Serephita presents for an interpretation of "Solòminka" is to be seen in the fact of her dispute identity. To Minna, a young girl, she appears as a youth . . . but to Wilfred and to Pastor Becker she appears in female form as Serephita. Ultimately, the character is neither and both, for its essence is ethereal and angelic. . . ." (Clarence Brown, "On Reading Mandelstam," in Osip Mandelstam, *Sobranie sochinenii,* 3 vols. [Washington, D.C., 1967], 1:xiii)

In his essay "The Word and Culture," Mandelstam writes: "In the stillness of night, a lover pronounces one tender name instead of another and suddenly realizes that this has happened before: the words, the hair, the rooster that just crowed underneath the window, crowed once before in Ovid's *Tristia.* And he is overcome by the deep joy of recognition. . . ." (Ibid., 2:224-25) Victor Terras, in "Classical Motives in the Poetry of Mandelstam," *Slavic and East European Journal* 10, no. 3 (1966): 259, points out that the reference is really to the *Amores* 1.4.65, not to *Tristia.*

No. 88.   "Petropolis." Saint Petersburg, or Petrograd.

No. 90.   This poem is dedicated to Marina Tsvetaeva. See *Sobranie sochinenii,* 3:306-47.

No. 91.   Black and yellow are colors often, and especially by Mandelstam, associated with Judaism. This poem, as well as the funeral imagery of no. 93 (the asphodel, though among the first flowers of spring, is the flower of the dead) may refer to the death of someone close to Mandelstam while he is in the Crimea, which for him is always redolent of Greece and the Mediterranean. Victor Terras suggests there are overtones here of the *Odyssey* 4. 219-84; Menelaos telling how Odysseus and Diomedes tried to restrain the Greeks from answering when Helen addressed the Trojan horse in the voices of their wives ("Classical Motives in the Poetry of Mandelstam," pp. 261–62).

No. 92. "Taurida." The Crimea.

Obviously a poem of many voyages, Jason's as well as Odysseus'. And so the spinning wheel suggests not only Penelope (and Helen), but also Medea and the Parcae.

No. 93. "Meganom." A peninsula to the southwest of Theodosia in the Crimea; 44°48′ N and 35°.06′ E. See also no. 91 above.

No. 94 "The Decembrist." Someone who participated in the attempted coup by some members of the Guards Regiments in Saint Petersburg to prevent the enthronement of Nicholas I. It took place on 14 December 1825 and was a complete failure. The conspiracy included plans for a constitutional regime and reflected the influence of nationalist-liberal movements in Western Europe, such as the German Tugenbund.

No. 100. "A. V. Kartashev." Anton Vladimirovich Kartashev (1875–1960), who had been minister of creeds in the Provisional Government had been released from imprisonment a short time before the publication of this poem. The poem was apparently written earlier, while Kartashev was still in prison. The poem is actually Jewish in theme, with the "yellow-black" Jewish motif typical of Mandelstam. Its dedication to Kartashev at the time of the latter's release from prison has a demonstrative character. Kartashev had just returned to publicistic activity and was at work helping prepare for a church council. Russia was soon to be plunged into the throes of civil war.

No. 103. In the Russian, this poem has the title "Freedom's Twilight." A striking use of the "ship of state" *topos*, as Victor Terras points out. The Romans called the fenced-in space where people voted the *ovile*, or sheep pen ("Classical Motives in the Poetry of Mandelstam," p. 266).

No. 104. "Tristia." Lyric poem on sad or elegiac themes. More specifically, Ovid's *Tristia*, in which the great Latin poet tells the story of his exile, recalls his life in Rome, his life among the barbarous Scythians where he has been exiled, and wishes his return. Mandelstam's identification with Ovid is very close, as was Pushkin's: partly because of their shared exile, for political reasons, in the same part of the world; but more importantly for the condition of exile itself, exile as the poet's fate, and for the theme of metamorphosis, with the implication that metaphor *is* metamorphosis, and life is the incarnation of metaphor, of the Word. As opposed to this particular poem, the volume of which it was a part was called *Tristia*, not by Mandelstam himself but by the poet M.A. Kuzmin, who saw it through the press in Berlin.

"Delia." Tibullus' lady. Also, an inhabitant of Delos, where the maidens speak many tongues and are close to the goddess Artemis. Tibullus, *Elegies*. 1. 3. 90–91.

"Greek Erebus." The land of darkness. Erebus is the son of Chaos, brother of Night, but also the father of Day.

No. 105. "bees." The word incarnate as a bee, the poet as a bee that makes honey, is a recurrent image in Mandelstam. For Pindar, the soul is a bee (Pythian. 4. 60). Bees were sacred to Persephone, and Athens was famous for its hives and honey.

"Terpander." Founder of Greek classical music and lyric poetry. Whether he or Hermes made the first lyre depends on the source.

No. 107. "Uspensky . . . Blagoveshchensky . . . Arkhangelsky . . . Resurrection . . . Churches within the Kremlin walls.

No. 111. "Theodosia." A town in the Crimea, once the outpost of the Genoese. See "Theodosia" in Clarence Brown, *The Prose of Osip Mandelstam* (Princeton, 1965), pp. 133–48. For all its exotic connections with the Near East, its most powerful associations for Mandelstam are with the Mediterranean, with the Europe of classical culture.

"Apple song." A revolutionary song, in which the "bourjuee" is depicted as a round little apple. It goes, "Ah, you little apple,/ where are you rolling to? . . ."

"nomads . . ." These are really "pilgrims" in the Russian original.

No. 112. See the tale of Psyche and Eros, from Apuleius, *The Golden Ass*.

No. 115. "Sazandaries." From the Persian, *sazandar*, an Azerbaijani folk musician.

"*dukhan.*" A kind of Near Eastern popular restaurant, like a trattoria.

No. 116. "dead bees." Reference to Gumilev's poem, "The Word" (Nikolai S. Gumilev, *Selected Works of N.S. Gumilev* [Albany, 1972], p. 107), with which Mandelstam prefaces his essay "On the Nature of the Word." The last lines of the poem read, "and like bees in a deserted hive/ the dead words rot and stink." Mandelstam did not agree with Gumilev, however, either about words or about the ideas on "numbers" he also expresses in that poem. For Mandelstam, even "dead" words could be reconverted into sunlight by a poet, mechanized speech could be redeemed. The word was fundamentally immortal.

No. 121. "cuckoos weep." One of many allusions by Mandelstam to the "Tale of Igor's Men." See the translation by Sidney Monas and Burton Raffel (*Delos,* no. 6 (1971), p. 13), where, however, the translators for benefit of the English reader have transmogrified the "cuckoo" of the original into a dove. The image has to do with Iaroslavna, Igor's wife, mourning her prince who has been taken captive by the pagans.

"pale woman." Persephone *and* Psyche.

No. 125. "Concert at a Railway Station." See the first section, entitled "Music in Pavlovsk," of Mandelstam's brief autobiography, "The Noise of Time," in Clarence Brown, *The Prose of Osip Mandelstam,* pp. 69–72. See also Victor Terras, "Classical Motives in the Poetry of Mandelstam," p. 259.

No. 126. "salt." For Mandelstam a symbol of *conscience,* though clearly also with a strong flavor of blood.

No. 130. "Yeast-dough." Yeast for Mandelstam means poetry, as do "moving lips" in the previous poem.

"Cathedrals." In the Russian, literally, "Sophias."

No. 136. In its original publication this poem bore the subtitle, "A Pindaric Fragment."

"Not by the Bethlehem carpenter, but the other one . . ." Probably, Apollo, god of embarkations; but possibly, also, Noah.

"Neyera." Possibly Neaera, a sea nymph, mentioned in Milton's "Lycidas": "Were it not better done as others use,/To sport with

Amaryllis in the shade,/Or with the tangles of Neaera's hair?" i.e., the land adjacent to Neaera's sea.

No. 137.  "A Slate Ode." The title, and a number of images and motifs in the poem refer to the famous "last poem" of Gabriel Derzhavin (1743-1816), the greatest Russian poet of the eighteenth century. The poem was written with a slate stylus on slate, and was, possibly, part of an intended ode "On Perishability." There are eight lines; translated literally, they read:

> The river of time in its flowing
> Carries away all the works of men
> And plunges into the abyss of oblivion
> Peoples, kingdoms and kings.
> And if something should remain
> Through sounds of the lyre and trumpet,
> Eternity seizes it by the throat
> Nor does it escape the common fate.

The movement is slow and stately and conveys a sense of doom and inevitability. As Professor Morris Halle of the Massachusetts Institute of Technology once pointed out to me, many years ago, the first letters of each line, read downward, form the phrase "ruin of honor." Mandelstam uses the "river of time" image in a different sense: the river as teacher to the "pupil," flint—creator, therefore, as much as destroyer. The first line of Mandelstam's poem is also an allusion to the well-known poem of Michael Lermontov (1814-1841), which begins "I walk out along the high-road," and the first stanza of which ends with the line, "And star speaks with star." Mandelstam thus begins by contrasting the eighteenth and the nineteenth centuries. (See the interesting essay by Victor Terras, "The Time Philosophy of Osip Mandelshtam," *Slavonic and East European Review* 47, no. 108 [January, 1969], pp. 344-54. See also his "Grifel'naia oda Mandel'shtama," *Novyi Zhurnal,* no. 92 [1968], pp. 163-71.)

No. 140.  "January 1, 1924." A crucial "new year." Lenin is mortally ill, suffering a paralysis from which he will not recover. In the political struggle, the ascendancy of Stalin is already fairly clear.

"straw-boards on roofs" means (literally) "along the eaves."

"peel off everything" means (literally) "keep stripping the scales."

"vows marvelous to the point of tears . . ." means (literally) "the wonderful pledge to the fourth estate and oaths enormous to the point of tears. . . ." Mandelstam as a *raznochinets,* or classless intellectual, identified himself with the fourth estate, an identification that persisted in the title he gave to the therapeutic prose essay called "Fourth Prose" (see Nadezhda Mandelstam, *Hope against Hope* [New York, 1970], pp. 177-78).

No. 144. In one of his autobiographical writings Mandelstam notes that the street by the theater, during theater-time, in Saint Petersburg before the revolution, with its horse cabs and coaches standing around and waiting, reminded him of a gypsy camp (Clarence Brown, *The Prose of Osip Mandelstam,* p. 95).

No. 180. "A fatal handshake . . ." The Treaty of Tilsit, 1807, between Alexander I and Napoleon, concluded on a raft in the middle of the River Niemen between the two Emperors. The treaty was a failure, ended by Napoleon's invasion of 1812.

No. 189. "An angel prays . . ." means (literally) "towers." Famous landmark behind the Winter Palace, now the Hermitage.

"Trouble-makers." An allusion to the seventeenth-century "Time of Troubles."

No. 191. "Ivan the Great." Reference is to the Bell Tower of Ivan the Great within the Kremlin walls, from which the bells had been removed.

No. 192. "October's favorite." The Russian word means "favorite" in the eighteenth-century sense, i.e., somebody elevated to power by virtue of more or less accidental personal relations with the emperor or empress; in the sense that Potemkin was a "favorite" of Catherine. Reference is probably to Kerensky.

No. 193. "dilatory Patriarch . . . Tikhon." A church council was called in 1918, under Bolshevik auspices, and it elected a patriarch—Tikhon. The Russian Church had been without a patriarch since Peter the Great created the Holy Synod in 1721, or rather since the death of the last patriarch in 1700. Tikhon died in 1925 and the patriarchate was again not filled for some years.

No. 196. Georgy Ivanov seems to think this a poem Mandelstam wrote to his "daughter." Nadezhda Mandelstam claims there was no such daughter and that the tale is as apocryphal as the suicide attempt Ivanov attributes to Mandelstam. Professor Struve, in a note to the poem (*Sobranie sochinenii,* 1:482) points out that, although signed by Mandelstam, the poem was actually written by Sergei Klychkov, a friend of Mandelstam's, and does not belong to Mandelstam at all (see Nadezhda Mandelstam, *Hope against Hope,* p. 260).

No. 203. "Armenia." In 1930, thanks to the intercession of Nikolai Bukharin, Mandelstam was allowed to undertake a long trip to Armenia, during and after which he wrote "Fourth Prose" (an English translation of which may be found in M. Scammell, ed., *Russia's Other Writers; Selections from Samizdat Literature* [New York, 1971], pp. 130-45), "Journey to Armenia" (which contains a number of separate essays, not all of them directly relevant to Armenia, though clearly inspired by the trip; for instance, the essay "Around Naturalists" [*Vokrug Naturalistov*] in Mandelstam, *Sobranie sochinenni,* 2:162-68; an essay on the French impressionists, ibid., pp. 159-62; and others. The entire sequence is in ibid., 137-76) and the cycle of poems entitled "Armenia." Mandelstam, who became very close to the young biologist, B.S. Kuzin, during his Armenian sojourn read and thought much about evolutionary theory and the life sciences in general. He was fascinated also by the works of the linguist Marr on the Japhetic languages. Armenia, as the earliest Christian kingdom, and for so long a tiny isolated Christian state in a pagan sea, fascinated him for historical and symbolic reasons as well as the obvious charms of a grape-growing land dedicated to Dionysos. In "Journey to Armenia" he quotes "the manner in which most Armenian fairy tales end: 'Three apples fell from the sky: the first is for him who has been telling the tale; the second, for him who listened; the third is for him who understood'" (ibid., 2:171). Mandelstam was also steeped in nineteenth-century European and Russian travel literature on the Caucasus.

No. 204. "Hafiz." Mohammed Shams-ud-din (c. 1300-1388), Persian poet and mystic, lived and died in Shiraz, where he is buried. He was a lover of life, and especially of wine, a satirizer of hypocrisy and false askesis, and thus altogether in what Mandelstam conceived to be the spirit of Armenia.

"far beyond the hill." An echo of the presumably twelfth-century Russian "Tale of Igor's Men," where it signifies "away from the familiar"—in the country of the Polovtsy.

No. 205. "musk-shop." Shop that sells things that *bring out* color, taste, smell. A dye shop that also sells spices.

No. 218. This is culled largely from Mandelstam's reading in nineteenth-century travel literature. In the nineteenth century, the Caucasus for Russians represented something like the Wild West for Americans; it was not merely an exotic place, but a proving ground for manhood, a breeding place for mythologies, and a return-to-nature kind of place, where "real" human qualities, as opposed to the artifice of civilization, the position in a bureaucratic hierarchy, or accident of birth, were brought out; and where the "artificial" ones were quickly erased from sight.

No. 220. See no. 218 above.

No. 222. "childishly tied to the mighty world." See Clarence Brown, *The Prose of Osip Mandelstam*, pp. 72–76, the section entitled "Childish Imperialism." "It always seemed to me," Mandelstam writes of his childhood, "that in Petersburg something very splendid and solemn was absolutely bound to happen" (ibid., p. 75).

It is perhaps not always remembered that Lady Godiva's famous bareback ride through a Saxon English town was propitiatory—she did it to induce her husband, the Earl, to relent on taxes. Everyone stayed behind shuttered windows, except Peeping Tom, who was struck blind.

No. 224. "sit in the kitchen." It is the Russian custom, before a departure, for the company to sit quietly together on a bench.

"where no one can find us." Mandelstam and his wife, fearing arrest, used to spend time in railroad station waiting rooms, where the political police would not think of looking for them.

No. 226. "Angel Mary, drink . . ." From Pushkin's "Feast in Time of Plague," written in 1830, based in turn on John Wilson's dramatic poem, "City of the Plague" (1816), depicting the London plague of 1665.

No. 229. This poem is based on a convict song. Mandelstam was much moved by Russian convict songs and felt very close to their spirit, as Blok did to the gypsy ballad.

No. 233. "star flowers." Literally, asters. Officers' epaulettes, abolished by the Revolution.

No. 235. "Novgorod." The medieval Russian merchant-republic, conquered and repressed by Ivan III in 1478, with terrible destruction, losing its former autonomy. It was destroyed again by Ivan IV (the Terrible) for dealing with the state of Poland-Lithuania and severely repressed once more in 1650 for protests against the coinage. Novgorod, which in its heyday as an independent republic had been a member of the Hanseatic League, came to represent the Western orientation in Russia, and its aspirations to democracy. This was the significance it had for the nineteenth-century Decembrists and later liberals. It was also the home of religious heresy, and the scene of repression of religious dissent by Muscovy. All these connotations are present, as well as the prophecies proclaiming the resurrection of Novgorod. The poem has other associations with political tyranny, repression, and the suffering of oppression: punishment inflicted by the Tartars during the period of the Mongol Yoke on those Russian princes who failed to obey their edicts or meet their tax quotas or resisted them in any way.

The iron shirt—a quaint form of medieval torture; also a form of askesis practiced by the *iurodivye,* or "Fools in Christ."

Croquet in the garden—a favorite sport, not only of the old upper classes, but also of the emergent Soviet elite.

"executions like Peter's." Peter the Great was a do-it-yourselfer and learned how to shave beards, pull teeth, and also to chop off heads; he performed several of his own executions. In the face of oppression Mandelstam seems to assume the role of the *iuridovy,* the Holy Fool, the imitator of Christ.

No. 247. "out on the trotting track." See Dante's lines on Brunetto Latini, *Inferno.* 15. 121-24.

No. 251. *"Dzenkuye, pane!"* Polish for "Thank you, sir!"

"Play savage games of cards . . ." means (literally) "play with miniature card decks."

No. 252. "S.A.K." Sergei Antonovich Klychkov (1889–1937), peasant poet and novelist, arrested in 1937. See note to no. 196. See also, Nadezhda Mandelstam, *Hope against Hope,* pp. 259–60.

No. 255. "gold-pieces rolling off . . ." Another allusion to the Igor Tale.

"Taras Bulba." Cossack hero of Gogol's novel of that title.

"Petropavlovsk . . . Tsusima . . ." Russian defeats.

"the young tsarevitch." Dmitry, son of Ivan the Terrible, murdered in Uglich at the beginning of the Time of Troubles.

No. 256. "Novellino." The novice, or the greenhorn. The title of a thirteenth-century Italian (vernacular) collection (anonymous) of tales of antiquity. See note to poem number 247.

No. 259. Fedor Tiutchev (1803–1873), Russian philosophical poet whom Mandelstam prized for his ability to render concretely an apprehension of the cosmos. Dmitry Venevitinov (1805–1827), poet, member of the Pushkin pleiade, as was Evgeny Baratynsky (1800–1844). Michael Lermontov (1814–1841), perhaps the one completely Romantic Russian poet. Afanasy Fet (1820–1892), lyricist, friend of Leo Tolstoy. Alexei Khomiakov (1804–1860), lay theologian, Slavophile ideologue, who also wrote some remarkable civic verse. Sampling of these poets may be found in a number of English anthologies; the first, third, fourth, and fifth may be found in Burton Raffel, *Russian Poetry under the Tsars* (Albany: State University of New York Press, 1971).

No. 260. "Middle-class intellectuals." The Russian word *raznochintsy,* which implies "intellectuals," but means literally "men of no particular class," so that perhaps "classless intellectuals" would be more precise. Mandelstam repeatedly refers to himself as a *"raznochinets."*

"Marya Ivanna." Tsvetaeva.

No. 261. "Batiushkov." See note to no. 31. Pushkin's older contemporary and friend; like Mandelstam, deeply immersed in the Greek and Roman classics.

"Zamostye," or Zamosc. Literally, "beyond the bridge." A small provincial town in Poland in the Duchy of Lublin.

"Zaphne," or Zaphna. From Batiushkov's poem, "The Source" [*Istochnik*], in K.N. Batiushkov, *Polnoe sobranie stikhotvorenii*

(Moscow and Leningrad, 1964), pp. 122-23. The poem when first printed in 1810 had the subtitle, "A Persian Idyll." It is a free reworking of Parney's idyll in prose, *Le torrent. Idylle persane.* Contrary to the French original, Batiushkov introduced the motif of the destructive force of time.

No. 262. "Derzhavin." See note to no. 137.

"Iazykov," Nikolai M. Iazykov (1803-1846), a member of the Pushkin pleiade, Gogol's favorite poet; Pushkin thought him intoxicating, but not so effective for quenching ordinary thirst.

No. 264. "S.A.K." See note to no. 252.

No. 266. "B.S. Kuzin." A young biologist, whom Mandelstam met in Armenia in 1930. Kuzin was much interested in Goethe and the German Romantics, who were also at the center of Mandelstam's interests at the time. They became friends. Mandelstam attributes his renewed and enlivened knowledge of Goethe, Hoelderlin, Moerike, to Kuzin, with whom he remained friends after his return from Armenia, a time when his "literary" friends considered him too dangerous to associate with. (See Nadezhda Mandelstam, *Hope against Hope,* pp. 227-28.) Kuzin also, apparently, gave a new impetus to Mandelstam's interest in biology and evolutionary theory. In Russian, this poem is written in sounds whose repetitive use is rather uncharacteristic of Russian but typical of German. The poem also refers directly and indirectly to the German Romantic poets. And the seven-year war, during which Russian troops occupied Berlin, is associated with the five-year plan.

No. 267. Having lost the manuscript of this poem, Mandelstam wrote no. 268 years later. Later, a manuscript version turned up.

No. 271. "Wrangel." Peter N. Wrangel (1878-1928), Russian general who served in both the Russo-Japanese War and World War I. He joined the anti-Bolshevik forces of Denikin early in 1918 and, after Denikin's defeat late in 1919, was left in command of the disorganized White army. He occupied the Crimea, from which he finally withdrew, leaving from Sevastopol in 1920. Mandelstam had wandered into the Crimea at the time of Wrangel's occupation and, for a brief time, was arrested.

No. 272. "Komsomol." The League of Young Communists, roughly equivalent, except for its strong and systematic ideological indoctrination, to our upper-age-group Boy and Girl Scouts. Since almost everyone belongs, even the indoctrination turns out to be rather banal. This poem, as Nadezhda Mandelstam tells us, was written as a rejoinder to Pasternak. See Nadezhda Mandelstam, *Hope against Hope,* p. 150.

"Nekrasov." Nikolai A. Nekrasov (1821–1878), poet and editor. Nekrasov was the poet of Russian populism. In spite of his sometimes errant taste, Nekrasov had genuine poetic energy, vitality and creativity.

No. 275. "racing-boat-arcs." These are sailboats in racing formation. For an interesting essay on these "Octaves," see Clarence Brown, "Mandelstam's Notes Toward a Supreme Fiction," *Delos,* no. 1 (1968), pp. 32–66.

No. 286. This is the poem on Stalin for which Mandelstam suffered greatly. He and his wife were sent first to Cherdyn in the Urals, then, after a softening of their punishment, to Voronezh, most likely as a result of this poem's having been reported. (It must of course not be confused with the later attempt to write a "positive" Stalin ode, the by-products of which were the poems written in Voronezh between 16 January and 9 February 1937.)

"Georgian munching a raspberry." Literally an Ossetian. The Ossetians are Moslem tribesmen of Georgia, of legendary ferocity, said to celebrate an enemy's death by munching a raspberry. Stalin, who was of course a Georgian, was rumored at times to be of Ossetian ancestry.

No. 288. "Andrei Biely." Pseudonymn of Boris N. Bugaev (1880–1934). His father was a well-known mathematician, professor at Moscow University, and conservative. Biely was a major symbolist poet, novelist, and critic. He was a mystic, and disciple of Rudolph Steiner. Before the Revolution, Mandelstam respected him but regarded him as a literary opponent. When Mandelstam met him in Koktebel in 1933, he was enormously impressed by him and began to rethink his views on Biely's achievements. Biely's death a year later inspired a series of poems. See Nadezhda Mandelstam, *Hope against Hope,* pp. 155–57, 230.

"gold-bird." In Russian *gogol',* or "golden-eyed duck." Biely identified very closely with Gogol, on whom he had written a wild, brilliant book, just before he died. In this book he makes explicit his own debt to Gogol. Like Mandelstam, Biely had chosen to remain in the USSR, rather than emigrate. He had had an important influence on young writers in the early 1920s but had been often attacked, and more and more violently. At the time of his death, he was, like Mandelstam, officially hounded and virtually isolated.

No. 290. "Favorsky." Vladimir A. Favorsky (1886–    ), artist and illustrator. Favorsky drew a portrait of Biely in his coffin.

No. 294. "a little Gogol." *Gogol'*, literally, is a species of wild duck, sometimes called the golden-eyed duck. One of the last works published by Biely was his marvelously playful, insightful, and brilliant little book on Gogol.

No. 295. "Kidnapped Turk." A Janissary. See note to no. 319.

No. 298. "Marina Mnishek." Daughter of the Polish magnate who supported the cause of the first pseudo-Dmitry against Boris Godunov in what was to be the beginning of Russia's *smuty*, or "Time of Troubles," at the turn of the sixteenth to the seventeenth century. Marina married Dmitry, and appears in both Pushkin's play, *Boris Godunov*, and Mussorgsky's opera, in which she sings a beautiful Italianate aria.

No. 299. See the section from Nadezhda Iakovlevna's memoir reprinted here as Appendix 1, p. 339.

No. 300. "ear-flaps." Slang for "informers."

No. 301. There is an untranslatable play of sounds and meaning in this brief poem, which the translators have cleverly approximated. The last line reads, in the Russian, *Voronezh—blazh', Voronezh—voron, nozh!* Literally, this means, "Voronezh—whim, Voronezh—crow, knife!"

No. 311. "Chapaev's rope drew tight . . ." Literally, "Chapaev's rifle was lassoed." Dmitri A. Furmanov (1891–1926) had written an epic novel about a Civil-War hero, Chapaev, from which an impressive sound movie was made. One of the scenes in the movie that clearly struck Mandelstam showed the officers of the Whites advancing on Chapaev's cavalry unit with cigarettes in their mouths, being mowed down by a machine gun and being replaced by others with cigarettes. There is another episode in the film that shows the shaving of a White colonel—and the admiral's cheeks of Supreme Commander Kolchak. Another theme of the film is the relationship of an elemental leader of revolutionary troops like Chapaev to the Bolshevik party, the difficulties of bringing him under the control of party discipline.

No. 312. "The Tale of Igor's Men." See the note to no. 204. Mandelstam uses numerous allusions to this remarkable twelfth-century work. See the English translation by Sidney Monas and Burton Raffel in *Delos,* no. 6, pp. 5-15.

No. 313. "G.P.U." State Political Administration, or the Secret Police.

"Chapaev." See note to no. 311 above.

No. 315. "Saint Isaac's." Along with the Kazan Cathedral, one of the two largest and most monumental churches in Saint Petersburg.

No. 318. This brief poem is typical Mandelstam, with its dense allusions and resonant associations. Translation is virtually impossible.

"smoky ritual." Smoke for Mandelstam has the connotation of "sacrifice," something sacrificial, often self-sacrificial, as in no. 235.

For Mandelstam's ideas on stones, mineralogy, see his essay, "Talking about Dante," *Delos,* no. 6 pp. 102-3, where he acknowledges also his debt to Novalis. For Mandelstam, a man, a poet, like a stone, was shaped out of "matter" and "the weather."

"opal disgrace," a valiant attempt to render in English the Russian *v opale; opal* being the same as our "opal," *v opale* would mean opalescent, irridescent, a play of color (*upal* is Sanskrit for "precious stone," i.e., the Ur-jewel. But *-pal* in Russian also suggests "I have fallen." One might thus read the line, "In a fallen state before me there lies . . ." What "I see" are *zemlianiki*. These are literally "strawberries." But *zemlia* alone means "earth." And *zemlianiki* can also mean "earth-creatures." With the accent shifted it can also mean people who live in shelters dug into the ground, as happens in time of war or catastrophe. "Doublesparked red quartz," in Russian, *serdoliki* means "cornelian," "sard," quartz of a rusty red or reddish white color, used for official *seals*. The adjective translated brilliantly as "doublesparked" is *dvuiskrennie,* which means as well "doubly sincere." More of this in a moment. In Russian, the words "agate" and "brother" are placed next to each other and rhyme strongly: *agat/brat,* a rhyme further reinforced in the next line by *soldat* ("soldier"), and again a somewhat weaker rhyme in the last line, *rad* ("glad"). Agate is typically of clouded or cloudy colors. To return for a moment to the adjective "doublesparked": the association with seals may suggest the Imperial Seal (the two-headed or doublesparked eagle) and hence the Imperial as opposed to the "simple," or ordinary soldier at the end. The antlike brother, the agate, is therefore a transition —somewhere between the royal cornelian and the simple soldier; hammered and notched into the poem by the rhymes. These colored stones are associated by Mandelstam with Koktebel in the Crimea, and the Crimea with Greece and the Mediterranean and classical world. These stones are, therefore, biographies from the history and legends of Greece and Rome that Mandelstam offers to eternity!

No. 319. "mercenary's forced abyss . . ." Literally, Janissary's. A Janissary (until 1826 when the Corps was abolished) had a high place in the Turkish army, but at the price of permanent exile. Young boys were drafted—kidnapped would be a more accurate term, since they never again had any contact with their parents or home —for special service. Many of these reached high rank, and yet remained in a sense both "exiles" and "slaves."

"Abyss." The Russian word means also, "bottom of the maelstrom," or "the depths."

No. 322. "Sadko . . . Novgorod." Sadko was a legendary merchant of the medieval merchant-republic of Novgorod, who appears in the *byliny,* or "epic ballads," in one of which he is entertained by the King of the Sea in his underwater kingdom.

No. 324. "Goldfinch." A bird with which Mandelstam closely identified. The bird also had special associations with Voronezh.

No. 327. "A forest university . . ." Literally, in the text, Salamanca which of course has particular associations with the Inquisition, the Jesuits, casuistry, Don Quixote, the Bachelor from Salamanca, etc.

No. 330. "fat necklaces." Reminiscent of the "thick fingers, fat like worms," of the Stalin poem, no. 286.

No. 337. "immortal Koschey," or "Kashchey." A fairy-tale character, whose name suggests "cat." He is usually the enchanter-guardian of a treasure, not necessarily or entirely evil, but who must be placated before access can be gained.

No. 338. "Anna, and Rossosh, and Gremyachye . . ." These names, which clearly suggest the rhythm of the train are in themselves obscure. "Anna" is possibly Anna Akhmatova.

"*sovkhoz.*" A state farm, more rigorously administered from the center than a *kolkhoz,* or "collective farm."

"Koltsov's step-mother . . ." Alexei V. Koltsov (1809–1842), a poet who made especially fine use of folk-song styles and motifs. He was born in Voronezh (clearly his "stepmother"), the son of a cattle dealer. He felt lonely and miserable in Voronezh, where he finally died, unable to break away.

No. 340. 'Spruce?/—No, lilac!" In English "lilac" may be a bush; the Russian word here *lilovy* refers only to the color; and is suggested by the word for spruce, *elovy.*

No. 341. "Hillocks of human heads." Pyramids of skulls outside towns that resisted them were the "warnings" set up by the Mongol terror against any notion of resistance.

No. 343. "circular Koltsov." Koltsov's name suggests, in Russian, a ring; Mandelstam puns this with the ritornelle effect of many of his poems.

No. 346. This is the first of the poems written by Mandelstam after he had decided to write a "positive" ode to Stalin. None of these poems of course is "positive" about Stalin or even deals with him directly. But his chill presence may be felt, as, in this poem, in the image of someone walking obliquely across a grave.

No. 350. According to Nadezhda Iakovlevna this poem, in spite of the date, was not part of the Stalin cycle, but came to Mandelstam between the goldfinch cycle and the Stalin cycle. But the figure on the horizon is clearly Stalin. See Nadezhda Mandelstam, *Hope against Hope,* p. 199.

No. 355. "Elbrus' volcanic snow." Mount Elbrus, the highest peak in the Caucasus.

"The people need . . ." Ironic repetition of the Soviet newspaper cliché.

No. 357.  "a disgrace." *Opal,* also "opal," i.e., a jewel. See the note to no. 318.

No. 316.  "Finnish words . . ." i.e., Someone speaking a Finnish dialect, on the train somewhere between Cherdyn and Voronezh.

No. 362.  Lermontov, too, was a soldier.

"The way the grave straightens a hunchback . . ." Reference to a Russian proverb, "Only the grave can straighten a hunchback," which the late Nikita S. Khrushchev made internationally famous by quoting it to assembled writers and artists at the Manége Exhibit in 1961. See also poem no. 234, and others.

No. 363.  "Mount David." Mountain near Tiflis (Tbilisi) in Georgia. There is undoubtedly an echo of the Stalin obsession in this poem. "He" is a personification of the city, which Mandelstam loved. But Stalin was a Georgian.

No. 364.  There was a small painting of Golgotha by Rembrandt in the Voronezh museum.

No. 365.  "Colchis." The Caucasus, home of Medea. Also, Georgia.

No. 366.  This poem is remarkable in Russian for its "slow-motion" effects through meter and phonetic patterning.

No. 367.  "Wasp." In Russian, *osa;* "axle," *os'*. Both suggest the name Joseph, which may be either *Osip,* or *Iosif*.

No. 368.  This is the last poem of the so-called Stalin Cycle. Nadezhda Iakovlevna points out that "stars" tended to appear in Mandelstam's poetry whenever one particular current of inspiration or cycle was running out. In this case, perhaps happily.

No. 369.  "Favorsky." See note to no. 290. Favorsky's most commonly used medium was the woodcut.

No. 372.  Although this is *not* the "positive" Ode to Stalin, the last two lines were originally written differently: as "awaken" reason and "arouse" life. But this was an obvious ploy for the benefit of snoopers, as Nadezhda Iakovlevna and Clarence Brown make clear. In any case, the last two lines seem artificially tacked on and do not really belong to the poem. See Clarence Brown, "Into the Heart of Darkness: Mandelstam's Ode to Stalin," *Slavic Review* 26, no. 4 (December, 1967), p. 602.

No. 387. "The "p" and "q" of a Greek flute." Literally, *theta* and *iota*. These were Greek musical notes, and the flute was a funeral instrument; the instrument of transcendance. *Theta* was the letter (or note) of death; *iota* of small or minuscule beginnings. See Victor Terras, "Classical Motives in the Poetry of Mandelstam," p. 263.

# Appendix 1
# Two Chapters by Nadezhda Mandelstam

*Translated by* SIDNEY MONAS

The first chapter, "cycle," appeared as chapter 41 in *Hope against Hope,* but in severely abridged form. The second, "Double Runners," which followed it in the Russian, was omitted on the grounds that the poems referred to were unfamiliar to the English reader.

## Cycle

The word "phase" refers to a person's view of the world. It has to do with his growth, and how, as he grows, his attitude to the world and to poetry changes. The poems of *Tristia* came to M. as he was expecting the revolution, and during his initial awareness of it. *New Poems* came as he broke a long silence by writing "Fourth Prose." A phase might contain more than one book. It seems to me that *New Poems* and the *Voronezh Notebooks,* books separated from each other by arrest and exile, represent a single phase. In the former, there are two sections called "notebooks," in the latter, three. To M., a "book" meant a biographical period, while a "notebook" was a section of poems with a certain unity of atmosphere and subject matter.

A "cycle" was a smaller unit. In Notebook 1 of *New Poems,* there is the "wolf" or convict cycle, for example, and the Armenian cycle. "Armenia" itself, however, is essentially not a cycle. It is a selection. M. had two such selections—"Armenia" and "Octaves." There and there only he violated the order of composition, consequently the quality of a lyrical diary that was, for example, characteristic of the *Voronezh Notebooks,* but not so evident in the work of earlier periods, when M. made his selections very rigorously and destroyed numbers of poems he considered immature.

In the *Second Voronezh Notebook,* one cycle begins with the poem "The Honk" (*Gudok,* no. 322) and another with "Precious World-Yeast" (no. 346). In each of these cycles, there is a "central" poem from which the others emerged; not necessarily the first, but generally longer than the others. There were cycles in which the poems followed each other like links in a chain, and others where they were wound around each other into something like a ball of yarn and where they all emerged from a single poem as from a matrix.

It is easy to show that "The Wolf" (no. 227) was the matrix of the whole convict cycle, because the drafts have been preserved. Poems of a common origin sometimes go such different ways that at first glance they seem to have nothing in common: shared words, lines that echo each other, have disappeared in the work process. In general, M.'s work on one of those cycles I have tried to characterize as resembling a "ball of yarn" concentrated on differentiating the threads, separating one organism from another, giving each its proper set of significations. His work reminded me of the movements of a gardener, pruning a tree.

In the wolf cycle, the line, "And only my equal can kill me," came last, although it contains the conceptual key to the whole cycle. This cycle has its source in Russian convict songs, the only folk songs M. loved. He refers to a particular song in no. 229, and in the variants of no. 227. He rarely did that. Except for the drafts of "The Wolf" and "The Man in Stripes," in his last period it is found only in "Abkhazian Song" (no. 365: "I sing when my throat is damp, when my soul is dry . . ."). In the first two instances, the song in question and M's poem which made use of it were not identical in spirit, and M. could not stand that. When he happened to open the current issue of *Zvezda,* M. would always be struck by the fact that Soviet poets (especially Leningraders) were invariably proclaiming they were young and sang songs. He would count up the number of times in a given issue these attributes appeared. It came to an imposing sum.

One can trace the emergence of the poems of the wolf cycle from the draft versions. The variants ("and my mouth is distorted with untruth," and "Let it not be said I hastened to the hut where six-fingered falsehood lies," lines dropped from no. 227) were worked into a different poem, no. 231: "Holding a smoking stick I enter/ the hut where six-fingered falsehood lies . . . " The line, "Having heard that voice I'll go for the axblades . . ." led to the ax in no. 235, "Preserve my words for their after-taste of misery and smoke . . ." The idea of "my words," "my speech," which it was necessary to preserve come what may, was united with the idea of the ax handle used in a Petrine execution. In "The Wolf" (no. 227) there appeared briefly the phrase "the cherry-tree of Moscow's wooden pavements," while immediately beside it there was written "a streetcar-cherry in a terrible time" (see no. 232).

"Alexander Herzovich" (no. 228) and "Soldiers' Star-Flowers" (no. 233) might be said to make up the periphery of the cycle. A clue to their connection with it is the word "fur-coat." In "Soldiers' Star-Flowers" it is the nobleman's fur-coat for which he had been reproached, and in "Alexander Herzovich—. . . we hang on a peg/ like a crow-skin coat." Both are connected with "Siberia's fur sleeves . . ." (no. 227). The fur-coat is one of M.'s most frequently repeated images, having made its appearance as far back as *Stone:* the doormen in heavy fur-coats, a woman in a fur-coat, and an angel in a golden sheepskin . . . . M's first prose work, which got lost in the Kharkov publishing house belonging to Rakovsky's sister, was called "The Fur-Coat." And finally the chapter heading, "In a Fur-Coat Above One's Station," from *The Hum of Time,* and that "literary" fur-coat from "Fourth Prose," which in that work M. tears from himself and stamps into the ground. A fur-coat is one of those solid, everyday things. It is the Russian frost. It is the social position to which a *raznochinets* dares not pretend.

The fur-coat from "Soldiers' Star-Flowers" reminds me of an amusing incident. At the end of the twenties, a certain formerly aristocratic lady since fallen on hard times complained to Emma Gerstein that Mandelstam had always seemed to her a very strange man; she couldn't forget, she said, the chic fur-coat in which he used to stroll around Moscow at the beginning of the New Economic Policy. . . . We merely caught our breath. We had bought this fur-coat straight off the back of an impoverished church deacon at the flea market in Kharkov: a brownish, moth-eaten raccoon that smelled of the cassock. The old deacon sold it for bread, and M. had purchased this luxury while we were on our way from the Caucasus to Moscow, so as not to freeze to death up north. This first literary fur-coat above his station was later presented to Prishvin, a writer who was spending his nights in a flophouse on Tver Boulevard, and it served him as a mattress. At one point, a small caliber primus stove blew up, and Prishvin stifled the flames with the coat. It charred the few remaining hairs on the brownish raccoon, so M. didn't even have the chance to tear the coat from his shoulders and stomp on it as would have been appropriate . . . Wearing a coat off a strange back . . . For M., wearing a fur-coat was out of his class. . . .

That kind of complication always came up in connection with fur-coats. At one point we saved our money and went to buy an ordinary Soviet fur-coat in a department store; then we had it explained to us the only ones they had for sale were made of dog fur. Now, M. simply couldn't bring himself to betray man's best friend in this way. He preferred to freeze. And so, he went around in a thin little coat right up to the last year of his life, when we were always having to travel in unheated trains to and from the hundred-mile zone. Shklovsky couldn't stand it: "You always look as if you'd arrived on flatcars," he said. "We'll have to get hold of a fur-coat. . . ." Vasilisa remembered that an old fur-coat of Shklovsky's was gathering dust at Andronikov's, who used to wear it when he went visiting, but who had by now managed to get hold of something a little classier. They invited Andronikov over, along with the fur-coat, and with great ceremony they draped M. in it. Throughout the Kalinin winter, it was great. M. was arrested in the spring. He didn't take it with him because he was afraid of the extra weight. The fur-coat remained in Moscow, and he froze in a thin, yellow, leather coat—also given him by somebody, in that last year of his "carefree life in a distant Moscow suburb." One-hundred miles distant, that is.

In the wolf cycle, Siberian forests, planks, logs are a kind of getting-ready for exile . . . The raw material of this cycle comes from the tree: the block, the tub, the pine, the pine coffin, the splinter, the ax handle, kittles, the cherry pit. . . . And certain epithets like "rough" would turn up here.

Even before "The Wolf" this cycle had its origins in images like the door chains rattling on the doors, the Petersburg fires and frosts, the sharp knife and the round loaf of bread, in the feeling that M. expressed, "Living in Petersburg is like sleeping in a coffin," in the need to run immediately to the railroad station "where no one can find us." What this cycle expressed was rejection, brotherhood unacknowledged. Once I read in Baudouin de Courtenay that the word "brother" didn't originally mean literally blood kinship but referred to somebody who had been "taken into the tribe." M. never did get taken into the tribe of Soviet literature, and so even the deacon's mangy fur-coat on his shoulders was presumed to bear witness to his bourgeois ideology. . . . Yet this cycle is also about the man who says no, and he who identifies himself with the common people. There are echoes of the year 1917 in a truck clamoring at the gates and in the common people who spread out to the palaces and the estuaries. . . .

From the rough wooden wolfish log cabin, these themes spread through the whole notebook. An attempt to find a second homeland in Armenia didn't work. Since he was forced to return to "Buddhist" Moscow, M. defined his place there, and he defined it with considerable precision.

In the "after asthma" poem (see the last stanza of no. 312), two surges are discernible: first, surprise at the sight of the new countryside, the black earth; then, recovering from his surprise, M. begins to recall how he happened to come there, and this evokes verses about the Cherdyn period of our life.

In both cycles of this notebook, each new poem was developed out of a life-bearing branch in a preceding poem. The buds (*pochki*)—"Ear-Flaps" (no. 300) "Don't ask how the buds are blooming . . ."—first appeared as a rhyme to *komóchki* ("clots," "clotting") in "Black Earth" (no. 299). At a certain point, *komóchki* were pulled out to the end of the line in order to link up with *pochki,* and then they departed to their proper place. And then, the name of the town Voronezh (no. 301) and "you will gape at" (*provoronish'*) [translated freely in this volume, see the note to no. 301] have the same root as "perforation" (*provorot*) in no. 299. [The phrase reads literally: "in the April perforation." Here: "as April does its quick work."] The instrumentation and the elaboration of meaning are so closely interwoven that it is virtually impossible to separate them. Was it accidental that a reference to "Land and Liberty" (*Zemlia i volia*) [1] appeared in "Black Earth," or that several rhymes in "Stanzas" (no. 312) like "mess" (*kuter'ma*) and "darkness" (*t'ma*) also happen to rhyme with the written, unpronounced word "prison" (*tiur'ma*)? And why do associations with "execution" slip through in the most unexpected places, in the poem, "Shearing the Children" (no. 302) for example: "There's a lot of life left in us?" [2]

This kind of train of associations entered very much into our way of life, and both in M.'s poems and in his prose there were repeated references to prison. The linking together of phrases like, "they've taken him," "he's sitting," "they've taken him away," "they've put him away," "they've planted him," has taken on a new significance in the Russian language as a whole and demonstrates how thoroughly our life has been drenched with thoughts of jail. One can see here, too, a certain diffusion and spread, a kind of mutual interpenetration between prison and the outside world, and this diffusion is convenient to those who rule in keeping those whom they rule properly terrorized.

I would like to conclude this prison discourse with a little scene from our daily life of the year 1937. In central Moscow, there was a house shared by writers and Chekists. God knows how the Chekists first got there. Maybe they moved in to replace those arrested from some other institution that had shared this house with the Writers' Union. They did live there, though, and their neighbors would occasionally discuss different things with them. There was once, for example, a drunken Chekist whose wife had locked him out of their apartment. He raged away on the stair landing. Deliriously drunk, he recalled how he had once cross-examined and beaten up his comrade during an investigation, and he wept tears of belated repentance. I rang up his wife in their apartment and urged her to let her husband in,

---

1. The first important organized underground revolutionary group in Russia, an offshoot of which, *Narodnaia volia,* was responsible for the assassination of Alexander II in 1881. In no. 299, the third stanza begins, "And yet the earth (*zemlia*) is. . . ." The title of the poem in Russian is *Chernozem.*
2. In the poem, literally: "We are still full of life *in the highest measure,*" which echoes the legal-official phrase *in the death sentence.* i.e., "punishment in the highest measure."

explaining that it wasn't likely he'd be congratulated for drunken rant of this sort. Then, all of a sudden, a group of wandering singers arrived in the courtyard. They sensed the need of the moment and started singing the best classical convict songs—Siberian, Baikal, thieves' songs . . . . People started pouring out into the balconies. I don't mean the writers, of course. They joined in the songs, they threw money to the singers. . . . This went on for about half an hour. Then one of the ideologically more reliable of the inmates was about to run downstairs to chase away the singers. But instead, somebody yelled to them from above: "Beat it!" And they beat it. M. and I stood on one of the balconies and tossed a coin or some paper money, wrapped in a scrap of newspaper and weighted with one of our Crimean stones so it would fall properly. This was our gift to Russian folklore.

Young Osia, as they now call Iosif Brodskii, was convicted for parasitism (actually, for poems, because life repeats itself, though in different forms)—anyway, he said once not long ago to Akhmatova that there was no folklore at all in Pasternak. Can this be so? It seems to me one of the basic questions in the investigation of a body of poetic work, this matter of its connection with folklore. You can see the convict folklore in M.'s work right away. Life reinforced it, and there it is on the surface. Nor is this M.'s only tie with the wealth of Russian and European folklore. From within folklore, there is nowhere to go. The whole problem is how to convert it into individual, contemporary poetry.

## Double Runners

The poem, "A Place in Dark Waters" (no. 338): M. worked on it slowly and with difficulty, for many consecutive days. He complained that "something" he almost perceived, something very important, just wouldn't come. This turned out to be the last line. It also came last. By no means the way it always happened.

M. stood at the table with his back toward me, and he was writing something. "Come here, look what I have." I was glad "Dark Waters" was finished and we could go for a stroll. It bored me. Like the plywood map of the Voronezh region at the telephone center on which little bulbs lit up tracing the points with which there were phone connections. But I was to be disappointed. On the piece of paper he showed me I read: "Landmarkstakes of a distant convoy" (see no. 340). "Wait," M. said, "that isn't all." And he wrote: "I sense winter/ like a tardy presence . . ." (no. 336). I said, "You've gone out of your mind!" I was disturbed. "We'll never get out at this rate. Come on, let's go to the market, or I'll go alone. . . ."

We went to the market together, though. It was only a few steps from our house. We sold something and we bought something. I think we sold a gray jacket that day of cheap, standard material. "That's the kind they put you in jail in," the buyer said—a clever, sly town-*muzhik*. "True," M. answered, "but this one's already been there, so it's safe now." The *muzhik* grinned and gave us what we asked for it. Right then and there we arranged a feast. That is, we got hold of an extra piece of meat or sausage if there was such a thing at that time. It's hard to remember what was in supply at different times. There was always some sort of "daily special," and everybody ate it. For Moscow, now, it's boiled sausage. At that time I think we were treated to bluish chickens, while the canned goods on the shelves were considered a luxury. There was a period of frozen pheasants and pigeons, but that soon came to an end. Cod held out quite a bit longer. Most of these "daily specials," it's true, never got to the provinces. For that very reason, we provincials knew how to value our daily bread.

The stanza with night's teakettle (no. 338) appeared practically that very day, while two little poems which had hatched out of the "Dark Waters" poem were only slightly elaborated. In "landmark-stakes of a distant convoy" (no. 340) the landscape from the window of the Tambov sanatorium is engraved. And this is the origin of the phrase, "a house, a real house . . ." (*osobniak,* no. 340). We did not live in "real houses." We lived anywhere we could, mostly in hovels. It is clear to me how the lines: "I sense winter/ like a tardy present . . ." (no. 336) helped find the last stanza of "Dark Waters." They provided the line: "bare steppe, without winter . . ." (no. 338). Suddenly the season's peculiarity manifested itself. Everything had gone stiff, waiting for the delayed winter. Nature was waiting for winter, but that winter of 1936, people already knew that 1937 was on its way. No special historical sense was needed. We'd been able to predict the coming trials from the radio announcements as far back as summer. M. wrote about the Voronezh countryside in this stanza.

> Where am I? What's wrong?
> bare steppe, without winter:
> Koltsov's step-mother—
> Sure, sure: it's the goldfinches' native-land.
>      —Oh, sure.—

That was a kind of synthesis of his mood at that time. The sense of calamity did not displace that wild, perpetual joy of life, that completely inexplicable gaiety of the poet locked in his cage.

Here are some small details of his life: toward night, tired of working, he'd go wandering around the deserted town where everything was sheathed in ice. After doormen disappeared, our provincial towns became a region of "eternal slipperiness. . . ." Akhmatova, too, has something about this in her Voronezh poem. She had a hard time walking on the slick ice: "gingerly, I tread on glass. . . ." But the teakettle in the last stanza of no. 338 was electric—an unheard-of luxury in those days! We allowed ourselves this one, because M. always drank a lot of tea when he worked at night. There were only two things he couldn't refuse himself: tea and cigarettes. Everything else, we thought, one learns to do without.

"Triptyches" appeared twice in Voronezh; that is, three poems with a single origin. The first triptych consisted of "Dark Waters" (no. 338), "I sense winter" (no. 336)—we called this poem "The Crows"—and "Landmark-stakes of a distant convoy" (no. 340). Another triptych was "I stare at the frost's face" (no. 349), "And what do we do with these crushed plains?" (no. 350) and his reminiscences of the Kama, "Oh these slow short-winded open spaces" (no. 351). In the first triptych everything was wound up like a ball of yarn, as in a cycle. In the second, all three poems developed independently from a common root. The lines,

> And what do we do with these crushed plains,
> the drawling hunger of this miracle?

and the phrase, "the steppe's breathing marvel" unite the first two poems. The third has to do with the theme of breathing, shortness of breath, which is also in the other two. "Short-winded open spaces" of the third poem echoes "the steppe's breathing marvel." In the Judas poem (no. 350) the very rhythm is organized to express shortness of breath: "And the question keeps growing—where are they going? where are they from?—" The shortness of breath that plagued M. was expressed that winter in the rhythm of many poems. For example: "Me—oh, that's me—and reality—that's reality!" (No. 359. In Russian: *"Ia—eto ia, iav'—eto iav'!"*)

The first triptych contains one more token of kinship: the rhymes "statefarm" (*sovkhoznyi*) and "terrible" (*groznyi*) and the violence of the sound z in two others, for example in the rhymes "frost" (*moroza*), "convoy" (*oboza*), "birch-tree" (*berioza*), "prose" (*proza*). The line that came to him first stands out in all M.'s poems, though one has to remember that it is rarely the line that begins the first stanza. Once it has been discovered —if it hasn't disappeared in the meantime, of course, having been dropped from the final text, as also happened—one can restore almost the entire sequence of work. Displacement from the final text of the first line that had occurred to him was something that happened frequently. In this connection, M. loved to recall Gumilev's words: "These are good verses, Osip, but when you're done—these lines you have now—you won't have a single one left. . . ." In such cases, of course, the history of the text cannot be restored; most of the work took place in the mind and in the lip movements and never took concrete form on paper.

The line that first started resounding and the word that was found last: these were also keys to the composition of a poem. They contain the impulse of the beginning and of the end. The underlined words in the following epithets are examples of words that came last: "the *conscience*-tar of labor" (no. 235, translated here as "honest tar"), *"tenfold-signifying* forests" (no. 349, translated here as "one forest is almost the same as any other forest . . ."), and *"lazy* epic hero" (no. 344).

A triptych was a rare event for M. Much more common were his "diptyches," double runners from a single root. The following among his published poems were characteristic diptyches: no. 131–no. 132; no. 140–no. 141. Quite a few were produced during the Voronezh period, too: two poems about the Kama, for instance (no. 308–no. 310) form an ordinary diptych while a third poem (no. 309) with the last line, "the river's rising! the river's rising!" connected with these two is a rare instance of a change that was made consciously with the censor in mind that poetically speaking actually worked. With regard to poems no. 347 and no. 348, a variant has been preserved (no. 346) in which both these poems are still interwoven. Poems no. 378 and no. 379 also form a diptych; they have a single source, though their development is different. Such a "paired structure" was very characteristic of M. He produced many other diptyches in addition to those already cited.

M. tried to preserve both runners of no. 378, and to print them side by side. Composers always do that, after all, and painters, too. If I live to see the free publication of M.'s works, I will of course see to it that it is done as he wished. As things are now, though, even if the promised book is printed —it has been rotting away in the offices of "The Poet's Library" (*Biblioteka Poeta*)—neither I nor Khardzhiev will be allowed to do this. We are, after all, people without rights. Some clever editor will explain very clearly to me that of two variants one must choose the better, that neither poets themselves nor those close to them are good judges in this matter, and that a poet's heritage belongs not to the person who shared his life for over fifteen years but to learned scholars and critics, competent to judge, who knew very well what was good and what was bad. In addition to correct ideology, the contemporary Soviet editor most values clarity, accuracy, a smooth texture, and luxuriant composition in which similes, metaphors and other figures of speech are laid out as on a plate. M. did not survive to witness this flowering of culture, but even during his lifetime he was taken by surprise more than once by the degree to which scholars seemed to dislike poems. And Anna Andreevna [Akhmatova] having learned that one poor lad had just been proclaimed "our future Pushkin," had commented: "It's because they dislike poems so." This particular lad wrote smooth poems in which they could recognize everything with which they were long familiar. Best of all they liked translations, with their glitter of prepackaged goods. There are such scholars and critics everywhere, but during Stalin's time they came to their fullest flower among us, and now they hold sway in painting, architecture, and film, as well as in literature. But to hell with them. . . . They were ordered to produce a renaissance, and the result was something on the order of the Café Renaissance. Dealing with them is no simple matter, though.

In his youth, M. would eradicate the traces of common origin from his poems or he would destroy one of the related poems. For a long time, he could not write down poems like no. 141 and no. 131 without at the same time saying something about their rights to independent life. In his mature period, his attitude changed drastically. He seems to have decided to acknowledge openly the principle of the double runners, and he no longer considered them as variants. "A single beginning? What of it? They're different poems, though." Or: "If it's noticeable, so much the better. . . . What's there to hide?" he would say. If in his youth M. had been secretive and showed the reader only distinct and separate units, in his mature and fully developed period he would reveal the entire flow, and he saw the main value in the poetic surge itself rather than in its separate manifestations. This expressed the inner freedom he had achieved. For many of his old admirers, it was a stumbling block. They tended to see incompleteness and imperfection in these poems of M. "He didn't actually prepare the book for publication, though. It needs trimming," the two Bernstein brothers said to me, the linguist Sergei Ignatevich and Ivich. "How many repetitions," said Orlov, "but they're simply variants." Slutsky, like Orlov, complained that while the published Mandelstam had been comprehensible, his unpublished work was extremely difficult. It's good we now have a new kind of reader, whose approach to poems and poetry is quite different.

A poet whose work goes through sharply differentiated phases is doomed to the fact that readers who have mastered one of his periods often will not grasp another. A good part of M.'s regular audience gave each new poem and each new poetic course a hostile reception, simply because they failed to recognize in it what they were used to. Emma Gerstein kept asserting long and stubbornly that after the wolf cycle M. ought not to have written anything at all. Kuzin, too, would react to new poems almost as though they were a personal insult. But both of them eventually got used to the poems, got acquainted with them, became their friends. Shengel, though, never could reconcile himself to the late poems, though he remained loyal to the old ones. In M.'s mature poems, he had a special aversion for the dictionary—for words from a dictionary that had nothing to do with poetry. On the other hand, M. now has a large number of readers who know his poems only from circulating manuscript copies, who have not yet had a good look at his books. There is no way of telling whether the early phase will please them. The reader's right to a choice, however, is just as unarguable as the poet's right to a printing press and to his views on poetry. "I wish you could be just as you are, and someone else, too," Akhmatova once said. . . . And so I've quite a different attitude to readers and their tastes, even their caprices, than I do to editors who have the right to veto and a love for bottlenecking manuscripts. As for the "imperfection" of M.'s last period—i.e., his wish to open up his inner laboratory—there's no such thing as a law superseding the author's own wish for his posthumous publications, any more than there is for those published during his lifetime. After all, he knew very well how to individuate his poems when he thought they needed it.

Probably these double runners were not peculiar to M. alone. Among Akhmatova's poems as well there are precisely such pairings: "Dante" ("Even after death he did not return to his tender Florence") and "Why have you poisoned the water and mixed my bread with mud?" These are undoubtedly a diptych. In many cases, such pairings may serve as commentary, one upon the other. "No, without the hangman and the gallows the poet cannot live on earth, we must have our hair shirts, we must march behind the candle and grieve—" that was the impulse the two poems had in common.

While he was putting his book together, M. saved all the diptyches, but while he was actually working, even during his last period, he had many doubts and hesitations. Thus, he wanted to reject no. 343, because he remembered how this poem had served as an impulse to another, no. 344. These two poems have no external resemblance, yet M. did not want to keep the first because it had come too directly, straight from his inspiration. The retrospective self-evaluation of a poet is more reliable than an attitude to his own poems he might hold during a given period of his work, which is always impassioned and apt to be conditioned and complicated by many things. A particular poem might be rejected simply because it was blocking a new one, whose pulse was already felt, but which could not somehow break through. Sometimes the old poem contains a potential bud of new growth, and when this new growth does make its appearance, the poet thinks the first was only a preparation, a prelude in the work process. This feeling figured especially strongly in the appearance of pairs of growths and the subsequent quick separation of the two runners. So it went with "The Smile" (no. 342; originally, no. 323 was the last stanza of no. 342) and "The Goldfinch" (no. 324, no. 325, no. 326, no. 327). In the finished texts, there is nothing in common between them, and yet "The Goldfinch" was hatched out of "The Smile." There is a stanza in which there is a childish mouth, chaff and a goldfinch (no. 325). . . . It was really the chaff that caught the goldfinch, while itself retaining only one of its original qualities, its prickliness, so that in this manner, and not by the cold of a terrible winter, it was turned into prickly frost. At first, though, M. considered "The Goldfinch" an illegitimate child.

The two poems on Ariosto (no. 267, no. 268) appeared in a completely different manner. The first was written during the summer of 1933 while we were guests of Grin's widow in Old Crimea, along with Kuzin who had just been released from prison. The manuscripts and drafts were taken away from us when we were searched in May 1934. In Voronezh, M. tried to remember the text, but his memory betrayed him, and instead the second "Ariosto" emerged. Soon after my return to Moscow, I found the 1933 "Ariosto" (no. 267) in its hiding place. This accounts in this instance for two poems on the same theme and with the same subject matter. One might call it a novella on the spirit of the time. I present it as such to future commentators.

# Appendix 2
# Finding-List of Poems with Titles

Most of Mandelstam's poems are untitled. The basic ordering of this book is by number, the numbers following those in the established Russian edition. Twenty-four poems which have been discovered and printed since Struve's and Filipoff's *Collected Works* follow; these are numbered separately, and consecutively, in lowercase roman numerals. However, for the convenience of those who may wish to find a particular poem to which Mandelstam gave a title, there follows an alphabetical listing by title. Note that the number which follows each title is a page number, not the sequential numbering of the poems, just referred to.

| No. | Title | Page |
|---|---|---|
| 74 | The Abbot | 76 |
| 195 | Actor and Worker | 173 |
| 48 | The Admiralty Tower | 158 |
| 59 | Akhmatova | 67 |
| 174 | American Bar | 162 |
| 52 | The American Girl | 62 |
| 203–215 | Armenia | 179–84 |
| 267 | To Ariosto | 218 |
| 268 | Ariosto [A Variant of 267] | 219 |
| 46 | Bach | 57 |
| 261 | Batyushkov | 212 |
| 342 | Birth of a Smile | 261 |
| 299 | Black Earth | 237 |
| 197 | But a Sky Pregnant with with the Future.... | 175 |
| 236 | Canzonet | 196 |
| 248 | The Carriage-Driver | 200 |
| 33 | Casino | 48 |
| 95 | To Cassandra | 96 |
| 38 | The Church of Hagia Sophia, Constantinople | 52 |
| 125 | Concert at a Railway Station | 123 |
| 94 | The Decembrist | 95 |
| 53 | Dombey and Son | 63 |
| 171 | The Egyptian: Inscription on a Rock of the Eighteenth-Nineteenth Dynasty | 160 |

| No. | Title | Page |
|---|---|---|
| 172 | The Egyptian [Poem 2] | 161 |
| 68 | Europe | 72 |
| 167 | Football Again | 157 |
| 180 | Fragment | 165 |
| 237–246 | Fragments from Discarded Poems | 197–200 |
| 103 | Freedom's Twilight | 101 |
| 266 | To German | 217 |
| 36 | Gold-Piece | 50 |
| 234 | The Grand Piano | 194 |
| 383 | A Greek Jug | 288 |
| 258 | Impressionism | 209 |
| 140 | January 1, 1924 | 137 |
| 289 | January 10, 1934 | 230 |
| 308–310 | Kama River | 241–43 |
| 298 | Lady Violinist | 236 |
| 254 | Lamarck | 205 |
| 86 | A Last Straw | 89 |
| 377 | The Last Supper | 284 |
| 221 | Leningrad | 187 |
| 37 | The Lutheran | 51 |
| 187 | Madrigal | 169 |
| 83 | Menagerie | 86 |
| 260 | Midnight in Moscow | 210 |
| 134 | Moscow Drizzle | 129 |
| 135 | My Time | 130 |
| 57 | 1913 | 65 |
| 70 | 1914 | 73 |
| 39 | Notre Dame | 52 |
| 256 | Novellino | 207 |
| 275–285 | Octaves | 224–28 |
| 72 | Ode to Beethoven | 74 |
| 41 | An Old Man | 54 |
| 189 | The Palace Square | 170 |
| 32 | Pedestrian | 47 |
| 42 | Petersburg Strophes | 55 |
| 326 | Poem on an Unknown Soldier | 272 |
| 262–264 | Poems on Russian Poetry | 213–17 |
| 176 | Poles! | 163 |

| No. | Title | Page |
|---|---|---|
| 71 | On Pope Benedict XV's Encyclical | 74 |
| 181 | Rheims and Cologne | 166 |
| 381 | Rome | 286 |
| 390–392 | Rough Drafts from the Second Voronezh Notebook | 295 |
| 26 | Seashell | 44 |
| 164 | Self-portrait | 155 |
| 302 | Shearing the Children | 238 |
| 50 | Silent Movie | 60 |
| 14 | Silentium | 37 |
| 137 | A Slate Ode | 134 |
| 166 | Sports | 156 |
| 69 | The Staff | 72 |
| 159 | The Street-organ | 152 |
| 194 | The Telephone | 172 |
| 51 | Tennis | 61 |
| 111 | Theodosia | 108 |
| 82 | Theseus, Hippolytus, and Phaedra | 83 |
| 104 | Tristia | 102 |
| 35 | Tsarskoe Selo | 49 |
| 136 | Whoever Finds a Horseshoe | 131 |

www.ingramcontent.com/pod-product-compliance
Lightning Source LLC
Chambersburg PA
CBHW030126240426
43672CB00005B/44